THE BRITISH AND THE GRAND TOUR

The British and The Grand Tour

JEREMY BLACK

CROOM HELM
London ● Sydney ● Dover, New Hampshire

© 1985 Jeremy Black
Croom Helm Ltd, Provident House, Burrell Row,
Beckenham, Kent BR3 1AT
Croom Helm Australia Pty Ltd, Suite 4, 6th Floor,
64–76 Kippax Street, Surry Hills, NSW 2010, Australia

British Library Cataloguing in Publication Data

Black, Jeremy
    The British and the Grand Tour.
    1. Travelers — England — History — 18th century
    2. Travelers — Europe — History — 18th century
    3. Europe — Description and travel — 17th–18th centuries
    I. Title
    914'.04253   D917

    ISBN 0-7099-3257-X

Croom Helm Ltd, 51 Washington Street,
Dover, New Hampshire, 03820 USA

Library of Congress Cataloging in Publication Data

Black, Jeremy
    The British and the Grand Tour.

    Bibliography: P.
    Includes Index.
    1. Europe — Description and travel — 17th–18th century.
    2. Great Britain — Social life and customs — 18th century.
    I. Title. II. Title: The Grand Tour.
    D917.855   1985   914'.0425   85-15005

    ISBN 0-7099-3257-X

Filmset by Patrick and Anne Murphy
Highcliffe, Dorset, England
Printed and bound in Great Britain
by Billing & Sons Limited, Worcester.

CONTENTS

PREFACE

I cannot omitt setting down here an adventure that happened to Mr Dixon at the Comte de Douglass assemblée: after he had played at cards some times with Madam de Polignac: a very handsome lady: she profered to sett him at home in her coach: which he very willingly accepted of: this young gentleman (who was a man of pleasure) finding himself alone with a fine young lady: could not forebear putting his hand where some women would not let him: after he had pleased himself thus for some time and she had bore it with a great deal of patience: she told him (in a pleasant manner) that since he had been so very free with her: she could not forbear being familiar with him: upon which she handled his arms: and finding them not fitt for present service: she beat him very heartily: he said all he could for himself: telling her that he had been upon hard duty for some time in the wars of venus: and if she would give him but one day to recruit in: he would behave himself like a man: she minded not his excuses but turned him out of the coach: and gave him this advice — 'Never to attack a young handsome lady as she was when his ammunition was spent.'

Lord Carpenter, Paris, 1717,
Bodl. Mss. Douce 67, pp. 74–6.

The Grand Tour has attracted attention for many years, and an apology is possibly necessary as a preface to this work. Most of the published work on eighteenth-century tourism has been based on printed sources. Many of these sources are extremely valuable and some are of great literary interest. However it could be suggested that excessive attention has been devoted to accounts that were intended for publication and insufficient notice has been taken of those that were never written for this purpose. There are problems with many of the latter, and it is easy to see why they have been often ignored. Many are poorly catalogued; some, such as the Wharton papers in Durham University Library, have never been catalogued. Much tourist correspondence is scattered in general political or family correspondence and is, as a result, difficult to find. A lot of the material that survives is anonymous, some of it is illegible and much of it constitutes isolated pieces of information concerning tourists about whom little else is known. As with the printed material, much of the unprinted material is repetitive. However it could be suggested that as a result of ignoring the vast bulk of unprinted material and concentrating on a relatively small number of familiar texts, a somewhat narrow conception of eighteenth-century tourism has developed.

The discussion of tourism tends to be dominated by literary considerations. To enable a wider range of sources to be consulted this book is based on an examination not only of a large number of printed sources, including some not hitherto used, but also of a considerable number of unprinted sources. Material from many archives has been used, including repositories in Aberdeen, Aylesbury, Bangor, Bedford, Bradford, Bristol, Bury-St-Edmunds, Cambridge, Carlisle, Chelmsford, Chichester, Durham, Edinburgh, Gateshead, Gloucester, Hatfield, Hertford, Huntingdon, Kidderminster, Leeds, Leicester, Lincoln, Maidstone, Manchester, Matlock, Newcastle, Nottingham, Oxford, Reading, Stafford, Taunton, Wigan and Winchester, and a large range of sources in London. It has proved impossible to consult all the available manuscript sources, but the number examined for this work is larger than that used for any comparable work; not that this entails necessarily greater comprehension of a complicated topic.

It was intended initially to confine this book to a study of the Grand Tour, the classic trip of a wealthy, young man to France and Italy for several years. However, it rapidly became apparent that although such trips could be differentiated readily from, for example, quick trips to Paris or visits to Spa for reasons of health, it was very difficult to distinguish the Grand Tour from the travels of many young men, not all of whom stayed abroad for so long or visited the same countries, but all of whom encountered the problems and experienced the joys of foreign travel. It was therefore decided to enlarge the scope of the work to include all British tourism in Europe. The limiting dates chosen, 1713 and 1793, reflect important events in British foreign policy which, particularly the latter, influenced British tourism: the Peace of Utrecht which ended Anglo-French hostilities and British participation in the War of the Spanish Succession, and the outbreak of war with revolutionary France. I have attempted not to repeat material published already.[1] As far as possible I have included large sections from the writings of eighteenth-century tourists, as it is by reading

Preface

them, rather than scholarly works, that one approaches most closely to their preoccupations, interests and attitudes. There is much research that still remains to be done in the field of eighteenth-century British tourism and many topics remain still to be examined. Hopefully this work will provoke further inquiry.

Note

1. J. Black, 'An Englishman Abroad in the 1730's', *Postmaster*, 6 (1980): 'British Travellers in Europe in the Early Eighteenth Century', *Dalhousie Review*, 61 (1981–2): 'The Grand Tour and Savoy Piedmont in the Eighteenth Century', *Studi Piedmontesi*, 13 (1984); 'France and the Grand Tour in the Early Eighteenth Century', *Francia*, 11 (1984).

ACKNOWLEDGEMENTS

I am grateful to a large number of archivists, colleagues, friends and owners of manuscripts, without whom it would have been impossible to carry out research on this topic. In the space available it is impossible to name more than a small number of those who have helped. The Duke of Beaufort, the Duke of Richmond, the Marquis of Salisbury, Earl Waldegrave and Lady Lucas permitted the consultation of their manuscripts. I am very grateful to a large number of archivists and particularly to Peter Barber, David Pearson and Beth Rainey. All or part of the work was read by Giles Barber, Eveline Cruickshanks, Grayson Ditchfield, Martin Fitzpatrick, and Hans-Joachim Possin and their comments have been of the greatest assistance. A large number of friends aided the course of research, particularly by providing invaluable hospitality. I would particularly like to mention Tony Brown, Peter Bassett, Richard Berman, John Blair, Roy Clayton, Jonathan Dent, Anthony Gross, Robert Gildea, Peter Hore, Harold James, James Kellock, Max King, James Lawrie, Jeremy Mayhew, Jon Parry, William Salomon, Peter Spear, Mark Stocker, John Tuckwell, Alan Welsford and Paul Zealander. Stuart Burrow, John Dyson, Libby Herbert and Catherine Newton gave valuable assistance. Richard Stoneman has been a very helpful publisher. The Staff of Travel and Research Fund, Durham University, provided useful assistance. I would finally like to thank two friends without whom this book would not have been written: John Lough, who read the entire work in manuscript and provided invaluable assistance and inspiration; and my wife Sarah for all her support.

NOTE ON CURRENCY

Prices are given in eighteenth-century British units of currency. £1 = 20 shillings (sh) = 240 pennies (d). Therefore 1 sh = 5 new pence. A guinea was £1 1s. The usual French units of account were sols/sous, livres and louis d'or. By modern standards exchange rates, particularly after the reform of the French currency in the mid-1720s, were remarkably constant. The following were usually quoted:

1 sol, sous	$\frac{1}{2}$d
1 livre	10d
1 louis d'or	£1 or 1 guinea

NOTE ON DATES

Until the 1752 reform of the calendar Britain conformed to Old Style, which was eleven days behind New Style, the Gregorian calendar used in most of the rest of Europe. In this work all old style dates are marked (os).

The convention by which the English New Year began on 25 March (os) has been ignored, and I have given the New Year as starting on 1 January even where (os) is used.

ABBREVIATIONS

Add.	Additional manuscripts
AE	Paris, Quai d'Orsay, Archives des Affaires Etrangères
Andrews, 1784	J. Andrews, *Letters to a Young Gentleman on his setting out for France*
Andrews, 1785	J. Andrews, *A Comparative View of the French and English Nations in their Manners, Politics and Literature*
Beds.	Bedford, Bedfordshire County Record Office
BL	London, British Library
Bodl.	Oxford, Bodleian Library
Chewton	Chewton Mendip, Chewton House, papers of James, first Earl Waldegrave
Christ Church	Oxford, Christ Church
CP	Correspondance Politique
Eg.	Egerton manuscripts
Ellison	Ellison papers, Gateshead Public Library
Essex	Chelmsford, Essex County Record Office
Gardenstone	Lord Gardenstone, *Travelling Memorandums made in a tour upon the Continent of Europe in the years 1786, 1787 and 1788* (3 vols, 1791)
Garrick, 1751	*The Diary of David Garrick being a record of his memorable trip to Paris in 1751* (New York, 1928)
Gateshead	Gateshead Public Library
Haggerston	Haggerston papers
Herts.	Hertford, Hertfordshire County Record Office
HMC	Reports of the Historical Manuscripts Commission
HP	R. R. Sedgwick (ed.), *The History of Parliament. The House of Commons 1715–54* (2 vols, London, 1970)
jnl.	Journal
Kent	Maidstone, Kent County Record Office
Leics.	Leicester, Leicestershire County Record Office
L	Lucas papers

MacLaurin	Aberdeen University Library, MacLaurin papers
Norfolk	Norwich, Norfolk County Record Office
Northumberland	Gosforth, Newcastle, Northumberland County Record Office
Orrery	John Earl of Cork and Orrery, *Letters from Italy, in the years 1754 and 1755* (1773)
PRO	London, Public Record Office, State Papers Foreign
RA	Windsor Castle, Royal Archives, Stuart Papers
RO	County Record Office
SRO	Edinburgh, Scottish Record Office
Stowe	Stowe manuscripts
Swinton	Oxford, Wadham College, Swinton journal
Thicknesse, 1768	P. Thicknesse, *Useful Hints to those who make the Tour of France* (1768), second edn, 1770
Thicknesse, *Païs Bas*	P. Thicknesse, *A Year's Journey through the Païs Bas and Austrian Netherlands* (1784)
Thicknesse, 1786	1786 edition is fuller
Wharton	Durham University Library, Wharton papers

1 NUMBERS, ROUTES AND DESTINATIONS

> To such an amazing pitch of folly is the rage for travelling come,
> that in less than six weeks, the list of Londoners arrived in Paris
> has amounted to three thousand seven hundred and sixty, as
> appears by the register of that city.
>
> *Daily Universal Register*, 29 August 1786

The eighteenth century witnessed a substantial increase in the
number of British men and women travelling abroad for pleasure.
Although it is difficult to ascertain exact figures, it is clear that the
number was a major increase on that of the previous century. In
addition, the widespread conviction that large numbers were travelling helped to widen the perception of the social importance of the
Grand Tour. Britain was not alone in this development: the
increase in tourism was a general European development, and, in
particular, large numbers of French and Germans travelled. However, it was generally agreed that the Grand Tour was dominated by
British tourists, and the fact of tourism by other nationalities rarely
played a part in the debate within Britain over the merits of
tourism.

In 1716 Henry Nassau, Viscount Boston, noted 'a great many
English gentlemen' in Geneva; the following year Alexander
Cunningham wrote of 'the abundance of English gentlemen' at
Venice. The future Bishop Berkeley provided quantification of a
sort from Rome in 1718. He noted, 'several of the nobility and
gentry of Great Britain, enough to fill two coffee houses'. The
'Etat des Anglois qui sont arrivés à Paris pendant le mois de
Decembre 1718' listed 25 tourists, in addition to merchants,
diplomats and domestics. Edward Southwell estimated the number
of English in Paris in September 1723 as 80, though the figure
included diplomats and Jacobite exiles. In May 1725 the British
envoy in Florence, Francis Colman, complained of an increase in
his expenses because of 'the number of English gentlemen who are
almost daily passing by here in their return from the Jubilee at
Rome'. The following month he provided a figure — 'I have hardly
had one hour to myself this last week by reason of the concourse of

English gentlemen that are here at present, of whom there have been above twenty.' That summer Francis Head wrote from Spa: 'Three quarters of the strangers here at present consist of the English and I believe there may be near an hundred of our nation who are most of 'em here for their health.'[1]

Paris attracted large numbers. In December 1727 Lord Waldegrave noted 'there are a good many English now in town'. Five years later he wrote, 'the Town swarms with English. I had near upon a dozen newcomers dined with me yesterday, and shall have near as many more today', whilst in 1735 he observed, 'the town swarms with English'. When, in November 1728, Horatio Walpole, envoy in Paris, gave a magnificent feast to celebrate George II's birthday the company included 'fifty Lords and Gentlemen of the British Nation'. Diplomats, such as Thomas Robinson in 1729, and tourists, noted what seemed to them to be a large number of British tourists. George Stanhope in October 1734 wrote 'there are a great number of English here', whilst the following August Robert Knight noted, 'We have had a pretty many English gentlemen and some ladies, within these 3 months last past'. Waldegrave also observed the presence of numbers of women tourists, 'This town swarms with English of both sexes'.[2]

Italy also saw large numbers of tourists in this period. The Earl of Essex, the Ambassador in Turin, disliked his posting intensely and travelled as much as possible, arousing the fury of his superiors in London. In June 1733 he wrote to his English agent informing him of one such trip to Bologna, 'the finest opera that ever was heard, and vast deal of company, there was 32 English'. The following month Colonel Elizeus Burges, the hard-drinking Resident in Venice, wrote 'Italy swarms of late with English gentlemen and ladies'. Two years earlier Bagshaw, the Consul in Genoa, wrote of the 'vast number of English gentlemen' in Rome. In 1737 Arthur Villettes, the Secretary at Turin, commented on 'a great number of English in this town' and listed twelve travellers. Richard Pococke noted 40 English in Rome in February 1734. Given these numbers it might be suggested that newspaper comments on 'that fondness for gadding beyond seas, which is at present so epidemical in this country' were overstated. Diplomats emphasised the numbers of tourists because they had to entertain them, and often to present them at court, a major call on their finances and time. The numbers who travelled in the first half of the century, though large by seventeenth-century standards, barely hinted at the numbers who were to travel in the seond half of the century.[3]

The European conflicts of 1739–48 did not stop British tourism, but they limited the number of travellers. The end of war led to a revival. In 1751 the *Newcastle Courant* carried a report from Rome,

> The English Lords and Ladies which are in this City, are so numerous as to be able to form amongst themselves a society as considerable as that of the Roman Noblesse. They have hired for that purpose a Palace, where there is every Evening an Assembly for Play, a concert of musick, and a supper;

In one morning in Paris, the actor David Garrick 'made twenty visits of English Gentlemen'. In February 1753 Lord North wrote: 'There are about 40 travellers of our nation now in Rome reckoning females.'[4]

The early 1750s witnessed a return to the level of tourism in the 1730s. This level was not to be decisively passed until after the Peace of Paris of 1763 which ended the Seven Years war. Thereafter the level remained high, albeit falling when Anglo-French hostilities commenced over the American rebellion, until the French successes in the early stages of the Revolutionary war made Italy, the Low Countries and the Rhineland as apparently unsafe as the French Revolution had already made France. The numbers travelling were not solely for tourism. In April 1769 one London newspaper reported that the students at the University of Göttingen included 'above fifty English noblemen and gentlemen'. In July 1787 another paper noted 'Brussels is over-run by indigent Englishmen'.[5] The press also commented on a massive expansion in tourism,

> So great is the Traffick for passengers on the Dover Road, that the Inns are often forced to club an Horse each to make up the necessary number for a post-coach-and-four; and several gentlemen, we are told, have been forced to wait the return of a carriage, to pursue the rest of their journey.
>
> . . . no less than six boats being constantly employed in carrying over passengers there [Dieppe], and near a score well-built inns kept by Englishmen on the road to Rouen.
>
> A gentleman who lately came from Calais assures us, that there

are near 200 French remises to be sold there belonging to the English nobility and gentry, who leave them there at the end of their travels.

Large numbers continued to visit France and Italy. When St Vincent caught the diligence from Paris to Chalon in 1772 half the passengers were English. Robert Wharton found 'upwards of thirty' English in Dijon, and Geneva 'brimfull of English'.[6] In 1784 Joseph Cradock found Paris so full of English that he had little opportunity to practise his French. The following year Mr Davies wrote from Rome: 'This year indeed, the English themselves form a considerable body; being more numerous, than at any period since the nation has travelled. Already most of the lodgings are engaged at Naples, and scarcely half the company arrived.' Numbers varied greatly by season and year. By December British tourists in Italy would have generally left Rome for Naples, returning in the spring and then leaving Rome for northern Italy as the summer heat and risk of malaria advanced. In late December 1787 Philip Lloyd informed Lord Hawkesbury that there were 'near 50' British tourists in Rome. On 8 May 1792 Lady Knight wrote from Rome: 'We have had a hundred and fifty English here this spring, but few of them are left.' In March 1793 Thomas Brand noted Rome as 'full of English of every sort'; the following February he estimated the number of British tourists in Naples as about 130.[7]

Several regions saw a distinct expansion in the number of British tourists in the late eighteenth century. The Riviera became fashionable in the 1780s as a winter resort, though numbers varied. Three hundred British tourists spent the winter of 1784—5 in Nice, but in December 1789 Nathanial Green, the Consul in Nice, wrote: 'There are but few English, about twenty individuals.' Probably the disturbances in France dissuaded tourists from visiting Nice, a Sardinian possession. There was a marked increase in the numbers visiting Switzerland — Geneva had always been popular for educational reasons. Unlike Angers, Tours, Lunéville and Turin, Geneva (like Utrecht and Leyden) was a town with educational facilities that was Protestant and in the latter half of the century tourism in Switzerland developed. In 1770 one British traveller noted 'there were a good many English at Geneva'; in 1785 another wrote from Lausanne 'I suppose the English colony consists of about 80'.[8]

As tourism became less the monopoly of the wealthy, increasing numbers of less affluent tourists travelled. They preferred a shorter and less expensive alternative to the Grand Tour, and few of them visited Italy. Instead they tended to travel to Paris and the Low Countries, and the latter witnessed an expansion in British tourism. The journals of British tourists in the Low Countries noted frequently the presence of compatriots. In 1772 one traveller found two English gentlemen in the Hotel l'Impérial in Brussels; in 1773 James Essex wrote from Antwerp 'soon after our return to the hotel several English gentlemen arrived'.[9] Another area that saw a marked expansion in British tourism was east-central Europe, particularly Berlin, Dresden and Vienna. In 1769 Robert Keith, envoy in Dresden, complained: 'I have, within this month, had an inundation of English, who have nearly eaten me out of house and home. The nine and twentieth left me a week ago.' Five years later, transferred to Vienna, Keith complained, 'here come half a score of Etonians'; and in 1785 he wrote, 'I am to have a prodigious colony of John Bulls this winter: Lords Wycombe, Ancram, Guildford, Glasgow, Dungannon, etc., etc., and commoners by the scores'. He added that in twelve years he had presented four hundred 'young gentlemen at the Imperial Court', the same figure as that he gave Lady Craven. When Keith saw a chess playing automaton at Pressburg (Bratislava) in 1774 he noted the presence of another 16 British travellers. In December 1785 Craven noted at Vienna, 'there are so many Englishmen here, that, when I am at Sir Robert Keith's, I am half tempted to fancy myself in England'. Seven years later Brand wrote from Vienna, 'Here are but two or three English'.[10]

Numbers therefore varied greatly, and though British tourists could be sure of the company of compatriots in Paris and the major Italian cities, this was not the case elsewhere. By modern or even nineteenth-century standards there were very few tourists, but contemporaries had no doubt that they were witnessing a significant social revolution. Their overwhelming impression was of the numbers travelling. Brand wrote from Lausanne in September 1783: 'I mean to be at Rome Decr. the 1st. There is such a shoal of English upon the road thither that "the like was never known".'[11]

Itinerary

The Grand Tour involved essentially a trip to Paris and a tour of the principal Italian cities: Rome, Venice Florence and Naples, in order of importance. Around this basis a variety of possible itineraries could be devised. Personal preference, fashion, convenience and the impact of external factors — war, political disorder and disease — were all of importance. The first stage of the journey was that to the British coast. The overwhelming proportion of tourists went to Dover in order to cross to Calais. There were, however, other crossings. At times of Anglo-French tension tourists could cross from Dover to Ostend, or, more commonly, Harwich to Helvoetsluys. This Dutch port was also the destination for those intending to tour the United Provinces, and possibly to go on to Germany (the Holy Roman Empire) or France. Very few tourists sailed directly to the Baltic or Mediterranean. In the absence of passenger ships it was necessary to rely on a warship, a merchantman or a privately hired ship, such as the yacht in which Lord Baltimore cruised round the Baltic in 1739. The terrors of a Channel crossing in poorly stabilised ships encouraged British tourists, most of whom had never been to sea before, to plump for the shortest crossing. After 1763 an increasing number of tourists chose crossings further west. Sailings from Brighton or Weymouth to Dieppe or Cherbourg became more common. However, the Dover-Calais crossing retained its dominance. One newspaper, commenting on the increased popularity of the Dieppe route, observed in 1769, 'however this may suit the trading people, Calais will always be the port for our Gentry, who had rather go thirty leagues more post by land, than cross twenty leagues of water instead of seven'. William Grenville preferred to return from a diplomatic mission to the United Provinces 'through Flanders, and by Calais, partly from curiosity, and partly to avoid the necessity of passing at least 24 hours in the tortures of the damned'.[12]

The three principal difficulties connected with a crossing were adverse winds, seasickness and problems of disembarkation. Total dependence on the wind led to irritating delays. John Leake waited five days at Harwich in September 1759 and was becalmed for a complete day on his passage to the United Provinces. Eight years later Lord Fife complained from Calais 'Here have I been three days, tired to death, detained with contrary winds, now going aboard at eleven o'clock at night, but likely to be drove back again'. In 1784 John Aikin was delayed by contrary winds and calms on a passage from Harwich to Helvoetsluys. Three years later Robert Arbuthnot recorded 'We were detained so long at Ostend and had so tedious a passage to Dover, . . .'. Arthur

Young was delayed at Calais in November 1787 waiting 'three days for a wind (the Duke and Duchess of Gloucester are in the same inn and situation) and for a pacquet'. Two years later Young wrote 'Passage to Calais, 14 hours for reflection in a vehicle that does not allow one power to reflect'. Too much wind could be as trouble-some as too little. In March 1730 Charles Thompson embarked at Dover 'for Calais, but a strong easterly wind rising soon after we had put to sea, drove us so far down the Channel, that the first French port we could make was Dieppe'. Five years later the Duchess of Norfolk was nearly drowned in a storm when crossing from Calais to Dover. Lady Craven made the same passage in a gale with her terrified mother and a sister who fainted. In November 1789 Brand crossed from Harwich to Helvoetsluys,

The wind was boisterous and changeable and the sea very high. We were obliged to lay to during 10 hours of the night under storm-sails for fear of approaching too near the coast of Holland. My poor young man all this while bringing to his recol-lection in much too lively colours every picture of shipwrecks and marine distress that he had ever seen. I did what I could to keep up his spirits . . . though I was neither frightened nor sick I was bitter sorry. We were 30 hours at sea.[13]

Seasickness was a major drawback to a Channel crossing. Despite a fine crossing to Calais the Duchess of Queensberry was sick in 1734. Making the same crossing in a brisk gale the poet Thomas Gray was very sick five years later. Leake was 'con-foundedly sick' in the 'rough sea' east of Harwich. 'Poor Mrs Carter' was a 'good deal' sick on the Dover-Calais crossing in 1763 though of her companions Mrs Montagu 'was not in the least sick; . . . Mr. Montagu and Dr. Douglas eat cold ham all the way. My Lord Bath was in gay spirits . . .'. Despite 'a most excellent passage' to Calais, Wharton was 'sea sick most part of the way. It is the most disagreeable sickness imaginable'. In 1786 Brand,

. . . had almost the quickest passage ever known, 2 hours and 40 minutes brought us to the gates of Calais — As usual I had no other amusement than to watch the Seagulls, Willocks and Porpoises unless I chose to pity the pale and wan faces of my fellow travellers or to listen to the splash of their evacuations which were most copious indeed as you will readily guess from the rapidity of our motion what immense billows we were tossed upon.[14]

It was hardly surprising that many found their Channel crossing a terrible ordeal. Spark Molesworth had to rest at Calais after 'the great fatigue of ye sea'. Fife spent 'two terrible days at sea' in the Channel in 1766. Pastor Stevens, returning from the Low Countries, was 'three weeks in a most terrible tempest', and driven to the Norwegian coast. Zachary Grey, taking a boat from Zeeland to Antwerp, ran aground. The boat floated off next tide, but sank as a result of being holed. Having struggled ashore Grey had to walk 14 miles to find lodgings. Terror gripped the Duchess of Bedford when the Duke planned a trip to Lisbon and Naples. She complained to her grandmother Sarah Marlborough: 'I have the greatest dread imaginable of it; going by sea I know would kill me, the least retching in the world gives me a pain in my side, and breast, and to be so sick as almost everybody is at sea, I should never go through; . . .'[15]

Having crossed the sea it was often difficult to land. The combination of wind, tide, and poor harbours meant that it was often necessary to transfer to a rowboat, a hazardous operation that left travellers prone to extortion. Sacheverell Stevens's boat was prevented by the tide from anchoring in Boulogne harbour in 1738 and he found the demands of the rowboat excessive. Lady Mary Coke was drenched in a little boat in 1764 and could be landed no nearer than four miles from Calais. William Cole was injured in 1765 changing boats in a rough sea in the dark off Dover.[16]

Once ashore tourists had a choice of routes. From Calais the majority travelled to Paris, a short journey along reasonably good roads with inns that were prepared for tourists, if only to charge them too much. A number travelled east from the Channel ports. Some, such as the Duchess of Queensberry in 1734 and the Earl of Bath in 1763, travelled to Spa, in the Ardennes, the most popular European watering place for British tourists. In August 1732 there were nearly 100 'English gentlemen and ladies there'.[17] The route to Spa was a good one, going along excellent roads through Brussels to Liège, although from Liège onwards the road deteriorated. It was possible to continue from Spa into Germany, travelling through Aachen to Cologne. Another route from the Channel ports ran through Lille, Rheims and Laon to Lorraine, where Nancy and the academy at Lunéville attracted travellers. Some tourists, such as the anonymous author of a journal of 1720–1, who attended the Lunéville academy, or Robert Trevor, who made a brief tour from the international peace congress at Soissons,[18] went no further. Others pressed on to Strasbourg and thence into Germany, or to Switzerland. From Calais, Ostend and Helvoetsluys it was possible to tour the Low Countries and then enter Germany, either in order to travel up the Rhine towards Munich, Innsbruck and Italy, or eastwards across Westphalia to Hanover.

Hanover had been visited by very few British tourists in the late seventeenth century. Its subsequent popularity owed everything to the accession of the Hanoverian dynasty in 1714. George I and George II frequently revisited the town, though George III never went there. It was the royal presence that encouraged British tourists eager for patronage or concerned to appear loyal. John Hervey was sent to Hanover in 1716 to ingratiate himself with George II's son, Prince Frederick. His father, the Earl of Bristol, wrote to him, 'when you see and are sure ye foundation in Prince Frederick's favour . . . is laid as indelibly as you know I would have it, . . . you may think of returning homewards'. The Duke of Manchester hoped that his son, Lord Mandeville, would benefit from his stay by acquiring a knowledge of German that could be useful. George I's visit to Hanover in 1716 was matched by that of the sons of the Dukes of Bolton, Kent and St Albans, and by John Clavering, who complained of the Hanoverian reception. Edward Finch's search for preferment led him from an Italian trip to Hanover in 1723 whilst the Marquis of Carnarvon visited Hanover on his way home in 1727 in order to solicit the post of Lord of the Bedchamber to Prince Frederick. Lord Strathnaver was told to do the same. Charles Fane was advised by his father that 'it would be both pleasant and proper to go to Hanover to pay his court to ye Prince of Wales', a course of action decried by Sarah Marlborough. In 1785 Sir Grey Cooper sought to turn the presence in Hanover of George III's son, the Duke of York, to some advantage. He decided that his son should return from Vienna to London via Berlin, Hanover, Brussels and Ostend, and he wrote to Keith,

> If you will honour him with a letter to his Royal Highness the Duke or to General Grenville, his reception at Hanover will repay him for his deviation from his road, and perhaps may procure him the distinction of being the bearer of any letters

which their Royal Highnesses may at the time of his arrival have occasion to convey to London.[19]

The reception of British tourists at Hanover was not always good. Lord Gage was denied access to the court in 1723; Lords Nassau Powlett and Burford complained of their treatment in 1716; and George II was extremely rude to aristocratic British tourists in 1750. Lord Nunehan found the court far from entertaining. And yet other tourists praised their reception. Nicholas Clagett, Pococke, John Baring and Sacheverell Stevens praised the courtesy and hospitality of the Hanoverians.[20] After September 1755 no British Monarch visited Hanover, and the need for aristocratic tourists to visit the town diminished. However, the number of tourists remained high. This reflected the increased popularity of central Europe for British tourists in the second half of the century. Tourists who followed, or hoped to follow, a military career attended the important Prussian military reviews and visited Hanover en route for Berlin, Magdeburg or Silesia (the locations of these reviews). In 1787 Captain John Barker, having attended reviews at Berlin, Potsdam and Magdeburg, visited Brunswick and Hanover on his way back to Britain. Mr Lyttleton, son of Lord Westcote, met Colonel Gordon in Silesia in 1787 whilst visiting the battlefield of Leuthen. Sir James Murray attended the Austrian reviews, and Charles Stewart those of Prussia and Austria.[21]

Hanover also benefited from the growing popularity of Dresden and Vienna. In the first half of the century few British tourists visited Saxony. Charles Cottrell visited Dresden in June 1741, but his route was a highly unusual one for the first half of the century. He sailed to St Petersburg and then travelled by land to Königsberg, Dresden, Bratislava, Vienna, Munich, Basle and the United Provinces. In 1751–2 Lord North, the future Prime Minister, and his step-brother William Legge, second Earl of Dartmouth, attended lectures at Leipzig, given by 'the celebrated Mr. Mascou'. Dartmouth was very pleased with the journey to Saxony, and he left an interesting account of the lectures he attended,

I really think it well worth anybody's while to travel so far, for the sake of a few months instructions from him. He begins a course upon the *Droit Publique* after Michaelmas, in the meantime he is giving us a system of modern history, from the latter end of the fifteenth century, which is inexpressibly instructive and entertaining. He is most thoroughly master of the subject, by which he is enabled to select such events as are most interesting and important, to dwell upon: he delivers himself in Latin, but he speaks so slow and distinct, and makes use of so elegant and pure a style, that notwithstanding the disguise of a German pronunciation, he makes himself clearly understood; as he goes along he makes many lively and judicious remarks, interposes little amusing anecdotes, and recommends to us the best writers on the several parts of history of which he treats.

Dartmouth liked Leipzig, though he did not approve of all the social customs,

This town is situated in a flat, but it is one of the richest and pleasantest spots I have met with in the country; in point of buildings, it is undoubtedly, much the handsomest of any town we have yet seen (I mean in Germany) and the inhabitants are reckoned more lively than their neighbours. This is a week of diversion . . . we dined one day in a tent with a large company of gentlemen and ladies, for the most part neither young nor handsome; as very few of them could talk anything but German, it was disagreeable enough. There were no dishes set upon the table, they were all carved without and sent round one by one, so that we were 3 hours at dinner, though we had not above half a dozen dishes: in the meantime bumper glasses came round to loyal healths, but everybody filled as they pleased, and there were none that seemed inclined to drink to excess. When these were over a long German sentence came round for toast, which I did not in the least understand, but as soon as the first gentleman had drank it, to my great surprise, he got up, went round the table and kissed all the Ladies. I happened to sit next so had no time to deliberate, but was obliged to follow his example; not without some reluctance; the weather was hot, and it was sad clammy work. The novelty of the thing surprised me, and the indecency of it shocked me; however agreeable it might prove in particular cases, I never wish to see the custom prevail in England.

The following spring the two friends visited Dresden,

We spent a fortnight in a sort of little London, in a continual hurry of amusements; as they have no publick diversions any part of the year except during the carnival, which begins upon twelfth-day and ends upon Shrove-Tuesday, they make all the use of that time that is possible and crowd diversions, upon the back of another, every day of the week, Sunday not excepted . . . We have danced a great deal, and have been at 3 balls of a night. I did not expect to see English country dances so well danced, out of England; but I find they are universally esteemed and practiced in all the courts of Europe, and here there are a great many, who dance them extreamely well, both men and women; in one respect I think they exceed us that they dance them slower than we do, and yet not too slow . . . We are extremely happy here in the fine weather we have enjoyed . . .[22]

In the second half of the century an increasing number of tourists visited Saxony and, in particular, Dresden. The beautification of the city and the purchase of the bulk of the Duke of Modena's collection of Italian paintings attracted tourists. Dresden was less forbidding than Berlin and more cosmopolitan than both Berlin and Hanover. In 1786 Muir Mackenzie thought the sights 'well worth the pains of going to see'. The first Marquis of Lansdowne's illegitimate son Mr Petty spent the winter of 1786–7 at Leipzig with his wife and daughter,

We have passed our winter in this place and I do assure you *extreamely well* and *agreably*; and forgetting that the first people here are merchants, have found their society very pleasing and on a very easy footing — I have made some valuable literary acquaintances and found the society of men of letters very advantageous, and as I am neither too old nor above instruction have profited much by attending those Professors who lecture on my favourite sciences — I have hired a pleasant house out of the town where we shall pass most of the summer with making only sometimes little journeys to Berlin.

Captain Barker, returning home from Vienna, wrote: 'The more I see of Dresden the better I like it; gaiety perhaps does not prevail quite so much as at Vienna; but here are some very good people.'
Thomas Brand was very impressed by the pictures though he was unimpressed by the entertainments,

. . . we expected to have found much amusement and gaiety at

Dresden but we had not a single invitation anywhere and there
was not so much as a theatre . . . a beautiful town with a
magnificent bridge over the Elbe with sentinals who make you go
on one side and come back on the other, a restraint that Englishmen are very refractory about. I must own I never had so violent
a desire to walk up and down the same side of a bridge in my life.

Revisiting the city five years later he wrote, 'It was full of English
boys' — and commented on the 'treasures of art and literature'.[23]
The route from Saxony to Vienna went through Bohemia. Between
Dresden and Prague it was necessary to pass the Bohemian mountains. This was far from easy and the road, which ran through the
Elbe gorge, was a bad one. William Bentinck wrote to his mother
from Prague in January 1727, that he had not

had the least accident which very frequently happen to travellers;
when the roads are bad, and that we go up or down steep hills,
we walk it, which is the safest, and in such places, one loses no
time by it . . . between this and Dresden, coming along the
banks of the Elbe, where there is room but exactly for one chaise,
with a steep rock on one side, and a precipice on t'other, with the
river at the bottom.

Thomas Robinson wrote in 1744: 'at Aussig there is only a causeway, hardly broad enough for two carriages to pass, between the
foot of the mountain and the Elbe, where I myself have always
chosen to go on foot rather than to sit in my coach and see the river
howling under me, . . .' Paintings of the scene leave no doubt of its
dangers.[24]
The accommodation in Bohemia, outside Prague, was poor.
Travelling from Passau to Pilsen in April 1743 the Earl of
Crawford 'met with such miserable accommodation that he was
obliged to lie all the night upon straw, with a large family of
children in the same room with him'. Bentinck informed his
mother,

This is the best country in the world to use one's self to hardness.
Indeed in the towns, one meets with pretty good houses now and
then, but in all the villages, one must lie upon straw, very often
stinking, because there is no fresh to be had, and when with a
great deal ado, you have got one truss, if you ask for a second,

they stare at you, like mad, being not used to so much magnificence. Add to that bugs, and flees, and the vermin that grows in the straw, and it will make a very pretty bed, but I have one suit of cloaths, which is condemned to serve me upon the road, which is already dirty as it can be and in that I lye down and sleep as comfortably as in a bed. In the beginning I did not like it a bit, but now, I do not mind it . . .[25]

Bohemian roads were not particularly good, though, as with most of Europe, they improved during the century. Most tourists spent very little time in Prague, though those that did spend a few days tended to like the city. In Vienna, on the other hand, tourists tended to stay for more than a few days. Opinions of the city and of its society varied greatly. The Earl of Sunderland informed his grandmother, Sarah Marlborough: 'Though this place is not usually the most agreable in the world to strangers, yet for my part I can't complain of it, for everybody has shewed me a vast deal of civility here.' The Duke of Grafton was not sure that his son, Lord Euston, would benefit from a visit to Vienna — 'it is just come into mind that Vienna and what our young man will see there will not be a great addition to his education.' The 'hard drinking' of Viennese society was attacked by Francis Panton in 1726 and by Robinson 15 years later: 'Society here is most dull and inanimate. Few men are to be found, and though one resolves to pass time well, it all amounts at last to eating and drinking, cheering the mere animal which is true Austrian life . . .' Brand wrote in 1792: 'I wish I were away from Vienna. Here are but two or three English . . . and they are of a bad sort. They are of the two idea sort. The bottle is one. *Davus* can tell the other.' The etiquette and ceremony of the court and of Viennese society was attacked by travellers, by the German Baron Pöllnitz, whose travels were widely read in Britain (they were excerpted by the *Daily Gazeteer* in the late 1730s), and by Petty. In 1786 Keith informed the Marquis of Lansdowne that his son Lord Wycombe and Wycombe's companion, Major Green, had not enjoyed their stay in Vienna: 'I am afraid that from the stiffness of Austrian manners and the cold uninteresting style of conversation which prevails here, their stay at Vienna has, in point of amusement as well as of instruction, fallen short of their expectation, as well as of my wishes.'[26]

Alexander Thomson was unimpressed by the town,

In the number of superb structures Vienna is doubtless remarkable; yet after all, I must abate from this general eulogium of its grandeur. The streets, excepting those in the suburbs, are narrow and dirty; the houses and furniture of the citizens are greatly disproportioned to the magnificence of the palaces, squares, and other public buildings; but above all, the excessive imposts laid by the house of Austria upon every commodity in its dominions, must always keep the manufacturing part of their subjects in a state of poverty, as is but too visible in the capital itself.[27]

Other tourists praised the town. Lady Craven visited Vienna in December 1785 and was delighted by the affability of Viennese women and the range of food available — large crawfish, delicious pheasants, artichokes and asparagus. The numbers visiting the city never approached those who visited Paris. Vienna involved a longer and more expensive journey, its court society did not attract non-aristocratic tourists. Lord Torrington, envoy in Brussels, wrote to Keith in 1786, 'the English who go to Vienna, are a very different and superior class of people to those who come to Bruxelles . . . fewer in number and more respectable personages . . .'. The numbers of British tourists to Vienna increased during the century.

Early in the century a trip to Vienna involved a certain amount of hardiness. Of the three prominent travellers who were in Vienna in October 1730 — the Duke of Portland, the Earl of Radnor and Sir Francis Dashwood — the latter two could better be described as intrepid travellers rather than tourists. The private papers of several of the British envoys in Vienna, Waldegrave, Robinson and Keith, reveal a marked increase in the number of tourists. In 1788 Lord Townshend could refer to 'the Vienna Club' in London, a group of friends who had enjoyed Keith's hospitality. Interest in Austria was increased by Joseph II's policies, and the improved facilities for travellers encouraged more tourists to travel to or from Italy via Vienna. To a certain extent the German alternative, the route to Italy that did not go through France, became less a matter of the Rhineland, Frankfurt, Munich and Innsbruck, and more one of Hanover, Dresden and Vienna. The shift received royal approval. In 1783 George III told Lord and Lady Courtown, 'You cannot do better than send your son to Vienna'.[28]

Whatever the appeal of the German route, the bulk of British travellers to Europe preferred to visit France, or rather Paris. It is true that some British tourists did not wish to see Paris, or did not enjoy their visit. John Pelham wrote from Nancy: 'I have heard such an account of Paris that I am quite out of conceit of going there. Everything is insufferable dear, and will be I am sure according to the character that I hear of it very disagreeable.' Robert Trevor left Paris in 1729 'without the least regret, being heartily tired of it'. Lord Boyle disliked the Parisians. Lord Grosvenor 'tired so soon' of the city that he 'returned posthaste to London'. Nevertheless, whatever the complaints, large numbers of travellers visited the city. Their activities varied greatly. George James Cholmondeley ran a gaming table; Hans Stanley studied international law; the Duke of Kingston returned to London in 1736 with the wife of a Parisian civil servant.[29] 'The joys of Paris'[30] were those of a metropolis that could offer all the adventures and activities of social life and all the facilities for comfort and yet be different, exciting, foreign and new.

Most British tourists saw little of France aside from Paris, the road to it from Calais and the routes from it to Italy. Few toured provincial France and those who travelled through it tended to do so for a specific reason: to attend the academy at Lunéville, to go for medical treatment at Montpellier, to travel between Paris and Germany, or, like Arthur Young, to travel for reasons of scholarship. The Loire valley was fairly popular in the first half of the century. At Angers and Tours (as at Besançon, where Richard Lyttleton studied in the academy in 1737, Lunéville and Geneva) young travellers could learn French and acquire expertise in some of the attributes of gentility, such as dancing, fencing and riding, without, it was hoped, being exposed to the vices of the metropolis. Simon, second Viscount Harcourt and Edward Mellish, both in the Loire Valley in the early 1730s, noted the presence of other British visitors. Lord and Lady Berkeley visited Bolingbroke at his seat at Chanteloup near Amboise in 1735. Lord Balgonie stayed at Tours in 1774. However, the Loire was not visited by large numbers of tourists and by the late eighteenth century its relative popularity had fallen sharply. Joseph Cradock noted that 'Blois, though particularly interesting, is not, even now, much frequented by the English; indeed it lies out of the general route'.[31] Possibly the gentle beauty of the Loire did not appeal to a generation increasingly obsessed by mountains and the raw beauty of nature. Probably the towns of the valley suffered from the fact that, in tourist terms, they led to nowhere. Dijon, Chalon-sur-Saone, and Avignon did not appeal to eighteenth-century tastes more than Angers, Blois and Tours; that they were visited more reflected the popularity of Italy and the unpopularity of Spain and south-western France. Travelling in provincial France was made less attractive by the poor state of the roads. The fifth Earl of Leven noticed this when he left the St Omer-Lille road in 1749 and Lady Craven complained of bad cross-country roads in Touraine in 1785.³² And yet a number of tourists did travel through provincial France. St Vincent went on a circular tour from Paris to Toulouse and back via Bordeaux. Balgonie visited Brittany in 1774, and Brand Toulouse in 1783. Provincial France was not dangerous to travel through, but its appeal was limited. St Vincent in his tour did not visit Italy. Few would have copied his decision to visit provincial France instead.

From Paris to Italy the route was clear to Lyons. Travellers went, either by the Lyons diligence or in other vehicles, to Dijon and then to Chalon-sur-Saône. At Chalon they would usually embark on the *diligence par eau* for a two day trip down the Saône to Lyons. Most travellers found this very pleasant. Andrew Mitchell observed: 'this way of travelling is expeditious and would not be disagreeable if one was sure to find good company: The charming prospects along the banks of the river are very entertaining.' Praise was also voiced by Sacheverell Stevens and Charles Thompson. Robert Wharton, travelling as far as Mâcon, whence he was to take a coach to Geneva, found pleasant company on the boat: 'we talked and chatted till the cool of the evening when we went on deck above the chamber and enjoyed the prospect. The river is as large as the Thames at Dachet; its sides covered with rich pastures abounding in cattle. At a distance are seen the mountains of Bresse and Bugey . . .' At the end of November 1772 St Vincent took the boat to Lyons,

> . . . a very convenient passage boat and must be a very agreable way of travelling in a more favourable season, being attended with no fatigue and affording a delightful prospect of the country on the borders of the river. This boat stops to dine and lye, at different places in its course. They have the bad habit of rewarding their coachmen and boatmen before they arrive at their place of destination whereby the passengers are entirely neglected and left a prey to a crowd of canaille under the name of porters, many of them sharpers and all imposters — which we had full demonstration of on our arrival at Lyons — the boat being constantly filled with these people, who but for the friendly

interposition of a French gentleman, would have fleeced us handsomely — This mode of travelling, so apparently commodious to weakly people has one great inconvenience, the want of a necessary, which indeed may be supplied by a portable close stool.[33]

From Lyons, 'the pleasantest city in France',[34] the problem of the Alps had to be confronted. It was necessary to cross them or to circumvent them by sea. It was impossible to follow a coastal route on land. It was possible to go on land from Marseilles and Toulon to the Sardinian border. There was an absence of good roads in the Sardinian county of Nice, though it was possible to reach Nice and Monaco by land. However these roads were not good. An anonymous journal of 1776–7 noted of the area near Nice,

These torrent-courses are the roads, and, in some parts, the only roads of the country . . . A road has been formed from Nice over Montalban to Villafranca, just practicable for a carriage, but so steep and so rough that it is scarcely safe; and a carriage is very seldom seen on it . . . The road to Monaco is practicable only for mules, asses, or mountain horses; and in some parts is scarcely safe with any of them.

The writer found the road to Monaco so bad that he got off his mule and went on foot. Lady Craven wrote from Antibes in 1785: 'Most part of the road from Hyeres to this place is very mountainous and narrow.'[35] East of Monaco the Ligurian mountains fall sheer to the sea and it was impossible to go by land to Genoa via Oneglia, Finale and Savona. The corniche road on the Riviera was not opened until Napoleon's time. It was possible from Nice to enter Italy by crossing the Alps to Turin through the Col (pass) of Tenda. The anonymous writer just quoted also noted,

the road is utterly impracticable for a carriage; and scarcely to be travelled by an ordinary horse; mules are chiefly used on it: and tender ladies and infirm men have no succedaneum but a sedan chair. It is three days journey over the mountains to the plains of Piedmont for a mule, and five for a sedan chair. The narrow rugged path which is called the road, is conducted up the courses of different torrents . . .

Galley slaves were then building a carriage road to Turin. This was to be opened the following decade: the first complete opening of an alpine pass to wheeled traffic. The writer, concerned more with the convenience of tourists than the interests of Victor Amadeus III, regretted that the road was not being built from Nice to Genoa.[36]

Tourists had to choose between the Alps and the Mediterranean. Neither was an attractive prospect. By sea there was the risk of storms, and the lesser risk of Barbary pirates, as well as the major inconvenience of contrary winds or being becalmed, and the minor inconvenience of the quality of accommodation available on the maritime trip. The boats used, the feluccas, were small, vulnerable to storms and dependent on the wind. In 1723 John Molesworth wrote: 'No mariners in the world are so cowardly as the Italians in general, but especially the Genoese; so that upon the least appearance of a rough sea, they run into the first creek where their feluccas are sometimes wind-bound for a month.' He also commented on the impact of storms on the feluccas. Francis Head was very impressed by the beauty of the Ligurian coast. In 1734 Andrew Mitchell had a troublesome passage from Genoa: 'I was detained some weeks longer at Genoa than I intended, and that by bad weather, for if it blows the least or if there is anything of a sea, the feluccas won't go out. I hired a felucca with 3 men from Genoa to Antibes for 3 pistols and a half.' On 1 November Mitchell left Genoa and got that night to Savona. The next contrary wind obliged Mitchell to put into Laon and have the felucca hauled onshore as there was no harbour. 'I was detained here a whole day by the laziness of the Italian sailors who chose rather to lie in the port and take their chance for a wind afterwards than to put to sea in fair weather. If there is the least swell in the sea they will by no means venture out.' Later in the trip he was delayed for another two days by adverse winds and indolent sailors.

Five years later Stevens sailed from Marseilles to Genoa,

On Sunday, May 31, I embarked in a felucca for Italy, having first laid in a good stock of provision, as cold tongues, ham, bread, wine, etc. This precaution will be of service to those who may perform this voyage; for in these feluccas it is uncertain where you may by drove to, which was my case; for we had not sailed above a day and a half, when the weather began to be extremely bad, and the sea became so rough and boisterous, that the waves very often beat over us; the mariners were now terribly daunted, the boat being half full of water; and for want of pails, etc. to fling it out, we were obliged to make use of our hats; . . . I grew so sick, that I could do no service . . .

After this storm between Marseilles and Antibes there was another between St Remo and Savona. At Savona Stevens was detained three days by contrary winds. The stage from Savona to Genoa saw another bad storm and at Genoa they were nearly driven by waves on to the breakwater. Stevens determined 'never to trust myself any more in a felucca'. Lady Knight sailed from Marseilles to Civitavecchia in 1778, 'our voyage was somewhat tedious, as we were, after seven weeks waiting for a wind, thirty days on our passage, putting into different ports'. In August 1785 Lady Craven hired a felucca 'a long narrow boat with three shoulder-of-mutton sails, and ten oars' — to take her from Antibes to Leghorn (Livorno). Told of the danger from Barbary corsairs, she observed: 'I cannot say I am the least afraid, since the very fears of my Italian sailors will prevent them from going farther from the shore than what is absolutely necessary for sailing.'[37]

The majority of tourists preferred to cross the Alps. This was less hazardous and unpredictable than the maritime route, though it was also dependent on seasonal factors. The most common route into Italy was from Lyons through the Duchy of Savoy, over the Mt Cenis pass to Susa and thence to Turin. As the pass was not suitable for wheeled vehicles it was necessary to dismantle the carriages near the foot of the pass. These were then carried over the pass on mules whilst the tourists were carried in a type of sedan chair by porters. Crossing in 1734 Richard Pococke was 'carried down in a chair without legs, with poles to the sides, carried by two men'. He was delighted by the speed of the crossing and observed 'it is nothing at all'. In 1719 Sir Carnaby Haggerston had 'a very pleasant passage of Mont Senis'. Thomas Brand crossed the pass in October 1783,

We passed Mt. Cenis after bad weather and it was covered with snow six or eight inches deep but even in that state we could not help shrugging our shoulders and shaking our heads at the extravagant exaggerations of danger which most travellers indulge themselves in describing that famous passage. It was indeed a little cold in going up but once on the plain the air was temperate enough and at the descent it was mild beyond expectation. We rode up upon mules and were carried down by porters: you sit in a kind of chair carried on poles like a sedan with a piece of wood or a cord to press your feet against and a little elbow to rest your arms on. In this manner with your legs and thighs in a straight horizontal position and in the plane of the poles the porters whisk you with incredible strength and celerity down a steep stony road with sharp angles at each turn. Perhaps for the first five or six minutes I was under some fright but the firmness of their steps soon set me at ease and the beautiful cascades that present themselves on every side and the majesty of the hoary mountains that surrounded me furnished me with sufficient matter of admiration and astonishment.

Thomas Pelham crossed in early 1777,

. . . crossing Mount Ceni is certainly a great undertaking in point of conveying the carriages etc., but as to our own persons there is neither danger nor inconvenience; it was so hard a frost that when we came to the top of the mountain we left our chairs and descending in sledges which though very trying to the *nerves* was not unpleasant. It was the clearest day imaginable and our view beyond all description.

In early 1764 Henry Ellison junior 'passed the Alps without danger and almost without difficulty'.[38] The Alpine passages were not always so easy. In 1732 Edward Raddon, a royal messenger, had to cross the Cenis 'on foot on account of the violent rains that had then lately fallen'. Pöllnitz wrote of the difficulties of the Brenner, and in 1738 the Reverend Patrick St Clair noted, 'it is dismal passing the Alps, when they are covered with snow'. In November 1729 George Lyttelton crossed the Alps in terrible weather. Heavy snow, a sharp cold, high winds, a thick mist and slippery precipices combined to make him very frightened. He thoroughly disliked the Alps. The contrast between Lyttelton's passage and that of Brand in 1790 — 'We had a most delicious passage of the Mt. Cenis' — summarises tourists' varied experiences of crossing the Alps.[39]

Turin was the first major Italian town reached after crossing the Cenis. Some tourists rushed through on the way to other Italian towns,[40] but many lingered. The third Duke of Grafton spent six weeks there in 1761. Some attended the academy — there were seven there in September 1737; and the fifth Earl of Berkeley was there in the early 1760s. St Clair hoped that Ashe Windham's son would 'stay a fortnight at least at the King of Sardinia's court, which is now the politest in Europe'. Many English travellers liked the town, the rectilinear street plan, and the architecture, though some found the amusements there limited. The second Earl Stanhope wrote of 'so mournfull a place as Turin'.[41]

From Turin there were two routes, one into Lombardy, the other to Genoa. There was no set course for the Italian section of the Grand Tour. Tourists were influenced by their point of arrival and of expected departure, the season of the year, the inclinations, if any, of their travelling companions, their desire to meet friends and their wish to attend specific events — the opera in Reggio, Bologna and Milan, the Carnival in Naples and Venice, and religious ceremonies in Rome. En route from Venice to Geneva in 1784 Brand 'went by Mantua on purpose to hear Marchesi in the opera of the Fair . . . all fell asleep during the performance! The heat was intense and we were fatigued beyond all conception, I can give no other excuse'. Six years later Brand went to Bologna partly to hear a famous tenor perform.[42]

Much depended on how long the tourist had to spend in 'the land of ancient virtue and modern virtu (otherwise called taste)'. Francis Head observed that Italy was 'like a fine mistress which is always the more agreeable on a longer acquaintance'. The purposes of travel to Italy varied. Charles Thompson presented respectable reasons,

> . . . being impatiently desirous of viewing a country so famous in history, which once gave laws to the world; which is at present the great school of music and painting, contains the noblest productions of statuary and architecture, and abounds with cabinets of rarities, and collections of all kinds of antiquities.[43]

For others the appeal of Italy was composed of various factors: the opportunity for sexual adventures, the climate, devotional reasons for Catholics, and the variety of occasions for enjoyment that the tolerant and civilised society of Italy presented.

Though the vast majority of tourists followed predictable routes and visited the same places a few travelled to other areas: Iberia, Italy south of Naples, eastern Europe, the Balkans and the Baltic.

The numbers visiting these areas increased during the century, though they never attained widespread appeal. The accommodation for travellers and roads south of Naples were both of very poor quality. Indeed this was true of most of southern Italy and it was only the volume of travellers that led to the improvement of the route from Florence to Naples via Rome. In 1772 Sir Philip Francis planned to travel down the east coast of Italy but he only got as far as Ancona,

> Our original intention was to have crossed the kingdom of Naples in order to avoid the Campania di Roma; but upon inquiry we found that the roads were impracticable, without posts or inns, and the people to the last degree brutal and barbarous. So we took the high road to Rome.[44]

Of the few that went further most were interested in classical architecture and archaeology. John, Lord Brudenell (1735–70) went in the late 1750s to such remote sites as Paestum, Taranto and Agrigento. St George Ashe, accompanied by George Berkeley as tutor, visited Apulia in the late 1710s. Sicily could be reached by sea from Naples or Rome. The fourth Earl of Sandwich toured the Mediterranean by sea visiting Sicily, Egypt, Cyprus, Greece and Turkey. William Dowdeswell and Sir William Gordon visited the island in the mid-1740s on a trip that also took them to Greece. Sir James Hall followed in 1785 though he was ' "stormstay'd" a week in Stromboli' on the way there. Lord Pembroke, another visitor in the mid-1780s, went on by sea to Gibraltar and Lisbon. Towards the end of an epic journey that had taken him from Vienna through the Balkans to Constantinople and thence to Cyprus, Crete and Greece, John Hawkins performed a thirty-day quarantine at Messina on his way from Zante to Naples. Brand accompanied Lord Bruce to the island in 1792. Their voyage from Naples to Palermo in 'nearly a perfect calm' took three-and-half days. From Palermo they took a trip to the classical remains at Segeste, before moving on towards Messina. Lord Bruce climbed Etna. Brand was unimpressed by the quality of Sicilian roads and of accommodation outside the cities: 'There is not a wheel in the whole country, the roads are mere paths for a single mule and the few huts scattered round are as bad as Hottentot kraals . . . we are sick of Sicilian roads and accommodations . . .' Of the road to Segeste he wrote 'it is rugged and precipice or mud'. Sir Richard Hoare visited the island the following year. Sardinia never enjoyed the vogue that Paoli's resistance to French occupation brought to Corsica. Greater interest in southern Italy in the second half of the century produced a limited number of guidebooks and journals. The most important was Henry Swinburne's *Travels in the Two Sicilies in the Years 1777, 1778, 1779, and 1780.* Swinburne (1743–1803), the fourth son of Sir John Swinburne of Capheaton Hall, Northumberland, was a Catholic educated in a monastic seminary in France. Also the author of *Travels through Spain in the Years 1775 and 1776,* he played an important role in spreading information about travel in southern Europe.[45]

Travel to Spain caused surprise. The Second Duke of Richmond's trip in the late 1720s aroused amazement. Viscount Townshend observed 'nor can I well conceive what curiosity should lead his Grace so much out of the usual road of travellers'. Lord Tyrawly, envoy in Lisbon, wrote to Richmond 'Point du point, I think Spain and Portugal excite ones curiosity more than any other countries, as being the least known, and quite out of the Old John Trott beaten, pack horse road of all travellers, and will make you as famous to later posterity as Dampier, Sir John Mandeville, Hacklyut, or Fernand Mendez Pinto.'[46]

When Theophilus, ninth Earl of Huntingdon (1696–1746) died, the *Gentleman's Magazine* noted: 'some part of his younger years he gave to Italy and France, and at last finished his travels with a tour, which few of our nobility, of late years, have had the courage to make, through Spain.' The *Worcester Journal* recorded his inscription: 'He visited France, Italy, and even Spain.' His successor visited Spain in 1752. Later in the century the numbers of travellers increased. In September 1788 William Eden, envoy in Madrid, could write that he had presented five or six British travellers that day to the royal family, including Lord Wycombe.[47] Spain was not regarded as the most interesting country to visit. Madrid lacked the cosmopolitan culture of Paris and Madrid society was regarded as dull.

Language was also a barrier, though most Spanish aristocrats spoke French. Outside Madrid there was little to see. There was no vogue for the beach, the mountains lacked the interest of the Alps, the Roman antiquities were less well known than those of Italy and there was little interest in the Moorish remains. William Stanhope, the diplomat, wrote from Madrid in July 1718: 'Lord Essex has been with me ten days, which I daresay is long enough to make him repent his expedition.' Stanhope's successor Benjamin Keene described Spain as 'the dullest country in Europe'. Travellers in Spain encountered major difficulties. The journey to Spain by land was a very long one and involved a passage of the Pyrenees; and facilities for travellers were limited. William Stanhope complained from Bayonne in 1729: 'it being impossible for me, or anybody else (without going post on horseback) to travel fast in Spain, where one is obliged to go on with the same setts of mules for a hundred leagues together. I have been forced to stay here two days waiting for mules, that had been sent for me to Pampaluna, and arrived here but this evening.' He subsequently complained of a lack of post horses between Bayonne and Paris.[48] The alternative approach was by sea, usually to Lisbon, and thence into Spain. Thomas Pelham chose this route in 1775 and Lord Pembroke in 1786. Pembroke disliked travelling in Spain — a dislike shared by Arthur Young, who travelled through Catalonia the following July. Young complained both of 'natural and miserable roads' and of the accommodation. He was often forced to walk. An interesting account of Spain was left by Thomas Pelham who travelled there in 1775–6. He stayed for many months in Madrid where he benefited from the hospitality of the Ambassador, Lord Grantham. From there he went on a trip to Andalusia and thence to France via Granada, Alicante, Valencia and Barcelona. This was a most unusual tour. In March 1776 he wrote to his father that he had decided to 'see the south of Spain, which is not only a very interesting tour from its having been the scene of so many transactions in the Roman History and consequently retaining many curious antiquities but likewise as being the most fruitful and commercial part of modern Spain'. It was necessary to prepare carefully for the journey,

My bed is repairing, and a boiler is making that may hang under my chaise to boil my dinner, for there are as many precautions to be taken for travelling in this country as if I were going into Arabia: my journey from Lisbon has taught me all the desagremens and how many of them are only imaginary ones for after two or three days travelling you fancy your boiled chicken or rabbit better than all the . . . ragouts from a French kitchen, . . .

Pelham set off for Cordoba in late September 1776. He took with him a lot of food and a Spanish copy of *Don Quixote*,

. . . the Inns we stop at being the same as those in which he met with so many adventures: the room I am writing in is worthy of one of his castles no window, a hole in the wall that admits light in the day and is stopt up with a board at night an indifferent door, a large pillar in the middle of the room that supports the roof, and round which we and our servants are to lay down our armour and set up our beds, and the walls naked except where some pedlar has left a few shabby prints, . . .

Pelham found Andalusia 'a most delightful country', but was delayed at Cadiz by heavy rainfall which swelled the rivers. The same cause delayed him at Lorca, whilst he was unimpressed by the quality of the roads near Gibraltar and Cartagena. His phlegmatic character enabled him to bear the difficulties of Spanish travel,

. . . it is really beyond all description but I make it a rule to go into a Pasada without asking any questions, have no wants, and as little intercourse with my landlord as possible who is never satisfied, with what you give him and will cheat whenever he has an opportunity: we buy our own provisions and that for our beasts all which excepting game are as dear and by no means as good as in England. After all this I can assure you with great truth that I never felt the least annoy or uneasiness, for the want of conveniences in the Inns makes one more active in providing them for oneself, and when found they give double pleasure from their rarity: I would never recommend a Spanish journey to a Lady, but it is by no means a bad beginning for a young traveller.[49]

Most travellers to Portugal went by sea, though the trip across the Bay of Biscay was not always a very comfortable one.[50] Many who travelled to Portugal were inveterate travellers — Radnor and Richmond in 1729, Pembroke in 1786. Those going to the Mediterranean by sea usually called at Lisbon; Dr Swinton left a good account in his diary of his visit in 1730. Some, such as the young Garrick, travelled to acquire commercial experience; Thomas Benson, MP for Barnstaple, fled there in 1753 after his fraud was discovered. An increasing number travelled to Lisbon for reasons of health. The air and the climate were regarded as among the best in Europe: Lady Craven noted that the climate 'made my hair grow very long and extremely thick'. Henry Fielding went to Lisbon for health reasons in 1754 and died there. Lady Tavistock died of consumption in Lisbon in 1768. The following year a newspaper reported: 'Died lately, in his passage between Bristol and Lisbon, whither he was going for the recovery of his health, Patrick Moran, Esq.' Five years later William Montagu, MP for Huntingdon, died at Lisbon where he had been sent for health reasons, and in 1781 Lord John Pelham Clinton died likewise. There was very little travel in Portugal outside Lisbon, except for those going to Madrid, who tended to follow the main road. An anonymous account of a trip from Lisbon to Badajoz in 1729 commented 'I never underwent more hardship in travelling'.[52]

Hardship also faced those who travelled in eastern Europe. The Balkans attracted very few British travellers in the first half of the century. Sir Francis Dashwood travelled from Constantinople to Warsaw in 1729. The following year the Earl of Radnor travelled from Vienna to Constantinople. Prince Eugene gave him letters to the governors of the Austrian garrison towns of Buda and Belgrade, and Radnor proceeded by boat to Belgrade, mooring in the middle of the river each night, in order to prevent an attack by brigands. A waterman was shot dead by Radnor's companion, Mr Green, when the latter was on watch. This led to a two day delay at Buda whilst the matter was adjusted. Having left Vienna on 25 October Radnor reached Belgrade on 10 November and Constantinople on 19 December. The journey so tired him that he had to spend five days in bed. In February 1731 he sailed for Smyrna having 'seen very little here', according to the Ambassador the Earl of Kinnoull. Sailing via Malta he reached Leghorn on 12 April, where Swinton recorded,

His Lordship saies yt. all the way from Belgrade to Constantinople he met with but very indifferent treatment amongst the Turks who inhabited yt. track of land, who are mortal enemies to the Christians, (which I suppose may in some measure be owing to the ravages of the Germans in the late war) so yt. they extorted from him extravagant and immense summs of money, and yet treated him with the greatest insolence, and accommodated his lordship with nothing scarce proper for him — His Lordship saies yt in his opinion Constantinople is larger than London, but withall a concourse of all nations, and so filthy and dirty yt in yt respect it exceeds all the cities he ever saw —[53]

In the second half of the century an increasing number of travellers visited the Balkans; some on their return from India. This was true of Lord William Murray in September 1787. Two years earlier Sir Robert Ainslie, Ambassador in Constantinople, wrote to Keith: 'to introduce the Honourable Captain Maitland, Captain Gardner, and Lieutenant Bresset, three officers of His Majesty's land forces in the East Indies, who, after crossing the desert from Bussara to Aleppo, and spending a short time at Smirna, arrived in this residence a few weeks since, and now proceed to Vienna on their way home.' On the same day Ainslie also sent letters of introduction to Keith for George Matcham, a civilian returning from India, and William Smith, a member of the Turkey Company. Letters of introduction sent later in the year included one for Captain Matthew Jenour on his way back from India and another for Willey Beverley, an artist who had accompanied Sir Richard Worsley Bt in his travels.[54] Worsley, an indefatigable traveller, visited Iberia, Asia Minor, Greece and Russia in the 1780s. Worsley was met in Constantinople in 1785 by two other impressive travellers, Lady Craven and Mr Cadogan. Needing to be out of Britain for personal reasons, Craven made an impressive journey in 1785–6 from Vienna through Cracow, Warsaw, St Petersburg, Moscow and the Crimea to Constantinople. From there she toured the Aegean before returning to Vienna via Varna, Bucharest and Transylvania. Cadogan visited Hungary, Poland, Egypt, Cyprus and Greece.[55] Worsley met another impressive traveller, Samuel Bentham, in southern Russia and Turkey the following year.

Travel between Vienna and Constantinople was doubtless increased by the Austro-Turkish peace of 1739–87. However, very few tourists visited the kingdom of Hungary which then included Croatia, Slovakia and Transylvania. The majority of tourists who visited Hungary did so an an excursion from Vienna. This was true of Keith in 1774, Wycombe in 1786 and Lord Granard in 1778. Wycombe set off to visit Belgrade but found the journey more than he had bargained for. He wrote to Keith from Peterwaradin (Novi Sad in modern Yugoslavia) of,

> . . . a very fatiguing journey of four days and an half from Pest, through a very fertile country which is at present as disagreable as incessant rain and bad communications are capable of rendering it. The roads are so much worse than we expected, and the disasters from place to place so much greater than we understood

they were, that our scheme of seeing Belgrade is likely to cost us more time than we originally intended to bestow upon it, . . . Wherever we have been we have met with the most hospitable and gracious reception imaginable.

Four days later Wycombe's companion, Major Green wrote from Semlin that they were unable to cross the river Sava because of very contrary winds.[56]

The Hungarian mines attracted visitors.[57] One visitor, John Hawkins, a Cornish gentleman interested in mineralogy, pressed on to Constaninople. His journey was not an easy one. He,

. . . staid severall days at Semlin and been more than usually detained by the badness of the roads and the severity of the season . . . I was detained four days at Belgrade untill the roads became passable and with difficulty reached Nissa in seven days. Instead of accompanying the Mail I took with me an extra Janissary . . . the new commander of Semlin to whom you favoured me with an official letter of recommendation, with much outward civility possesses neither the manners of a gentleman nor even understanding or activity enough to be of the least service to any traveller.[58]

At Constantinople he joined forces with the botanist Dr Sibthorpe and a Captain Imrie of the British army based in Gibraltar. They toured the Greek islands, including Cyprus, and the coasts of Greece and Asia Minor, Sibthorpe finding new species and Hawkins boasting 'few men have made a more compleat tour of Greece'.[59]

The route through Budapest, Belgrade, Nis, Sofia and Adrianople (Edirne) was the usual one between Vienna and Constantinople. Very few British travellers took any other route. Tourists did not cross from the Adriatic to the Aegean; Albania, Macedonia and mainland Greece were visited by very few, though Greece was becoming more popular by the 1780s. The Rumanian principalities — Wallachia, Moldavia and Transylvania — were visited by very few. In 1762 Sir James Porter returned from his embassy to Constantinople with his wife and children through Bourgas (Burgas), Galatz (Galati), Jassy (Isai), Cracow and Breslau. In 1786 Lady Craven followed a more southerly route. Ainslie was not impressed by the decision to travel through the Carpathians,

Lady Craven, and Colonel Vernon, by the advice of their friends departed on the 2d instant by the way of the Black Sea, in a Greek Boat for Varna, from whence they intend to proceed, through Moldavia and Walachia, to Transilvania in their way to Vienna. I hope they will meet with no considerable inconvenience in this new route, which I should not have recommended.[60]

This route was to be cut the following year by the outbreak of Russo-Turkish hostilities. In eastern Europe the effect of war on travel was more striking than in western Europe, for tourists could not rely on their passports being respected. The irregular forces in eastern Europe, Hussars, Cossacks and Tartars, were particularly feared. The Russo-Turkish war of 1768–74 witnessed hostilities in the Danube basin including the Russian capture of Bucharest and naval conflict in Greek waters. This dissuaded all but the most hardy tourist. Furthermore the unsettled nature of the Russo-Turkish border prevented the early development of the Moscow-Constantinople route that was to be used by Lady Craven and the prison reformer, John Howard.[61] This route only appeared reliable after the Russian annexation of the Crimea in 1781. The subsequent attention devoted to the area by Catherine the Great and the visit of Catherine and of the Austrian ruler, the Emperor Joseph II, to Cherson in 1787 raised British interest in Southern Russia. Difficulty of access restricted tourism both to the Ottoman and Russian empires. In the first half of the century travellers were so rare that their return to Britain merited a mention in the British press; such as that of William Lethullier who returned in 1723 from the Ottoman empire with a mummy.[62] The route to Russia was far from easy. The overland route was arduous. Edward Finch who made the journey in 1740 in order to take up his posting as envoy in St Petersburg wrote from Königsberg to Lord Harrington, Secretary of State for the Northern Department,

Courland, at all times a desart country . . . everything necessary for the subsistence of myself and servants must be carryed with me, since I am assured that it will be impossible even to find bread and salt in any place nor in many so much as water . . . there is no such thing as posting, so that I am reduced to make use of the same horses sixty four german miles from hence to Riga.[63]

Most tourists preferred to travel to St Petersburg by sea. This was the method used by Sir Francis Dashwood in 1733, by Lord Baltimore in 1739 and by Cottrell in 1740. However a Baltic trip was not without its hazards. Crawford, who sailed to St Petersburg in the late 1730s, recorded the hazards of fog, storm, rocks and bad navigation. St Vincent, who sailed to St Petersburg in 1774, was unimpressed with Baltic seamanship. Most who visited St Petersburg saw nothing more of Russia. This was true of Dashwood, Baltimore and St Vincent.[64] Distances were vast, the next most interesting town, Moscow, was a long way away in a direction in which further travel was not practicable until the Crimean route to Constantinople was opened up, the roads were poor and the spring thaw made many impassable. Sledge travel delighted some, such as Lady Craven, but it could only be used during the winter. And yet St Petersburg was different and interesting for that reason. Russian activities were on a different scale; Russian customs were very different: from the practices of the Orthodox church to the bathing which shocked St Vincent: 'went to see the baths, which represented such a monstrous scene of beastly women and indecent men mix'd together naked as our first parents without the least appearance of shame as to shock our feelings.' The general motive for visiting Russia was probably that of Finch's friend, Mr Meggot, 'whose curiosity brought him to see this country'.[65]

The Scandinavian lands saw few tourists. William Benson's trip there at the beginning of the century probably owed much to the fact that his father was a prominent iron merchant and Sweden Britain's principal source of iron. Lord Clinton visited Copenhagen in the summer of 1727 and having crossed to Sweden journeyed by land to Stockholm where he spent a week. Lord Bruce visited Denmark, Sweden and Russia in the early 1750s. Lord and Lady Effingham and Lord Howard travelled to Copenhagen, Stockholm and St Petersburg in 1769. In 1786 Sir Henry Liddell Bt, Matthew Consett and Stoney Bowes sailed from the Tyne on a tour of Sweden, Swedish Lapland, Finland and Denmark, that lasted three months. The tour was undertaken as a result of a wager by Liddell that he could go to Lapland and return with two reindeer and two Lapp women. He returned with a Lapland sledge, two reindeer that perished the following winter and two women, Sigree and Anea who 'remained for sometime at Ravensworth Castle, where they were considered as great curiosities . . . they were sent back to their native country at the expense of Sir Henry with about £50 in money, which they looked upon as great riches'.[66] An interesting journal of the trip was published.[67]

Norway was visited by very few. An astronomical expedition set off for the North Cape to view the transit of Venus in 1769; George Norman travelled in Norway and Russia in 1784.[68] Aside from Copenhagen, Denmark received few tourists. Most called at Copenhagen en route by sea, to or from the Baltic.

Poland was another area that was not popular with tourists. Facilities for travellers, particularly accommodation, were poor. The diplomat George Woodward noted in 1729: 'There is not an inn in Poland, that I have yet seen fit to lodge a dog, I'll only compare them to the worst in Westphalia and leave you to judge of them.' Petty visited southern Poland in 1785. He commented,

> the wretched inns kept by more wretched Jews, render travelling through this rich country very disagreeable and for several nights we had no other beds than straw laid on the damp floors of the nasty habitations . . . I never saw a finer or richer country than Galicia . . . yet after all the poor miserable cottager almost starves on sour bread and water, even the cabarets on the road, afford nothing to eat, and few of them even beer. The iron hand of oppression seems to reign throughout. Nor is there any encouragement for an inn to be well supplied, as the Poles always carry their own provisions with them, and their beds . . .

He added that his wife and daughters were well despite 'their difficulties of often going on foot where the badness of the way rendered it dangerous to stay in the carriage and the troops of vermin among these blest abodes of the sons of Israel'. Lady Craven on the other hand left a more positive account. She had Polish friends, was impressed by the King and wrote from Cracow, 'this journey is not so very formidable as it is represented'.[69]

There were few British travellers to the Balkans, the Baltic, eastern Europe and Iberia, and many of them could not be truly described as tourists. Fashion and convenience restricted most tourists to several well-worn routes, where the whims and wishes of those who travelled for pleasure were appreciated. Across much of Europe roads were poor and accommodation for travellers minimal. Thomas Pelham had to stay in a private house between Cadiz and Gibraltar. Good-quality food and bankers and merchants who were correspondents of London bankers could not be found throughout Europe. Language was also a problem over

most of Europe. The French known by most British tourists was
not very useful in eastern Europe where the lingua franca was
German. Aside from these negative factors there were reasons
encouraging travel to France and Italy. They were fashionable,
exciting and fairly pleasant to visit. The ardours of travel were
generally limited to the crossings of the Channel and the Alps. It
was not necessary to be well-connected to enjoy a visit to France
and Italy. This contrasted markedly with the position elsewhere.
Thomas Pelham's round trip round Spain was dependent on the
support of Grantham. Keith played a crucial role for many travellers in eastern Europe. These connections could not be so easily
utilised by those outside the nexus of aristocratic society. That most
chose to follow similar routes, however, did not mean necessarily
that their responses to travel and to the experience of European
culture and society were identical.

Notes

1. Boston to his mother, Countess of Grantham, 27 Nov. 1716, Herts. RO D/E
Na F8; Cunningham to Paul Methuen, Secretary of State for the Southern Depart-
ment, 8 Jan. 1717, PRO 99/61; Berkeley to Lord Perceval, 26 April 1718; 'Journals
of Travels in Italy in A. A. Luce and T. E. Jessup (eds), *The Works of Geoge
Berkeley*, 8 (1955), p. 110; 'Etat . . . ', BL, Stowe 246 fo. 188–9; Southwell jnl.,
BL, Add. 34753, fo. 31; Colman to Charles Delafaye, Under-Secretary at the
Southern Department, 4 May, 29 June 1725, PRO 98/93, 98/25; Head to
Archbishop Wake of Canterbury, 5 Aug. 1725, Christ Church Oxford, Wake Mss.
2. Waldegrave to Duke of Newcastle, Secretary of State for Southern Depart-
ment, 4 Dec. 1727, Waldegrave to Delafaye, 6 Dec. 1732, Waldegrave to John
Couraud, Under-Secretary at the Southern Department, 1 Oct. 1735, BL, Add.
32753, PRO 78/188, 78/210; [A. Boyer], *Political State of Great Britain* (1728)
p. 457; Robinson to Delafaye, 9 July 1729, PRO 78/197; Stanhope to his brother
Philip, second Earl Stanhope, 25 Oct. 1734, Kent RO U1590 C708/2; Knight to Earl
of Essex, Ambassador in Turin, 6 Aug. 1735, BL, Add. 27734; Waldegrave to
George Tilson, Under-Secretary at the Northern Department, 15 Aug. 1732, PRO
78/201.
3. Essex to Bowen, 30 June 1733, BL, Add. 60387; Burges to Newcastle, 17 July
1733, Bagshaw to Newcastle, 18 Dec. 1731, Villettes to Couraud, 4 Sep. 1737, PRO
99/63, 79/16, 92/41; Pococke to his mother, 4 Feb. 1734, BL, Add. 22978; *The
Nonsense of Common Sense*, 3 Jan. (os) 1738.
4. *Newcastle Courant*, 26 Jan. (os) 1751; Garrick 1751, p. 26; North to John
Hallam, fellow of King's Cambridge, 21 Feb. 1751, BL, Add. 61980.
5. *St James' Chronicle; or British Evening Post*, 4 April 1769; *The Times*, 3 July
1787.
6. *St James' Chronicle; or British Evening Post*, 6, 20, 23 May 1769; St Vincent
jnl., BL, Add. 31192, fo. 16; Wharton to his mother, 18 July, Wharton to Dr Baker,
26 Aug. 1775, Wharton.
7. Cradock, *Literary and Miscellaneous Memoirs* (1826), p. 162; Davies to

Keith, 30 Dec. 1787, BL, Add. 35535, 38222; Brand to Robert Wharton, 26 March 1793, 1 Feb. 1794, Durham, Wharton.

8. Green to Keith, 14 Dec. 1789, BL, Add. 35541; anonymous account of travels in France and Switzerland, 3, 9 (quote) April 1770, Leics. DG7/4/12b; Livingstone to Keith, 14 Sep. 1785, BL, Add. 35535.

9. H. Peckham, *Tour of Holland* (1772), p. 107; W. M. Fawcett (ed.), *Journal of a Tour through part of Flanders and France in August 1773 by James Essex* (Cambridge, 1888), p. 47.

10. Keith to his father, 30 Dec. 1769, Keith to Bradshaw, 24 July 1774, Keith to Andrew Drummond, 28 Sep. 1785, Mrs G. Smith (ed.), *Correspondence of Sir Robert Murray Keith* (2 vols., 1849), I, 123, 469, II, 180; *Memoirs of the Margravine of Anspach*, Lady Craven (2 vols., 1826), I, 135, 151; Brand to Wharton, 30 June 1792, Durham, Wharton.

11. Brand to Wharton, 25 Sep. 1783, Durham, Wharton.

12. *St James' Chronicle; or British Evening Post*, 20 May 1769; Grenville to Pitt, 3 Aug. 1787, HMC *Fortescue III* (1889), p. 413.

13. Leake jnl., Herts. 84595, pp. 1–2; Fife to his factor William Rose, 1 Feb. 1767, A. and H. Taylor (eds), *Lord Fife and his Factor* (1925), p. 39; J. Aikin, 'Journal of a visit to the Low Countries', in L. Aikin, *Memoir of John Aikin* (2 vols., 1823), I, 67; Arbuthnot to Keith, 15 May 1787, BL, Add. 35538; A. Young, *Travels during the Years 1787, 1788, and 1789; undertaken more particularly with a view of ascertaining the Cultivation, Wealth, Resources, and National Prosperity of the Kingdom of France* (2nd edn., 2 vols., 1794), I, 88, 116. The second is more complete than the first edition. *The Travels of the late Charles Thompson* (Reading, 1744), p. 2; *London Journal*, 30 Aug. (os) 1735; Craven, *Memoirs*, I, 20; Brand to Wharton, 24 Nov. 1789, Durham, Wharton.

14. Queensberry to Mrs Herbert, 4 Aug. 1734, BL, Add. 22626; P. Toynbee and L. Whibley (eds), *Correspondence of Thomas Gray* (3 vols., Oxford, 1935), I, 99; Leake, p. 1; R. Blunt (ed.), *Mrs Montagu 'Queen of the Blues'* (2 vols., no date), I, 47; Wharton to mother, 18 Feb., Wharton to Miss Raine, 26 Feb. 1775, Brand to Wharton, 10 Feb. 1786, Durham, Wharton.

15. Molesworth to Gregor, 24 March 1739, BL, Add. 61830; *Fife*, p. 28; *Original Weekly Journal*, 9 Jan. (os) 1720; Grey Journal, Bedford to Marlborough, [June (os) 1732], BL, Add. 5957, fo. 62–3, 61449, fo. 120.

16. Stevens, *Miscellaneous Remarks made on the Spot in a late seven Years Tour through France, Italy, Germany and Holland* (no date), p. 3.

17. James Dayrolle, Resident at the Hague, to Tilson, 9 Aug. 1732, PRO 84/319.

18. BL, Add. 60522, 61684, fo. 85.

19. R. Halsband, *Lord Hervey* (Oxford, 1973), p. 30; Manchester to the Hanoverian minister Görtz, 9 Nov. (os) 1718, Darmstadt, Staatsarchiv, F23 144/7; Clavering letters to Lady Cowper, Herts. D/EP F196; Captain Fish, Bearleader of Marlborough's grandsons, Charles and John Spencer, to Marlborough, 30 Oct.; Marlborough to Fish, 24 Oct. (os) 1727; Cooper to Keith, 17 March 1785, BL, Add. 61444, 35534.

20. Stephen Poyntz, diplomat, to Delafaye, 25 Sep. 1723, PRO 43/5; Clavering to Cowper, 9 Oct. 1716, Herts. D/EP F 196; HP II, 534; Lady Harcourt to Nuneham, 29 July 1755, E. Harcourt (ed.), *The Harcourt Papers* (7 vols., Oxford, no date), III, 74; Baring to Keith, 4 Aug. 1788, BL, Add. 35541; Stevens, p. 382.

21. Murray to Keith, 29 March, Barker to Keith, 9 June, Gordon to Keith, 8 Sep. 1787, Stewart to Hawkesbury, 31 Dec. 1786, BL, Add. 35538, 35539, 38221.

22. J. Vinogradoff, 'Russian Missions to London, 1711–1789'; *Oxford Slavonic Papers*, new series 15 (1982), p. 72; Dartmouth to Edward Stillingfleet, 13 Aug. 1751, 9 March 1752, BL, Add. 62114K.

23. Mackenzie to Keith, 23 May 1786, Petty to Keith, 10 May 1787, Barker to

Keith, 17 March 1788, BL, Add. 35536, 35538, 35540; Brand to Wharton, 10 Sep. 1787, 11 Sep. 1792, Durham, Wharton.

24. Bentinck to Countess of Portland, 18 Jan. 1727, BL, Eg. 1711; Robinson to Edward Weston, Under-Secretary at the Northern Department, 29 Aug. 1744, PRO 80/164; J.A. Thiele, 1685–1752, Die Elbe bei Sörnewitz in Reif und Nebel.

25. *Memoirs of the Life of . . . John Lindesay, Earl of Crawford and Lindesay* (1769), p. 357; Bentinck to Portland, 18 Jan. 1727, BL, Eg. 1711.

26. Sunderland to Marlborough, 5 May 1722, Grafton to Essex, 2 May (os) 1735, BL, Add. 61444, 27733; Panton to the Duke of Wharton, 21 Jan. 1726, RA 89/128; Robinson to Weston, 20 May 1741, PRO 80/145; Brand to Wharton, 30 June 1792, Durham, Wharton; *Lettres et Memoires du Baron de Pöllnitz* (5th edn., 3 vols., Frankfurt, 1738), I, 213; Petty to Keith, 26 Nov. 1785, Edward Southwell junior to Perceval, 27 July, Perceval to Southwell, 7 May (os) 1726, Harry Digby to Sir Charles Hanbury-Williams, 25 Dec. 1751, Lord Pelham to Thomas Pelham, 10 Aug., 5 Oct., Thomas to Lord Pelham, 18 Dec. 1777, Earl of Pembroke to Keith, 17 June 1777; Keith to Lord North, 21 July 1779; Keith to Landsowne, 25 March 1786, BL, Add. 35535, 47031, 51393, 33127, 35512, 35517, 35536; Lord Nuneham to sister, Lady Elizabeth Harcourt, no date (1755), Bucks. RO D/LE/E2/24; journal of Sir William Lee, CUL, Add. 4377, p. 83.

27. A. Thomson, *Letters of a Traveller on the Various Countries of Europe, Asia, and Africa* (1798), p. 166.

28. Torrington to Keith, 3 March 1786, Townshend to Keith, 2 May 1788, Duke of Montagu to Keith, 6 Sep. 1783, BL, Add. 35536, 35540, 35529; Lord Pelham to Thomas Pelham, 16 Nov. 1777, John Strange, Resident in Venice, to Keith, 5 March 1779, BL, Add. 33127, 35516.

29. Pelham to Thomas Pelham of Stanmer (no date, pre–1721), Trevor to Thomas Trevor, 24 May 1729, BL, Add. 33085, fo. 41, 61684; Orrery, I, 43, 48; Inigo Thomas to Keith, 25 Feb. 1788, M. Vallet de la touch to Lord Hardwicke, 4 Jan. 1737, BL, Add. 35540, 35586.

30. Lord Gower to Essex, 20 July (os) 1732, BL, Add. 27732.

31. Knight to Essex, 6 Aug. 1735, BL, Add. 27734; W. Fraser, *The Melvilles Earls of Melville and the Leslies Earls of Leven* (3 vols., Edinburgh, 1890), II, 278; Cradock, *Memoirs*, p. 165.

32. Fraser, *Melvilles*, I, 326; E. Craven, *A Journey through the Crimea to Constantinople* (Dublin, 1789), p. 14.

33. Mitchell jnl., BL, Add. 58314, fo. 50; Stevens, pp. 69–70; Thompson, I, 46; Wharton to Thomas Lloyd, 14 Aug. 1775, Durham, Wharton; St Vincent jnl., BL, Add. 31192, fo. 17–18.

34. Thompson, I, 47.

35. Anon. jnl., BL, Add. 12130, fo. 113, 125–6, 130; Craven, *Journey*, p. 76.

36. BL, Add. 12130, fo. 122–3.

37. Molesworth to Carteret, 10 Feb.; Molesworth to Robert Walpole, 18 Aug. 1723, PRO 92/31; Head-Wake correspondence, Christ Church Wake papers, vol. 264, p. 9; Mitchell BL, Add. 58319, fo. 61–7; Stevens, pp. 82–91; E. Eliott-Drake (ed.), *Lady Knight's Letters from France and Italy 1776–1795* (1905), p. 47; Craven, *Journey*, pp. 77–8.

38. Pococke, BL, Add. 22978, fo. 90; Haggerston to his mother, 9 April 1719, Northumberland, Haggerston; Brand to Wharton, 24 Oct. 1783, Durham, Wharton; William Windham, 'Journey through France and Italy', Leigh (Wigan) RO D/DZ; Thomas to his father, Lord Pelham, 5 Feb. 1777, BL, Add. 33127; Robert Ellison to Henry Ellison senior, 26 March 1764, Gateshead, Ellison, A12.

39. Edmund Allen, Secretary in Turin, to Newcastle, 26 April 1732, PRO 92/33; Pollnitz, II, 68, 71–2; St Clair to Ashe Windham, 5 Oct. (os) 1738), Norfolk RO WKC 6/24 401X; M. Wyndham, *Chronicles of the Eighteenth Century* (2 vols.,

1924), I, 27; Brand to Wharton, 27 Oct. 1790, Durham, Wharton.

40. Robert to Henry Ellison senior, 26 March 1764, Gateshead, Ellison, A12.

41. W. Anson, *Autobiography . . . of Augustus Henry Third Duke of Grafton* (1898), p. 17; Villettes to Couraud, 4 Sep. 1737, PRO 92/41; St Clair to Windham, 26 Oct. (os) 1738, Norfolk WKC 6/24 401X; Pococke, BL, Add. 22978, fo. 89; Brand to Wharton, 24 Oct. 1783, Durham, Wharton; Thomas Pelham, BL, Add. 33127, fo. 171–95; Stanhope to Essex, 6 Jan. 1733, BL. Add. 27732.

42. Brand to Wharton, June 1784, 6 Dec. 1790, Durham, Wharton.

43. Wharton to Brand, 19 June 1775, Durham, Wharton; Head to Wake, 21 Nov. 1724, Christ Church, Wake; Thompson, I, 67.

44. Francis, BL, Add. 40759, fo. 11.

45. Brand to Wharton, 13 July 1785, Durham, Wharton; Hawkins to Keith, 26 Feb. 1788, BL, Add. 35540; Brand to Wharton, 3, 22 April 1792, Durham, Wharton.

46. Townshend to Earl of Chesterfield, 17 Sep. (os) 1728, Keene, Minister Plenipotentiary in Spain, to Delafaye, 13 Dec. 1728, PRO 84/302, 94/99; Earl of March, *Duke and his Friends* (2 vols., 1911), I 171.

47. *Gentleman's Magazine* Dec. 1746; *Worcester Journal* 14 Sep. (os) 1749; HMC, *Rawdon Hastings*, III, 77–80; Eden to Lord Sheffield, 8 Sep. 1788, BL, Add. 61980.

48. Stanhope to Earl of Stair, 18 July 1718, Kent, Stanhope papers, U1590 0145/24; Keene to Waldegrave, 20 July 1733, Chewton; Stanhope to Horatio Walpole and Stephen Poyntz, 30 Sep., Stanhope to Keene, 12 Oct. 1729, BL, Add. 32763.

49. Lord Herbert, *Pembroke Papers* (2 vols, 1939, 1950), II, 315; Young, *Travels* (2nd. edn.), I, 33–43; [D. Defoe] G. Carleton, *A True and genuine History of the two last wars against France and Spain* (1742), pp. 326, 332; Pelham, quotes BL, Add. 33126, fo. 316, 404; 33127, fo. 67, 74, 96.

50. Craven, *Memoirs*, I, 398.

51. Craven, *Memoirs*, I, 378; *St James' Chronicle; or British Evening Post*, 1 April 1769; Cradock, *Memoirs*, p. 154.

52. *Political State of Great Britain* (1729), p. 177.

53. Robinson to Tilson, 25 Oct. 1730; Kinnoull to Newcastle, 5 Jan. (os), 5 Feb. (os) 1731, PRO 80/69, 97/26; Radnor to Robinson, 11 Nov. 1730, BL, Add. 23780.

54. Ainslie to Keith, 17 Sep. 1787; 1 Sep., 8 Nov., 3 Dec. 1785, BL, Add. 35539, 35535.

55. Cadogan to Keith, 31 July, 25 Nov. 1785; 11 April 1787; Ainslie to Keith, 25 Aug. 1785, BL, Add. 35535, 35538, 35535.

56. Wycombe to Keith, 12 April; Green to Keith, 16 April 1786; General Conway to Keith, 18 Jan. 1788, BL, Add. 35536, 35540.

57. Ainslie to Keith, 25 Aug.; Mr Williams to Keith, 2 Oct. 1785, BL. Add. 35535.

58. Hawkins to Keith, 21 Feb. 1787, BL, Add. 35538; Ainslie to Marquis of Carmarthen, Foreign Secretary, 10 Feb. 1787, PRO 78/8.

59. Ainslie to Carmarthen, 25 Aug. 1786, PRO 78/7; Ainslie to Keith, 24 July 1787; Hawkins to Keith, 26 Feb. 1788, BL, Add. 35538, 35540.

60. Ainslie to Carmarthen, 10 July 1786, PRO 78/7.

61. Howard to Keith, 23 Nov. 1789, BL, Add. 35541.

62. *Whitehall Evening Post*, 20 April (os) 1723.

63. Finch to Harrington, 9 May (os) 1740, PRO 41/24.

64. *Memoirs . . . Lindesay*, pp. 117–18.

65. St Vincent, BL, Add. 31192, fo. 98; Finch to Harrington, 5 Sep. 1741, PRO 91/29.

66. Robert Jackson, Minister Resident in Stockholm, to Lord Townshend, 7,

14 June 1727, PRO 95/49; HMC, *Rawdon Hastings*, III, 105; *St James' Chronicle*, or *British Evening Post*, 8 April, 13 May 1769; *Daily Universal Register*, 14 Jan. 1785.

67. M. A. Richardson, *The Borderer's Table Book . . .* (8 vols., Newcastle-upon-Tyne), I, (1846) p. 305; *The Monthly Chronicle of North-Country Lore and Legend* (1887, Newcastle), pp. 14–15.

68. *St James' Chronicle; or British Evening Post*, 16 May 1769; Norman, letters to his step-mother, Kent, U310 C3.

69. Woodward to Tilson, 28 May 1729, PRO 88/35; Petty to Keith, 1 Aug.; Craven to Keith, 27 Dec. 1785, BL, Add. 35535.

2 TRANSPORT

We left our chaises at Pont Beauvoisin, and came here post on horseback in about 10 hours after the most tiresome journey I have ever yet had, both from the badness of the roads and the places we lay at . . .

Charles Stanhope, Lyons, 1732.[1]

Roads

The bulk of tourist travel was by road, and a major difference between eighteenth-century and modern comment on European travel was the stress in the former on road conditions. A wealth of information about these can be found both in tourist accounts and in those of other travellers, particularly diplomats. A reiterated theme was the dependence of road conditions on the weather.

German Roads

. . . bad weather and impracticable roads from hence to Dresden, keep us at present . . . I would not travel the road from hence to Frankfort for all the coronations in Europe.

John Sturrock, Kassel, 1740.[2]

British tourists had a poor opinion of German roads. Sacheverell Stevens was critical. From Innsbruck to Munich, 'some heavy rains having lately fallen, we found the roads excessively bad, there being no sort of pavement as in France and Italy'. Between Munich and Augsburg 'we passed through some woods, where the roads were very bad', and on the way from Dönauwörth to Nürnberg, 'we passed two posts through such exceeding bad roads, that we were obliged to walk almost half the way'. Between Kassel and Hanover, 'The roads were very bad, occasioned by some late rains'. Colonel Charles Rainsford, who, as equerry, accompanied the Duke of Gloucester on his 1769–71 trip to Denmark, Germany and Italy, commented on the new turnpike roads being made near Hanover: 'in the manner of a causeway, and wide enough to march in division and cost about £1000 an English mile — These roads are very much wanted; the present ones being extremely bad, especially upon the least rain which we had now a full opportunity of knowing.' Nathaniel Wraxall travelled from Dresden to Vienna in 1777 'through very bad roads'. George Ogilvie, who travelled from Hamburg to the United Provinces in January 1779, was unimpressed by the quality of the Lower Saxon roads. Fortunately they were made more passable by a pretty severe frost. In December 1785 Matthew Jenour found that a hard frost 'made the roads exceeding good' on his trip from Vienna to Paris via Munich. That spring Dawkins had found the roads between Vienna and Prague 'in general extremely bad, . . . so much so, that we once held a consultation about returning'. Following the same route in the summer of 1787, Brand noted 'the roads are good'. Further west other British tourists were less satisfied by the German roads that year. Robert Arbuthnot informed Keith: 'The roads from Mainz to Cologne are so bad that we were advised to take a boat and sail down the Rhine.' Adam Walker, the prominent 'lecturer on experimental philosophy', complained of the roads on his journey through the Rhineland. Sir John Macpherson, former Governor General in India, 'found the roads so bad in Germany, that I directed my course to Italy'.[3]

The comments of tourists were supported by those of diplomats. In 1720 Lord Glenorchy, on his way from London to Copenhagen via Hanover, complained of the roads and his complaints were shared by John Molesworth, on his way from Paris via Strasbourg to Augsburg, and by Charles Whitworth en route to Berlin. Glenorchy criticised the roads in Lower Saxony again in 1723, and his views were reiterated by Sir Charles Hotham in 1730. The situation had not improved greatly by the second half of the century. Earl Cornwallis wrote from Hanover in 1785 of the prospect of going to Magdeburg, 'I grudge travelling 160 miles on the worst roads in Europe'. The roads in central Germany left much to be desired, and Waldegrave was unimpressed by those of Bavaria. The views of British diplomats were confirmed by those of foreign commentators. Count Dehn was unimpressed by the roads from Leipzig to Prague in 1726; Count Philip Kinsky by those from Prague to Frankfurt in 1733; Sainte Croix by those in Germany in 1787; De Löss by those between Dresden and Brabant in 1737; and Count Törring by those from Coburg to Leipzig in 1740. Pöllnitz was scathing about much of the German road system. The theme that emerged repeatedly was the dependence of the road system on the weather: bad in snow, rain or thaw, better in frost. The impact of the weather was more important often than the state of the original road, of which one commentator wrote in 1738, 'The roads here are not much better than what nature has made them'.[4]

Italian Roads

We have paid the usual tribute to Venetian roads that of broken carriages and broken *commandments*. A *curse* on all Republics say I.

Brand, Milan, 1792.[5]

The Italian road system was better than that of Germany and tourist complaints about the major routes — Turin-Genoa, Milan-Parma-Bologna, Turin-Alessandria-Parma — were limited. The road system was best in Lombardy and Piedmont. Further south there was a deterioration in quality both of the major and of the minor roads, a factor that reflected the relative poverty of these areas. The Appenine chain posed a problem for tourists. Those hoping to visit Tuscany could avoid the Ligurian mountains by sailing direct to Leghorn from Genoa or Marseilles. From northern Italy the usual crossing was the road from Bologna to Florence, though in the 1780s the routes from Modena to Pistoia and Lucca were improved. A popular route to Rome was from Ancona via Loretto, Spoleto and Terni. Opinions of the Appenine roads varied. Francis Head was very unimpressed by the Bologna-Florence road in 1723. Mitchell thought the road between Terni and Strettara 'extremely difficult, and bad' but those between Nova and Volaggio 'paved and well kept; there is often precipices on one hand, but there is no danger in passage'. Sacheverell Stevens thought the best way to travel from Florence to Bologna was 'in a litter' as the mountainous road was bad for wheeled carriages and it was necessary 'to get out so often to ease the horses'. Charles Thompson found the Bologna-Florence trip 'a very tedious journey' and wrote: 'This passage would be quite intolerable, did not the Italians take extraordinary care of their highways, in which particular they seem to outdo any nation in Europe; but the road over these hills is still so incommodious for wheel-carriages, that we were advised to hire mules to ride on, . . .' The Tuscan roads were not as good as those in Lombardy. Travelling from Siena to Rome in 1741, Lady Pomfret complained of a 'rough and dismal journey

. . . obliged to get out and walk several times for fear of breaking our necks'. Stevens had noted of the same road two years earlier that snow and rain affected its quality. In 1732 Mitchell commented on the impact of rain on the Ferrara-Bologna road which ran over poorly drained clay: 'very bad when it has rained . . . if one days raining in summer was enough to spoil the roads, what must they be in the winter?'

A major problem affecting road travel in Italy was the need to cross rivers many of which flooded during the spring thaw and the autumn rains. Furthermore, there were very few bridges. As was the case in most of Europe, rivers were usually crossed by ferries and these found it difficult to operate if the river was in spate. Pococke found the system working well on his way from Milan to Turin in 1734: 'before we came to Novara we passed over the Tessino, very rapid . . . a horse drew the boat half a mile up the river, then being carried down in crossing a horse drew us up again to the landing place . . . a boat goes down 12 miles an hour without rowing.' Mitchell was less fortunate crossing the Trebia near Piacenza 'by reason of a very small quantity of rain that had fallen the day before'. The river had a very wide channel and followed a varying course. There was no bridge as was the case with most of the rivers that flowed from the Appennines to the Lombard plain. Mitchell also observed that many Appennine roads followed river beds and often could not be used. In December 1785 Lady Craven found that the ferryman was unwilling to cross the Trevisa because of storms. Eighteen months later Lord Belgrave travelled from Trieste to Venice: 'The weather was so bad that we were obliged to give up all thoughts of going by sea, so continued our journey on a road, which was tolerably good, except where the rivers Tagliamento and Prava had overflowed their banks, and almost deluged the neighbouring country, which delayed us considerably.' Later that year Walker was forced to 'go seven posts about' almost as far as Lake Maggiore, because of flooding on the Milan-Turin road.

Aside from Rome to Naples few tourists travelled on roads in southern Italy. This road was of a reasonable standard. There were complaints about roads in northern Italy. Stevens thought the Bologna-Ferrara road 'generally very bad'; Lady Craven thought it was too easy to fall off the causeway on that from Cento to Ferrara. However, in general tourists praised the quality of northern Italian roads. Pococke was unhappy about the road west from Brescia, but noted that it was rare for him to be thus dissatisfied. Mitchell described the road from Voghera to Tortona as 'excellent'. Walker was very impressed by the roads from Ferrara to Bologna, Rimini to Fano, Siena to Florence and Bologna to Milan. He claimed that the road near Reggio was 'as good as our best turnpikes'. Swinton observed that the roads 'almost all over Italy' were good. Thompson praised the road from Modena to Bologna, and Orrery that from Bologna to Florence. There were complaints but no-one was put off a trip to Italy by the state of the Italian roads.[6]

French Roads

The only French roads that most British tourists saw were those from the Channel to Paris, and from Paris towards Italy. The road from Calais to Paris was a fairly good one. St Vincent noted in November 1772, 'The road from Calais to Montreuil is not extraordinary, but from the latter to Amiens for the most part extremely good, being paved and trees on either hand'. Bad weather however made the journey an unpleasant one. Sacheverell Stevens travelled along the mostly paved Abbeville-Beauvais road in September 1738, 'as it happened to rain very hard this day, it rendered the unpaved part like a quagmire, and made it excessively bad travelling'. Thomas Brand recorded of his arrival in Paris from the Channel in 1786 'arrived here . . . through bad roads'. The road from Paris to Dijon and Lyons was generally a good one, but Spark Molesworth complained from the latter of 'a very fateaguing journey from Paris of 6 days and a half, ye weather being all ye way very bad, and ye roads I believe in this country were never so bad, for where they could be bad they were so indeed'. The alternative to the road to Dijon and then the boat to Lyons was a road via Montargis, Nevers, Moulins and Roanne. Mitchell was not too pleased with 'the first 20 posts from Lyons' on this road, though Walker who took it in October 1787 found it acceptable. Between Lyons and Roanne he had to have a yoke of oxen added to the three carriage horses in order for the carriage to be dragged up a mountainous section of the road. Towards Paris he noted 'the roads improve, are very wide, level, hard'. From Lyons to Marseilles it was usual to go to Avignon by river and thence by road via Aix. Mitchell thought the roads from Avignon to Aix and Aix to Marseilles 'very good'. Robert Wharton was less happy with the latter road; 'Never in my life did I pass such bad roads though it is the passage between two such towns . . . I have not yet recovered the fatigue which made me really ill last night.' Probably bad carriages and bad weather played as large a role as bad roads in causing his fatigue.[7]

As was to be expected, roads in the rest of France varied. The importance of ferries, for rivers such as the Garonne and the Dordogne,[8] meant that heavy rainfall created difficulties.[9] However, there was less flooding than in Italy. The roads in northern France, particularly in areas of heavy clay, tended to be more affected by rain than those in the south. In July 1734 Pococke was able to travel 90 miles from Thil through Vitry and Châlons to Rheims in one day — thanks largely to the 'goodness of the road like a gravel walk, broad and lately made'. The following day, however, he went to Laon 'half of the way bad and the other very bad' and thence 'by indifferent roads . . . to Lafiere in Picardy'. Mitchell was unimpressed by the roads near the Pont du Gard, but thought the Nîmes-Montpellier road 'excellent' and observed 'the roads in Languedoc are generally good and kept in repair'. An anonymous traveller of 1776–7 was impressed by the fact that the whole Orléans-Paris road was paved. He observed: 'The wide strait roads of France are convenient and magnificent, but they fatigue the travellers eye.' Brand found the road from Orléans to Toulouse so bad in 1783 that the axletree of his carriage broke near Montauban. Lady Craven advised travellers not to go from Blois to Tours by night as the road was unfenced and it was easy to fall into the Loire or into low-lying meadows. Arthur Young was very impressed by the Orléans-Limoges and Limoges-Brive roads, the same road Brand had found so fatal, and by the 'incredible number of splendid bridges, and many superb causeways' in Languedoc.[10] Very few tourists visited areas of France where the roads were really bad: the Massif Central, or the Jura, for example. Those who did travel in provincial France found the roads in general reasonable, particularly in good weather. The road system improved during the century, but was already in existence between the major centres at the beginning of the period. In the first half of the century the system was good enough for people to consider a stay in the provincial French academies, particularly Angers and Lunéville.[11] The roads that linked Paris to the Channel, Rouen, the Loire valley, Dijon and Strasbourg constituted what was, by eighteenth-century standards, a good road system. That tourists did not tend to visit more distant areas of France reflected not so much the quality of their roads, as a lack of interest in these regions.

Roads: Other Countries, Conclusions

> The roads are excellent, and untaxed with turnpikes; but these the poor peasants are obliged to make and to repair by the sweat of their brow, without even the prospect of advantage accruing to them from their labour.
>
> Anon., Tour of Holland (1772) p. 230,
re French roads.

The roads in the United Provinces were well maintained, particularly in the provinces of Holland and Utrecht. Tourists tended to comment on the Dutch canals, though Stevens described the Utrecht-Amsterdam road as 'one of the most agreeable roads in all Europe' and claimed that it was 'the same as if going through the finest walk or avenue in the best laid out garden'. Roads in the Austrian Netherlands (Belgium) were often badly affected by rain, but the straight roads delighted many British tourists. The Duchess of Queensberry was very impressed in 1734, and, having travelled from Antwerp to Brussels, James Essex wrote in August 1773,

> The Roads are worth the notice of a Traveler being made through the most delightfull inclosed Country that can be imagined, it is paved in the middle, as well as the best streets in London, and kept in better repair, on the sides of the paved road they are sand or gravel, and through the whole way they are planted with two rows of trees, which forme a beautifull Avenue, and running straight farther than the eye can distinguish forme a delightfull arbour, which affords a refreshing shade for Travelers, many miles without interuption.

Lady Craven found Russia less delightful. She wrote from St Petersburg in February 1786,

> The road between Warsaw and this place is one insipid flat, except just in and about the town of Nerva, where I took a sledge and flew hither . . . I can conceive nothing so *ennuyant* as travelling in such a country as this, one flat plain; the view terminated by a forest, which you drive through, only to arrive at the same scene you have quitted, the frost was not hard enough to make the road good, till I came to Nerva.

Later in the year she wrote in Wallachia: 'There is no road made, and I saw no carriage track, but a fine soil without stones or ruts, made the journey very pleasant.'[12] The roads in Iberia, the Balkans, Poland and Russia were generally bad. There were often individual prestige roads, but an absence of a road system. However, the intrepid tourists who visited these areas were not put off by the roads, and the vast majority of tourists, who never visited them, had many reasons for not so doing besides the quality of the roads. The vulnerability of coaches and the relative ease with which they broke down must have made some tourists concerned about the state of the roads, though they appear, on the whole, to have borne the latter phlegmatically. Some compared British and European road conditions. Walker commented on the absence of charges for 'barriers or turnpikes in travelling through France'. Young thought European ferryboats better than those of Britain. In France it was possible to drive into and out of ferries rather than forcing the horses to leap in, as in Britain. Young also thought the Languedoc roads better than those of Britain though he was dissatisfied with the 'unjust taxation' that paid for them, and angered by the contrast between the roads and the accommodation available in inns. The final word can perhaps be left with the anonymous writer who claimed in 1738: 'There is no country, whose roads have more engaged the care of the Legislature, and upon which more expences have been bestowed, than the English; and perhaps there are few so bad . . .'[13]

Canal, River and Sea

> . . . embarked on board a Roman trading vessel bound to Ancona . . . passed the night in a hogstye, (which the captain called his cabbin) on a mattress, in the utmost misery. The vessel full of goods and stinking passengers. Calms or contrary winds all night . . . continuance of misery. Godfrey eating, Francis spewing.
>
> Journal of Sir Philip Francis, 1772.[14]

Waterborne travel by tourists in Europe was restricted largely to the canal network of the Low Countries. This was the area in Europe with the most highly developed system of water communications, and outside it tourists tended to travel by road. Canal and river travel in Europe suffered from major disadvantages. It was interrupted often by drought or ice; it was difficult to travel on many rivers against the direction of the current, and it was often a very slow and inflexible means of communication. Few rivers had been canalised and many suffered from rocks, shoals or shallows. Outside the Low Countries tourists tended to use only a limited number of rivers and canals; they were rarely used in Iberia or eastern Europe. The standard tourist routes in Germany ensured that the rivers were rarely used, with the exception of the Rhine. It was usual to approach Vienna from Prague, Munich or Venice and not down the Danube from Regensburg. In northern Germany tourists travelled between Dresden, Leipzig, Berlin and Hanover, and from Hanover to the United Provinces. The Oder, Elbe and Weser led towards the Baltic and North Seas, and did not constitute tourist routes. In Italy the only river that was used frequently was the Brenta from Padua to Venice. In France the routes used by tourists were the Saône from Chalon to Lyons, the Rhône thence to Avignon and the Canal du Midi from Béziers to Toulouse. Tourists generally praised their riverine trips in France. The anonymous traveller of 1776–7 arranged to travel from Lyons to Avignon, stopping when and where he pleased, for 4 louis and 6 francs (between £4 and £5), in a *bateau de poste*,

> These boats are flat bottomed and of very rude construction, the materials being always sold for plank and firewood on their arrival at Avignon. My cabriolet served me for a cabin: The wheels being taken off were laid flat at the bottom of the boat, and the body of the carriage being set upon them, was thus kept above the bilge water, which came in so plentifully as to require frequent bailing.

Impressed by the beauty of Viviers from the river, he discovered one of the limitations of river travel,

> On such occasions the rapidity of the stream, so convenient for the traveller who merely wishes for his journey's end, is a mortifying obstacle to those who would contemplate at leisure the beauties of the scenery they pass. It being such, in many parts, that there is no stopping those awkward machines the bateaux de poste, without reaching the shore, and that cannot be done but by the utmost exertions of the boatmen with their clumsy oars

for a considerable time together, during which the boat unavoidably drives a considerable way down the stream; and in some places rocks and shoals make it dangerous to quit a particular part of the channel.

Lady Craven was pleased by her trip from Lyons to Avignon in July 1785: 'Nothing can be more delightful than my last method of travelling by water. I have had high and contrary winds; but the Rhone's famed rapidity that I had heard so much of, was neither surprising nor terrifying — the shores on each side were rocks interspersed with vineyards and castles.'[15]

St. Vincent took the Post Boat on the Canal du Midi to Toulouse: 'which sets out every day backwards and forwards between Beziers and Thoulouse and is three days and a half on the passage stopping to dine and lie, is a very convenient, though slow conveyance, and the entertainment in the auberge very tolerable, good beds most of the way, the changing boats when there are double, or more locks appear tedious, on account of shifting the baggage.'[16]

When facilities existed for tourists, as on the Saône, Rhône, Brenta and Rhine, river transport was pleasant. Stevens took the *burcello*, which was drawn by two horses, from Padua to Venice. He enjoyed the prospect of villas and gardens and observed 'it is very agreeable travelling in this manner'. On the Rhine boats,

> . . . one travels at the rate of four or five miles for a penny; their accommodation by day is good enough, and in the evening they commonly put into a town, where passengers sleep in the inn. When there are floods, or contrary winds, the passage is somewhat tedious; but sailing down the river, or having the wind, they sail at the rate of five or six miles an hour, and it is extremely delightful.

In 1785 Captain William Gordon found the trip 'very pleasant only a little tedious and cold', and two years later Robert Arbuthnot found the weather a problem sailing from Mainz to Koblenz: 'There was a very high wind all day, with frequent hail showers. Once or twice I thought the boat would have overset.' As a result, despite having set off at 7 am, Arbuthnot and Lord Ancram had only reached Rheinfels by nightfall.[17]

In the Low Countries the canal system was best developed around

Ostend, Ghent and Bruges in the Austrian Netherlands, and in the provinces of Holland, Utrecht, Friesland and Gröningen in the United Provinces. Few British tourists visited Friesland or Gröningen, but the canal system was used fully in the other areas. It was not necessary to hire a boat. Rather, as on the Brenta, Rhine, Saône and Canal du Midi, tourists relied on an efficient system of public transport. As on those rivers, the boats that carried the tourists did not carry freight, other than baggage and mail. The horsedrawn barges (*trechschuits*) of the Low Countries were inexpensive and relatively comfortable. The provision of a kind of first-class compartment added to the comfort. Meals could be taken on many of the barges, and the service was frequent, once-hourly in the summer over most of Holland. The boats were punctual and reasonably quick. In 1784 it took Aikin two-and-a-half hours to get from The Hague to Leyden. Two years later Cradock gave some journey times that included The Hague-Leyden (three hours), Leyden-Haarlem (four), Haarlem-Amsterdam (two), Amsterdam-Utrecht (eight) and Utrecht-Gouda (six). The Flemish canals were praised,

> We left Ghent yesterday morning in a large boat drawn by two horses; this was still more agreeable than the Dutch trekschuytes, as it has an awning over the end of the deck, where you may sit very much at your ease; below, there are two separate apartments, the one elegantly fitted up for the better sort of people; add to these, a kitchen where they dress you a good dinner . . . I don't remember spending a more agreeable day, the weather perfectly fine, the view of the country delightful, joined to the conversation of a very pretty French woman, who was lively and good-humoured to a degree; we arrived here [Bruges] early in the evening . . .

James Essex enjoyed his travels on the Flemish canals in 1773. He travelled from Nieuport to Bruges in the best apartment — neatly wainscoted and the windows sashed — for 15d, and had a 'very good dinner for 15d'. Before he arrived at Bruges, he was forced to change barge, as there was too little water in the canal to pass a lock. The second barge was 'rather disagreable under deck having been used for carrying salt-fish' but Essex sat on deck in the fine weather and 'drank tea very merrily' with some people he had met on the boat. The journey from Bruges to Ghent also cost 15d with 15d for a dinner of '2 hot courses. 5 dishes each and a Desert of fruite and biskets'. In 1754 Oliver Goldsmith was very pleased with his journey to Leyden on the Dutch canals.

> Their ordinary manner of travelling is very cheap and very con-venient. They sail in covered boats drawn by horses and in these you are sure to meet people of all nations. Here the Dutch slumber and the French chatter and the English play cards, any man who likes company may have them to his taste. For my part I generally detached myself from all society and was wholy taken up in observing the face of the country, nothing can equall its beauty. Wherever I turn my eye fine houses elegant gardens statues grottoes vistas present themselves . . .[18]

Not everybody appreciated the Dutch boats. In 1763 James Boswell complained that they were sluggish and tedious. An anony-mous writer complained that travelling from Amsterdam to Utrecht he,

> . . . for the first time found a Trechschuyte disagreeable; We unluckily could not get the roof, and as it rains hard, we cannot walk upon the top; we therefore have no other alternative than to sit in the body of the boat, with upwards of twenty persons of both sexes, from whose mouths nothing has hitherto issued but volumes of tobacco smoke; which has made my friends sick, and me sulky.[19]

However in general comments were favourable. They were certainly far better than those for travel by sea. Aside from the Channel or North Sea crossing, tourist travel by sea can be divided into two categories, short hops, usually designed to avoid difficult sections of land, and long voyages. In the first category the most common journey was that between Marseilles and Genoa and/or Leghorn. Travelling to Venice was another cause of short voyages. In February 1721 Viscount Parker wrote from Venice to his father, the first Earl of Macclesfield: 'The roads between this place and Ravenna being most extraordinarily bad, we determined to go to that place by water, and have been obliged to stay here longer than we intended by the bad weather.' Viscount Harcourt sailed from Venice to Trieste in June 1734, en route for Vienna. Adam Inglis made the same journey in the opposite direction in 1786: 'a pleasant

journey where we were obliged to remain three days the wind tho'
fair being so high that we could not put to sea. We were two days
on the passage which was rather disagreeable. By what we now hear
of the new road by Clagenfurt we regret that we did not come by it
as we should then have shunned the incertainty of a sea passage.'[20]
The increased popularity of travel to Vienna and the improvements
at the port of Trieste ensured that the Trieste-Venice run which had
attracted few tourists early in the century was quite busy by the
1780s. Few sailed further south from Venice than Ravenna; the
Adriatic was toured by very few; facilities for tourists were scarce
and there were no famous sites south of Ravenna. The eastern
shores of the Adriatic were largely under the control of Venice, but
were an area of brigandage. The Roman antiquities on the
Dalmatian coast were not on the tourist itinerary. Short hops took
tourists to Sicily, or, as with the tenth Earl of Pembroke and the
son of the Earl of Bute in April 1769, to Corsica. In northern
Europe there was little short-hop coastal movement by tourists
aside from in Dutch coastal and estuarine waters, where, as Joseph
Shaw and Zachary Grey discovered, the effects of tide, wind and
shoals could be very troublesome.[21]

Long sea journey were made by few tourists. In 1739 the fifth
Lord Baltimore (1699–1751) sailed to the Baltic. From
Copenhagen he sailed in his own yacht to St Petersburg, thence to
Danzig, and from there, travelled to Dresden and Berlin. Having
set out in May 1739 he reached Hamburg on his return in late
September 1739. As he observed, his stay had been 'very short in
most places'.[22] His trip aroused so much surprise that it was
believed that he had been entrusted with secret negotiations. The
same was believed of the Duke of Richmond's trip to Madrid in
1728.[23] Lady Craven sailed from the Crimea to Constantinople to
Varna in 1786. Very few tourists reached the Black Sea. It was safer
probably to sail across it than to journey around the shores, though
Lady Craven was aware of the danger of drowning.[24] Some
travelled round the Mediterranean by boat, but the absence of
passenger services meant that it was necessary to rely on naval
vessels as Swinton in 1731 and Lord Pembroke in the 1780s did, or
on merchantmen, who usually lacked suitable accommodation, or
to arrange one's own transport as the fourth Earl of Sandwich did.
Such a course tended to require financial resources, whilst obtaining a passage in ships of the Royal Navy was easiest for those with
good contacts. As a result Mediterranean cruises were usually

enjoyed by aristocratic travellers, such as the Duke of Bedford, who planned a tour in 1732 to Lisbon, Naples and Turin.[25] Sea travel was hazardous and fairly unpleasant. Most tourists preferred to avoid it and to resort to it only for short hops or for journeys, such as that to Lisbon, for which there was no reasonable, comfortable alternative by land. Having crossed the Channel most tourists wished to avoid 'the mad, savage, tyger- and Leopard-like appearance and motions of the multitudinous sea'.[26]

Vehicles

My travelling will be but slow, as I go on horseback; having on account of the reviews principally bought one at Dresden: I find it much the best way of getting through this country for a man who has no carriage of his own; and beyond all comparison the most agreeable.

Captain John Barker, Brunswick, 1792.[27]

I was not hurried with the alarming rapidity of Italian postillions nor shut up in a close cramp carriage but mounted on a safe easy horse with a sober steady Florentine boy 'similarly situated' on another with a little valise holding three clean shirts and other necessaries that I might not be taken for that disgrace to the human species the sans culotte of France.

Thomas Brand, excursion from Florence to
Lakes Como and Maggiore, 1793.[28]

Tourists in Europe had two alternatives. They could take their own carriages to Europe or use vehicles that they found on the continent. In the latter case they could hire vehicles or use the transport available for the local inhabitants. Many took their own carriages, particularly later in the century. Lord Gardenstone travelled round Europe in his own carriage in the late 1780s and found this perfectly satisfactory, and the taxation of British carriages brought into France became an issue in the mid-1780s. The use of public transport was widespread particularly in France on the Lille-Paris and Paris-Lyons routes. Elsewhere, with the exception of the Low Countries, it was less common as there were fewer facilities for public transport. The diligence, or public coach, from Lille to Paris was described by many tourists. Opinion on it was divided. Some found it slow; others, such as Arthur Young, noisy.[29] However, it was praised both because it was less expensive than hiring a carriage, and because it provided an opportunity to meet the French.

> We . . . had no reason to regret having travelled in the diligence; as by it we avoided the insolence of the Post-Masters, and squabble with Postilions; who, like the barren womb, are never satisfied, and say not, it is enough. In respect to our company, we had much reason to be pleased; . . . Their behaviour was civil, and their conversation lively and entertaining.[30]

John Andrews in his guidebook praised the idea of always travelling,

> . . . in a public vehicle, where he might have a chance of conversing with a diversity of characters . . . People that meet on a travelling party, being usually total strangers to each other, and meeting together for the first and last time, are not fettered by any apprehensions of what may happen from the discourse that passes among them: they indulge themselves without any restraint, and speak of men and things with a latitude and freedom, which they would not dare to use elsewhere.[31]

It is not clear how far the sentiments in such guidebooks were shared by tourists. Whether many really wished to spend several days in a confined space practising their schoolboy French with strangers may be doubted. Robert Wharton, however, enjoyed his trip from Lille to Paris in 1775. Whereas his journey from Calais to Lille had cost about six guineas, 'the diligence from that place hither is only 3 Louis for which you are provided with supper the first night and dinner and supper the next days besides your journey'. He defended travel by diligence as a 'way of seeing the French people as much as possible and being sure not to be imposed on'.[32] Sacheverell Stevens praised the diligence he took from Paris to Lyons in 1739. He was impressed by the speed ('300 miles, which it performs in four days') and the cost: 'the fare for each passenger is 100 livres, and everything found you upon the road, or 70 livres without: this is the cheapest way, but not so expeditious and easy as a post chaise, but infinitely more diverting, occasioned by the odd assemblage of the passengers, such as monks, pilgrims, officers, courtezans, etc.' St Vincent, on the other hand, on the journey from Paris to Chalon in 1773, found the diligence full, slow and noisy, and disliked being confined in it. He was also inconvenienced by the absence of a toilet (the Flemish barges in contrast were shown as possessing one in Essex's plan).[33] An anonymous tourist took the stagecoach from Paris to Rouen. He found it inexpensive — 'being only half a Guinea' — but was angered by its slowness. Travelling at three miles an hour it took two-and-a-half days to travel 90 miles. Fed up with it, he determined to ride post back to Paris and never to take a stagecoach again. The writer revealed one principal disadvantage with taking public transport: the abrogation of tourist independence. He noted, 'the coachman as arbitrary as his monarch, and we the poor passengers were obliged to be as abject as his subjects'. The sentence was balanced doubtless for effect but, the inflexibility of public transport was a major hindrance. In the case of barges this was not much of a problem. They could not be expected to go on many detours and they usually travelled as fast as was possible. Neither was the case with land transport.[34]

Elsewhere in Europe some tourists took public transport. For the sake of company Stevens took the stagecoach from Florence to Bologna. Aikin took 'the Ostend diligence' from Bruges.[35] However, most tourists who did not take their own carriages preferred to hire them on the continent. Carriages were hired often at Calais, frequently at Dessein's, the leading inn. They could be purchased on a basis that allowed for the return of a deposit when the carriage was brought back to Calais at the end of the tour. Alternatively, carriages could be hired for shorter stretches of a trip. Whatever the means employed it was necessary to rely on the system of posting by which fresh horses could be obtained at regular intervals along the route. The quality of posting varied greatly throughout Europe and it was of major concern to tourists. The availability of horses, the cost and the speed with which the horses could be changed were of great importance. In Italy the price varied by principality. It was particularly expensive in the Papal States. Brand, travelling from Milan to Florence in 1790, was dissuaded from the Modena-Pistoia route because he was told 'that the posts were ill served and the accommodation very bad'. He was not, however, very satisfied with his alternative choice: 'Nothing can exceed the ill behaviour both of men and horses at the posts between Bologna and Florence. *Sa Sainteté* has certainly some Jewish ideas of retaliation and thinks it but right that as he gives us one grand tremendous annual curse, he should receive thousands of daily maledictions from all those unfortunate heretics who travel thro' his patrimony and territories.'[36] Swinton, on the other hand, was very impressed by the posting system in Italy. He praised the ease and speed of travelling in Italy. Possibly he could be accused of extrapolating unreasonably from his own experiences in Tuscany.

There were complaints about posting in the Low Countries. One writer wrote of a trip from Utrecht to Breda: 'our mode of travelling is now changed in all respects for the worse. This is not the country to go post in; for we were obliged to hire a coach and four from Utrecht, to convey us to Breda; the distance is only forty-two miles; notwithstanding which, we were eleven hours on the road, and paid five pounds sterling for this tedious, miserable conveyance.' Essex complained of his journey from Ghent to Antwerp in 1773,

> . . . in a miserable equipage called a carrosse (in English a coach) being an open chaise with two seats, to which was fixt a head with a buckram cover and curtains which could not keep out a little shower of rain. To this machine four miserable horses were tied with cart ropes, and dragged us to Antwerp, travelling at the rate of three miles an hour, through a heavy sandy road and baiting our horses every six miles.[37]

In northern France the posting system worked reasonably well and tourist demand led to improvements during the century, particularly from Dieppe to Paris. Early in the century there were gaps in the posting system. In 1722 Lord Polwarth, envoy at the peace congress at Cambrai, pressed for the establishment of a post 'about a league from Ardres betwixt Calais and St. Omer; for neither messengers nor travellers can get horses to go from the one place to the other, it being eight leagues, and no post established'.[38] Seventeen years later Thomas Gray was most impressed by the postchaise in which he travelled from Calais to Boulogne, and which 'will, upon occasion, go fourscore miles a day'. Tourists naturally compared travel in Britain and France. Lady Craven noted that the changing of horses was not as speedy in the latter. Arthur Young complained about the state of French stables, and having travelled from Calais to Paris in May 1787 observed 'that posting in France is much worse, and even, upon the whole, dearer than in England'. The previous September Lord Gardenstone noted, 'If the accommodations for travelling, in the articles of hired carriages, drivers, harness, are not yet so good here as in Britain, they are cheaper.' Young commented unfavourably on the difficulties of hiring carriages in provincial French towns, as compared to England.[39]

Whatever the comparisons, few tourists complained seriously of the posting system in northern France. In the south there was sometimes a reliance upon mules, which could be an irritating form of transport. Travelling in a mule-drawn coach from Avignon to Aix, Robert Wharton found himself going only at three miles an hour. Mules were also to be found between Lyons and Vienne. Walker was very impressed by the mules used to pull his coach between Viterbo and Siena in 1787,

Our mules held out very well; they will travel for twelve hours together without a bait; but this we did not suffer. Their pace is but slow; but then it is all alike, uphill or down, rough and smooth . . . When we arrive at the post, the driver takes them into an open place, spreads a little straw; the mules then lay down, and begin to tumble over their backs, in a diverting manner, for several minutes. They then get up, shake themselves, and after a small feed, are as fresh as the hour they set out. It is an excellent animal, and so sure-footed, that I find myself much more at my ease than when horses are in the shafts.[40]

Whatever their charms, mules were slow. Invaluable as they might be in mountainous regions and difficult terrain, it is possible that their lack of speed was yet another factor discouraging tourists from visiting such areas as Iberia, Italy south of Naples, inland Provence and the Massif Central. Whatever the region, tourists faced several problems in common. Exposure to the elements made transport inconvenient and in some circumstances miserable. High winds and heavy rainfall were particular problems.[41] Many tourists had quarrels with postilions, drivers and postmasters. The fifth Earl of Leven was dissatisfied by his visit to Paris in 1749 and in particular disliked the trip from Lille to Paris,

Oh! its miserable posting in this country, 5 or at most 6 miles in one hour . . . They yoke 3 miserable beasts all in a breast, just

as we do in harrows, and an old surly rascal as post boy, who will
do nothing but what he pleases. One of them had the impudence
this day to tell us, after we had given him sixpence to drink, that
we payed like Frenchmen and not like Englishmen, and gave us
names, upon which Sandie thrashed him.[42]

Some tourists found their drivers and postilions fraudulent.
Others found them simply troublesome. Lady Craven commented,
'I might just as effectually argue with a horse as with a French
postillion'.[43] A few tourists were dissatisfied with the opportunities
that coaches provided for seeing the countryside. In May 1787
Arthur Young noted: 'Being in a post chaise I travelled to Paris, as
other travellers in post-chaises do, that is to say, knowing little or
nothing.' An anonymous tourist commented, on his trip through
Provence: 'A country at all fruitful in beautiful scenery, can
scarcely be known without being travelled twice; forward and
backward, and least if travelled in a carriage . . . travelling in a
chaise, from which retrospects are seldom taken in the most advantageous point of view.'[44]

In eastern Europe tourists made do with the vehicles that they
could find. Most, such as Lady Craven, tended to take their own
carriages. In Germany posting was fairly well organised on the
major routes. Tourists in the United Provinces found that the
quality of travel on land did not approximate to that on Dutch
canals. Thomas Brand left two vivid accounts of the journey, taken
by many British tourists, from Helvoetsluys to Brill,

> . . . we were equipped with a thing called *coach* and a pair of
> horses without shafts with such machinery thereto belonging as
> you would suppose the very first inventor of carriages would not
> have used and the coach itself infinitely more ugly clumsy and in
> every respect inconvenient than you can imagine. The basket of
> the blue fly is worth a 1000 such. But in this as in most other
> things they are at least a century behind us in England.

> From Helvooitsluis to the Brill there is still no other conveyance
> to be had than an open wagon which carries you and your
> baggage to the annoyance of one and the utter destruction of the
> other unless it is packed with the greatest care and address. Two
> of the most stupid looking animals of our species on this side the
> Cape of Caffres sat in the front and each drove his own pair of

horses which every now and then dropped down in a muddy hole and were almost suffocated.[45]

Difficulties with posting encouraged some tourists to use their own horses,[46] whilst several were happy to ride on horseback.[47] However, it is necessary to put tourist difficulties with transport in perspective. Few cut short their trips because of transport problems, and most accepted, albeit with grumbles, whatever they found. The principal difficulty affecting transport was the weather, and this was watched with great concern. As most tourists tended to follow those routes that were of great importance for domestic travel, they benefited from the greater concern of eighteenth-century governments for transport — a concern that was motivated by commercial and military interests, not by tourism. Many regions did not benefit from this development, but whilst travel for most tourists was a matter of moving at speed from one major city to another this was not too much of a problem.

Notes

1. Stanhope to Essex, 18 Oct. 1732, BL, Add. 27732.
2. Sturrock to Richard Neville Aldworth, 19 Dec. 1740, Essex D/D By C1.
3. Stevens, pp. 369, 370, 372–3; 381; Rainsford, BL, Add. 23646, fo. 29; Wraxall to Mrs Montagu, 10 Dec. 1777, *Montagu*, II, 40; George Ogilvie of Aucheries jnl., Aberdeen University Library, Ogilvie-Forbes of Boyndlie Mss., box 46, 24 Jan. 1779; Jenour to Keith, 30 Dec. 1785, Dawkins to Keith, 27 March 1785, BL, Add. 35535, 35534; Brand to Wharton, 22 Aug. 1787, Durham, Wharton; Arbuthnot to Keith, 30 April 1787, BL, Add. 35538; A. Walker, *Ideas suggested on the spot in a late excursion through Flanders, Germany, France, and Italy* (1790), pp. 63, 69; Macpherson to Keith, 19 June 1790, BL, Add. 35542.
4. Glenorchy to Duke of Kent, his father-in-law, 15, 22 Nov. 1720, Beds., Lucas papers, L30/8/10/4-5; Molesworth to Stanyan, 27 Nov., Whitworth to Viscount Stanhope, Secretary of State for the Northern Department, 9 Nov. 1720, PRO 92/30, 90/12; Glenorchy to Kent, 7 Dec. 1723, Beds., L30/8/10/66; Hotham to Tilson, 8 April 1730, PRO 90/27; C. Ross (ed.), *Correspondence of Charles, First Marquis Cornwallis* (2nd edn., 3 vols., 1859), I, 212; Richard Sutton, envoy in Kassel, to Townshend, 1 May 1727, Woodward to Harrington, 14 Jan. 1733, PRO 81/122, 88/41; Waldegrave to Newcastle, 24 June 1730, BL, Add. 32767; Dehn to Duke of Bevern, 5 Nov. 1726, Wolfenbüttel, Staatsarchiv, 1 Alt 3 Nr. 26; Kinsky to Prince Eugene, 4 Feb. 1733, Vienna, Kinsky Palais, correspondence of Philip Kinsky 3(b); Sainte Croix to Montmorin, French foreign minister, 7 Sep. 1787, AE, CP, Russe 122; De Löss to Brühl, 7 Feb., 1 March 1737, Dresden, Hauptstaatsarchiv, GK, 639; Törring to his father, 5 Aug. 1740, Munich, Hauptstaatsarchiv, Bayr. Ges., Berlin 10; Sutton to Townshend, 14 Feb. 1729, Robinson to Harrington, 10 April 1735, Robinson to Weston, 16 Jan. 1737, PRO 81/123, 80/125; Anon., *The Present State of Germany* (2 vols., 1738), II, 382.

5. Brand to Wharton, 5 Oct. 1792, Durham, Wharton.

6. Mitchell, BL, Add. 58319, fo. 8, 49; Stevens, pp. 324–5; Thompson, I, 98–9; Lady Pomfret to the Countess of Hartford, 15, 16 March 1741, Leics., D67, Finch D5; Stevens, p. 156; Mitchell, BL, Add. 58316, fo. 16; Pococke, BL, Add. 22978, fo. 89; Mitchell, BL, Add. 58319, fo. 47–8, 51; Belgrave to Keith, 19 May 1787, BL, Add. 35538; Walker, pp. 381–3; Stevens, p. 331; Pococke, Mitchell, BL, Add. 22978, fo. 86, 58319, fo. 48; Walker, pp. 186, 339, 341, 366, 369, 373; Swinton, 8 June (os) 1731; Thompson, I, 92; Cork and Orrery, p. 71.

7. St Vincent, BL, Add. 31192, fo. 3; Stevens, p. 8; Brand to Wharton, 10 Feb. 1786, Durham, Wharton; Molesworth to Gregor, 8 April 1739, BL, Add. 61830; Mitchell, BL, Add. 58319, fo. 103; Walker, pp. 422–3; Mitchell, BL, Add. 58319, fo. 83–4; Wharton to Thomas Wharton, 7 Oct., Wharton to Miss Raine, 7 Oct. 1775, Durham, Wharton.

8. St Vincent, BL, Add. 31192, fo. 31; Young, I, 18, 58, 62.

9. Waldegrave to Keene, 18 Nov., BL, Add. 32796.

10. Pococke, BL, Add. 22978, fo. 92; Mitchell, BL, Add. 58419, fo. 93, 97, 101; BL, Add. 12130, fo. 188, 193; Brand to Wharton, 12 March 1783, Durham, Wharton; Craven, *Journey*, p. 5; Young, I, 14, 16–17, 54.

11. Lunéville was in Lorraine, but the Lorraine roads were of a similar standard to those in neighbouring areas of France. For military reasons this region of eastern France had roads of a good standard.

12. Stevens, pp. 386–7; Queensberry to Mrs Herbert, 4 Aug. 1734, BL, Add. 22626; Essex, p. 55; Craven, *Journey*, pp. 164–5, 386.

13. Walker, p. 438; Young, I, 18, 35, 44, 47, 54; *Present State of Germany*, II, 382.

14. BL, Add. 40759, fo. 10; Francis and Godfrey embarked at Venice.

15. BL, Add. 12130, fo. 51, 61–2; Mitchell, BL, Add. 58313, fo. 50; Stevens, pp. 69–70; St Vincent, BL, Add. 31192, fo. 17–18; Wharton to Thomas Lloyd, 14 Aug. 1775, Durham, Wharton; Craven, *Journey*, p. 37.

16. St Vincent, BL, Add. 31192, fo. 26–7.

17. Stevens, p. 342; *Present State of Germany*, II, 289; Gordon to Keith, 23 March 1785, Arbuthnot to Keith, 30 April 1787, BL, Add. 35534, 35538.

18. L. Aikin (ed.), *Aikin*, I, 74; Cradock, p. 265; Peckham, *Tour of Holland* (1772), p. 121; Essex, pp. 10–11, 21–4; K. C. Balderston (ed.), *The Collected Letters of Oliver Goldsmith* (Cambridge, 1928), p. 24; J. Shaw, *Letters to a Nobleman from a Gentleman travelling thro' Holland, Flanders and France* (1709), p. 43; *Daily Universal Register*, 28 Aug. 1786.

19. F. A. Pottle (ed.), *Boswell in Holland 1763–1764* (1952), pp. 6, 11, 93; *Tour of Holland* (1772), p. 72.

20. Macclesfield, BL, Stowe Mss. 750; Pococke, BL, Add. 22978, fo. 84; Inglis to Keith, 4 March 1786, BL, Add. 35536.

21. Shaw, *Letters to a Nobleman*, p. 56; Grey, BL, Add. 5957, fo. 62–3.

22. Harrington to Walter Titley, envoy in Copenhagen, 18 May (os), Baltimore to Titley, 20 June, 19 Sep. 1739, BL, Eg. 2686; Guy Dickens, envoy in Berlin, to Harrington, 15 Sep., Cyril Wych, envoy in Hamburg, to Harrington, 29 Sep. 1739, PRO 82/60, 90/46.

23. *Northampton Mercury*, 8 Oct. (os), 5 Nov. (os) 1739; Chesterfield to Townshend, 21 Sep. 1728, PRO 84/301.

24. Craven, *Journey*, p. 202.

25. Duchess of Bedford to Sarah Marlborough, [June (os) 1732], BL, Add. 61449, fo. 120.

26. L. Temple (really by John Armstrong), *A Short Ramble through some parts of France and Italy* (1771), pp. 4–5.

27. Barker to Keith, 9 June 1787, BL, Add. 35538.

28. Brand to Wharton, 24 Sep. 1793, Durham, Wharton.
29. Young, I, 116.
30. *Tour of Holland* (1772), p. 131.
31. Andrews, 1784, pp. 477–8.
32. Wharton to —, 27 Feb., Wharton to Dr Baker, 12 March 1775, Durham, Wharton.
33. Stevens, pp. 66–7; St Vincent, BL, Add. 31192, fo. 16–17; Essex, p. 22.
34. *Tour of Holland* (1772), pp. 201–5, 208.
35. Stevens, p. 324; L. Aikin (ed.), *Aikin*, I, 92.
36. Brand to Wharton, 6 Dec. 1790, Durham, Wharton; Pococke, BL, Add. 22978, fo. 86.
37. Swinton, 8 June (os) 1731; *Tour of Holland* (1772), p. 85; Essex, p. 36.
38. Polwarth to Whitworth, 7 Sep. 1722, BL, Add. 37389.
39. Gray, I, 99; Craven, *Journey*, p. 7; Gardenstone, I, 15; Young, I, 52.
40. Wharton to Thomas Wharton, 4 Oct. 1775, Durham, Wharton; Thompson, I, 54; Walker, pp. 334–5.
41. Brand to Wharton, 7 April 1780, Durham, Wharton.
42. Fraser, *Melvilles*, I, 326.
43. Craven, *Journey*, p. 11.
44. BL, Add. 12130, fo. 102, 147.
45. Brand to Wharton, 11 July 1779, 24 Nov. 1789, Durham, Wharton; L. Aikin, *Aikin*, p. 68.
46. Petty to Keith, 30 Oct. 1785, BL, Add. 35535.
47. *Fife*, p. 23; Pococke, BL, Add. 22978; 12 May 1734; Brand to Wharton, 9 Aug., 1 Sep. 1780, Durham, Wharton.

3 ACCOMMODATION, FOOD AND DRINK

We are to sleep this night at a very good or rather fine house erected by Cosimo the first for the reception of strangers, I wish he had furnished it, for 'tis without windows and with very few doors, the furniture just enough to sit down to supper and lie down to sleep, for which our rough and dismal journey has prepared us . . .

Lady Pomfret, Radiocofani (Tuscany), 15 March 1741.

Accommodation

In ye article of good eating, and drinking, France goes far beyond us; and we exceed them as much in ye good accommodations of our inns. I hardly remember one place where some of us did not sleep in the same room in which we supped; — for it was generally furnished with two or three beds, and those beds almost as generally occupied with troops of bugs, and whole armies of fleas. The nightly excursions, and attacks of those hopping, and creeping gentry were a great annoyance to all ye company except myself, who happily have not ye honour of being to their taste.

Walter Stanhope on the journey from Paris to Berne, 1769.[1]

An important factor encouraging tourists to spend as much time as possible in major towns and to rush from one to the next, was the nature of the accommodation available elsewhere. Over most of Europe small towns, villages and rural areas could not offer acceptable accommodation for tourists accustomed in Britain, since having left school, to a modicum of comfort. There were no networks of inns or hotels to match the post roads of Europe, and accommodation outside the major towns was only provided on any scale on a few of the major routes. The two-day boat trip from Chalon to Lyons always broke at Mâcon and there was plenty of accommodation available there, though some tourists disliked the town as old and ugly. Radicofani was an accepted night-stop, with accommodation provided, on the Rome-Siena route. However many tourists experienced bad accommodation on at least one stage of their journey. Tourists who wandered far from the usual routes could hardly have been surprised at the nature of their accommodation. It was bad in Spain: Thomas Pelham had a travelling bed made; Arthur Young in his brief trip in the Catalan Pyrenees in 1787 was forced on at least two occasions to pass up unsatisfactory inns for the dubious pleasures of the private houses of a *curé* and a shopkeeper. Possibly the desire for effect led him to exaggerate conditions at the former, but he is worth quoting as contemporaries would probably have seen it as an accurate description. Of one bed Young wrote, 'the bed and a pavement might be ranked in the same class of softness'. Young's friend had to make do with the table 'and what with bugs, fleas, rats, and mice, slept not'.[2] Sir James Porter took furniture with him on his trip from Constantinople to London via Cracow in 1762, which was just as well given the nature of the accommodation available. Lady Craven was able to sleep in her coach: she had a travelling bed with her; though in 1786 on her way from Moscow to the Crimea her excellent contacts were of use: 'At Soumi I was indebted to Mr. Lanskoy and a brother of Prince Kourakin, who were both quartered there, for a lodging, as they obliged a Jew to give me up a new house which he was on the point of inhabiting.'[3]

Colonel Gordon and Lyttleton spent the night 'on straw in the famous village of Leuthen' in Silesia. George Ogilvie found the lodging in post houses en route from Hamburg to Osnabrück unsatisfactory. At Leese he recorded, 'our beds stink abominably and half the panes of glass in the windows were broken, so that we were almost froze to death'. The post house at Boompt was so dirty that he continued to Osnabrück, though it was January and he had to travel by moonlight.[4]

The position was little better outside the major towns in Italy, France, Germany and the Low Countries. Richard Pococke was dissatisfied with the inns on his descent from the Alps into Savoy in 1734. Andrew Mitchell commented on Ancona, 'the inn is exceeding bad'. Sacheverell Stevens was unimpressed by the situation in Italy. On the way from Rome to Naples he stayed at Piperno — 'the town affords but bad accommodations for travellers' — and on the way from Florence to Bologna he spent a night at Scarparia where he 'found but very indifferent accommodations'. David Garrick informed his brother in 1764 that at Munich, 'eating, drinking, and beds exceed those in Italy'. Returning from an Italian excursion with his pupil, Duncombe, Thomas Brand wrote: 'We met with some distresses from abundant vermin and from the indifferent accommodations of the *castles* of Piedmont.' On his way from Siena to Viterbo Walker stopped the night at Aqua Pendenta and complained of 'the bugs and fleas of this filthy town'.[5] Fortunately the situation was very different in the major Italian towns. In these good accommodation was available, though some tourists, such as Walker in Milan, were angered by the cost. Pococke found 'a very good English publick house' in Venice; Pomfret 'a very good inn' in Siena. Stevens was impressed by the accommodation in Naples. In general tourists were satisfied by the quality of their accommodation in the Italian towns. Difficulties could arise if it was impossible to get into the best inns, as happened to Viscount Nuneham and Lord Bulkeley at Trieste, but the wealthy British tourists in Italy rarely had problems in the major towns. Possibly the situation would have been different had the number of tourists approached Parisian figures, but until the end of the period Italy remained a largely exclusive area of tourism and most of the British tourists there were reasonably wealthy and did not share Walker's concern with the cost of accommodation.[6]

'In Germany . . . a man may travel many days and not find a bed to lie upon' observed one British newspaper in 1722, and the situation in Germany, outside the major towns, was generally regarded as fairly bleak. Travelling from Cologne to Lorraine in 1711, Sir Carnaby Haggerston was 'often content with straw to lie on'. Nine years later John Molesworth complained from Augsburg of 'scurvy accommodation, but yet which I wonder at, as dear as at London or Paris'. Pöllnitz's memoirs, published in English in the 1730s, were full of damning comments.

Whoever would be well accommodated at Carlsbad must carry 3 things thither with him, his own bed, wine and cook . . . 'Tiz surprizing that so plentiful a country as Saxony should have no better ordinarys. I don't mean Leipsic and Dresden, where considering one is in Germany, we come off pretty well; though were it so in Holland, the Netherlands, or in France, we should not think ourselves well used. I mean the little towns and villages in a road so frequented as that from Leipsic to Dresden. There's provision to be had at these ordinaries, but then 'tis so ill dressed, and the house so nasty, that 'tis enough to turn one's stomach.

Sacheverell Stevens left a full account of his accommodation in various parts of Germany, and it is clear from it that he was unprepared for the type of accommodation and bedding provided there,

The manner of lodging in this country seems odd, for on going to your bed you perceive neither quilt, blankets, nor sheets on it, and are apt to conclude that the maid had forgot to put them on, when she turns down a down-bed and discovers the sheets, for the custom here is, instead of quilts, etc. to lay a bed on them, which is very disagreeable, and almost smothers those not used to this method of lodging.

On his trip from Nürnberg to Württemberg he wrote,

. . . night coming on, we were obliged to put up at a little ordinary town; but the inn to outward appearance, looked to be a good one, the provisions were tolerable, and the wine excellent; we ordered the maidservant to shew us to our beds, who conducted us to a long room, the sides of which were littered down with straw, but for what use I could not conceive, nor imagining that they had their stables upstairs; she then, to our great surprize, informed us that was the place where we were to lay, there being but one bed in the house, and that was occupied by her master and mistress, so we lay down in the straw, like so many horses, in our cloaths; in a short time came in ten or a dozen gentlemen — travellers, well dressed, who were used to the custom of the country, and very contentedly laid themselves down on the straw, and fell asleep; for my part I had but little, and was glad to see morning return . . .

Twenty miles from Hanover he came upon an inn where 'there were no beds in the house, so we were obliged to lie upon straw'. In Westphalia he was,

. . . under the necessity of putting up at an inn in a little dirty village, which consisted of only one large room; at that end next the fire place were several little places, like cloaths presses, or closets with folding doors, in each place was a bed, to which you ascend by a little step ladder; you are obliged to undress before the landlord and landlady, who see each passenger to his respective bed, and then shut the folding doors; but I begged to have mine left open, for fear of being smothered; at about ten yards from me, on one side of the room, there were several cows in their stalls, and on the other hogs in little pens; I never had so disagreeable a lodging, and began to wish myself again in my clean straw in Upper Germany.[7]

The bedding available was commented on by several travellers. Walker compared the method of sleeping in Germany to lying 'between two beds'. Walker, Wharton and the Scottish mathematician, Colin Maclaurin, were amazed at the height of foreign beds, Walker claiming that Tyrolean beds were at angle of 25 degrees and the other two that they literally had to climb into bed.[8]

Tourists were however generally satisfied with the accommodation available in the major German towns, such as Vienna, Prague, Dresden, Munich, Hanover and Frankfurt. Petty wrote from Prague in 1785: 'We are extreamly well lodged in an handsome suite of apartments in a very good street, and everything comfortable about us.'[9]

In Switzerland most tourists only ever stayed in the major towns, particularly Geneva and Lausanne. Here the accommodation was generally good. Walter Stanhope in Lausanne stayed with private families, but assured his mother that this was in order, and that he gained valuable introductions as a result, 'to take in Boarders is not ye least disgrace to ye best families here'. Equally there was concern if young men, abroad for their education, lodged in undesirable inns. Edward Mellish was forced to reassure his father and his uncle on his point when he stayed in Tours in 1730–1: 'being lately informed by an English Gentleman who was some time at Tours that he was obliged to lodge and eat in a publick house (as there were no private pensions for strangers) . . . Colonel Paget keeps house but as there is no such thing as private pension here, the rest of the English lodge and eat in a Publick House.' Mellish observed that it was the custom in France and the Low Countries to lodge in public houses.[10]

Accommodation in the Low Countries was generally satisfactory, though Porter complained that the post house at Amersfort was 'a most dirty, wretched hole'. James Essex noted at Ghent, 'our lodging was a piece with our supper having excellent beds fine clean sheets and everything answerable to them, but in this as in all other places where we baited, we eat drank and slept in the same room'. Aikin 'lodged . . . very well' at Ghent, and stayed in

Ostend in 'a very comfortable (but dear) English house'. Cradock's hotel at Breda was very clean, though expensive. At Gorcum he found 'an excellent hotel'.[11] Possibly tourists would have been less satisfied had they toured the landward provinces of the United Provinces, such as Gröningen and Gelderland, or the south and east of the Austrian Netherlands, particularly the Ardennes. George Tilson lumped part of the United Provinces in with Westphalia in his condemnation of 'ye heaths, marshes, barns and dunghills of Overyssell and Westphalia'.[12]

There was a wide choice of accommodation available in Paris. It was possible to lodge with private individuals. Sir John Blair did so in 1787 in order to learn French. His bearleader Arbuthnot wrote to Keith: 'I have within these few days removed to the house of a Mr de Ville a Secretaire du Roi, where we board. It is a situation attended with no other advantage, than its serving to forward Sir J. Blair in his knowledge of the French tongue, from his hearing no other language spoken at table.'[13] Most tourists stayed in hotels. The Hotel de l'Impératrice in the Rue Jacob was clearly comfortable: 'we have an elegant dining room, with two bed chambers on the first floor, and a bed chamber in the entresol, with an apartment for the servant, for three guineas per week. I confess the lodgings are dear, but the situation is good, and the furniture magnificent.'[14] Others were less satisfied. Jane Parminter, who toured France in 1785, arrived in Paris on 30 June: 'sup't and slept at the hotel de la ville de Rome près de la rue de poulers et de la Colonnade de Louvre a very dirty inn indeed, the staircase shaking, the maids bold and impertinent, the treatment sparing and the charge extravagant.' Lady Knight was pestered by bugs, a fate that also afflicted Jane Parminter at Chailly near Paris and Mrs Montagu.[15]

There is a mass of comment available on the inns between Calais and Paris. This was the first experience of foreign accommodation for most tourists, and not all found it agreeable. Sacheverell Stevens complained of the accommodation available at Abbeville and Beauvais and of 'the badness of the inns in general on this road', and a tourist, on his way from Lille to Paris, wrote of Péronne: 'We lodged at a dirty little cabaret, for it deserved not the name of an inn, where we met with very indifferent accommodations, did not therefore regret the early summons of the coachman.'[16] Smollett, on the other hand, praised his accommodation at Montreuil and Amiens and Arthur Young was 'well lodged, fed and attended' at the Hotel de Bourbon at Cambrai.[17] Young left a lot of information about the state of accommodation available for travellers. He was pleased with Dunkirk, a view shared by James Essex, Pont l'Evêque and Nîmes, though at Bordeaux he was dissatisfied with one aspect of his hotel: 'The inns at this city are excellent; the Hotel d'Angleterre and the Prince of Asturias; at the latter we found every accommodation to be wished, but with an inconsistence that cannot be too much condemned: we had very elegant apartments, and were served on plate, yet the necessary-house the same temple of abomination that is to be in a dirty village.' Near Limoges, Young stopped 'at an execrable auberge, called Maison Rouge, where we intended to sleep, but, on examination, found every appearance so forbidding, and so beggarly an account of a larder, that we passed on to Limoge'. In Pamiers the inn was terrible though on the way from Bayonne to Bordeaux 'everything at Aire seemed good and clean; and what is very uncommon, I had a parlour to eat my dinner in, and was attended by a neat well dressed girl'. However, though Young was soaked as a result of a downpour 'the old landlady was in no haste to give me fire enough to be dried'. Young was very dissatisfied with the Breton inns: 'sleep at the *Lion d'Or* at Montauban, an abominable hole . . . This villainous hole, that calls itself the *Grand Maison*, is the best inn at a post town [Belleisle] on the great road to Brest, at which marshals of France, dukes, peers, countesses, and so forth, must now and then, by the accidents to which long journies are subject, have found themselves. What are we to think of a country that has made, in the eighteenth century, no better provision for its travellers.'[18] Provincial French inns failed to satisfy many tourists, particularly on the score of cleanliness. Many claimed that they were full of bugs, whilst Mrs Montagu stated that 'inns are so little frequented in France one often meets with damp beds'.[19]

Faced with problems with accommodation tourists could always carry camp beds in their coaches. Sir Carnaby Haggerston, Thomas Pelham and Lady Craven all resorted to this expedient. This was an inconvenient method rarely resorted to except by those who travelled in regions not usually visited by tourists. Instead the nature of the accommodation was one of the factors that discouraged tourists from venturing off the beaten track. Furthermore it encouraged them to move from city to city as fast as possible for in the cities accommodation was generally of a better standard and less likely to be full, and there was more choice. In 1780 Thomas Brand learnt the miseries of a trip in the country. He went from Geneva, where he was staying, to see the Perte du Rhône, a section of the Rhône between Geneva and Lyons that ran underground. He endured: 'the miseries of bad weather, an open cabriolet . . . and a wretched inn. The *inn* having but one fire place we were altogether a goodly company of men women children hogs and poultry . . . You'll guess that the first glimpse of the morning made me quit the luxury of my couch.'[20]

Food

> I was helped to an excellent Fricassee, but was much puzzled to find out what it was, there being an uncommon quantity of bones and especially of small merry-thoughts . . . I found that I had been eating no small quantity of fricasseed frogs. I shall bring the recipt [sic] home with me. It will be at least a curiosity. They tasted exceedingly like white veal which you know is so much approved of.
>
> Wharton, Dijon, 1775.[21]

A common theme in eighteenth-century xenophobic English literature was that the contrast between free Britons and unfree Europeans, particularly the French, was symbolised by the difference in their food. British food was solid, substantial and good for you. Its eaters enjoyed vigour and character. French food, in contrast, was insubstantial, and in particular lacking in meat. The French sought to disguise the poverty of their food by showy sauces. The food was devoid of goodness. Ragouts were specifically attacked and the habit of eating frogs condemned. A standard critique of the Walpole ministry was that its members preferred foreign to British dishes.[22] The food symbolism could be mocked, but there is no doubt of its frequent reiteration. 'A true Englishman who loves roast beef and pudding cannot breath freely out of his own island' wrote Lord Boyle, whilst a pamphlet referred to,

> a certain Ald——n in the City . . . particularly fond of beef, which he calls Protestant victuals, and ascribes the glorious victories of La Hogue and Hochstedt to it; and says, there is

religion and liberty in an English sirloin: But foreign cookery is
like the Latin Mass, and wishes that soups and ragouts were out
of fashion, for that they savour strongly of Popery and wooden
shoes; Let us (us this magistrate) in the name of Liberty and full
bellies, stick to Beef and Pudding, . . .[23]

Yet most British tourists were happy with the food they found in
Europe and discovered that reports of continental cooking and
eating habits were often wrong. It was possible to obtain meat in
Paris in Lent.[24] Wharton did 'not find all their dishes stuffed with
onions . . . as I expected'.[25] When in 1787 the Irish tourist James
St John discussed with a Frenchman the eating of frogs the Frenchman told him that the British were unfair in criticising this habit as
they ate shrimps and cockles.[26] Furthermore much of the food
eaten in Europe was similar to that consumed in Britain. The
principal difference was not fricassees of frogs, but the wider range
of fruit readily available in Europe. Possibly the major novelty was
the different manner in which a lot of food was prepared. In the
major cities frequented by British tourists it was possible to find the
same dishes that they ate at home. Brand wrote from Naples in
1792, 'we eat roast beef and potatoes'.[27]

Food in the Low Countries was generally satisfactory. At Dort
Joseph Shaw found 'good Rhenish wine and salmon, and bad
cooks'. Zachary Grey was very interested in the salad he was served
when he ate in a village neat Antwerp: 'among the viands served in
for our supper, there was cabbage sallad made after the following
manner. A cabbage very finely sliced, an apple or two minced, one
large onion minced: mix well all together, and eat them with
pepper, vinegar, and salt.' James Essex was very disappointed at
Nieuport: 'when we sat down to dinner . . . at not being served as
usual with several sorts of dishes, there being nothing provided but
soupe maigre and two or three sorts of fish dressed in a plain way,
. . . it was meagre day on which nobody eats flesh meat in that
country, . . .' He cheered up however on the Bruges-Ghent barge,

> . . . our dinner consisted of 2 hot courses. 5 dishes each and a
> desert or fruite and biskets. for the first course
>   Beef Boiled
>   Peas stewed
>   Soupe
>   French beans stewed

Herrings pickled on Greens.
Secd. Course
Mutton Roasted
Veal
Fowls
Soals
Veal stewed.
Desert
Apricots — Plum
Pears
biskets — Crumplins
filberts
Butter Cheese.

After this 15d dinner (modern lunch) he had at Ghent a supper 'of 2 hot courses of five dishes each and after it a Desert of fruit and biskets with ice cream and our wine was served in ice'.[28] Cradock was pleased with Dutch food. After an 'exceedingly good' dinner at Utrecht he observed,

> The meat in Holland is not to be despised, but the flesh is not so firm as that in England; it is spongy, from the rankness or luxuriance of the herbage with which the cattle are fed. Very little beef is ever brought to table in Holland . . . The beef that you chiefly see is preserved in the winter, when they smoke a great quantity of it, to eat in summer with butter or salads . . . Their butter is of the best quality, but they cut off all the fat from their mutton or veal cutlets, and bring them congealed in no small quantity of it; for, from their long passages, and want of proper covers, it is difficult sometimes to raise them with a strong fork from their dishes. However, they make full amends by their puddings, which are pronounced to be good for the stomach, and they are amply fortified with the best spices, and very superior brandy.

One of the Dutch dishes he tried was a water-souchée: 'It consisted of a fish soup, with either a very large tench or perch in the middle of it; and it was surrounded with little plates, containing some necessary additions . . . black-rye cake . . . Gorgona anchories . . . and hot India pickles . . .'[29]

Travelling in Europe it was not always easy to get a good meal outside the major towns. Rushing from Lille to Brussels in 1734 the Duchess of Queensberry's party had to make do with 'two cold black chickens which from extream hunger' they found delicious. A dispute between some French officers and the master on the boat that Robert Wharton took from Lyons to Avignon led to the passengers being dumped for the night at an unscheduled stop: 'where we could neither get vituals, drink, nor beds. At last we got a few eggs, and a loaf or two and some vile wine.' On the way from Calais to St Omer, Colin MacLaurin noted: 'the country on the road seemed very poor and we would have dined very uncomfortably had we not carried wine with us. We could find nothing but eggs to eat being Friday.' Arthur Young 'dined, or rather starved, at Bernay'.[30]

Most tourists in France found something about the food to grumble about at some stage — the food itself or its preparation or service or cost could be attacked. Smollett complained at Boulogne that 'the meat is boiled or roasted to rags'. Boswell disliked the French custom of a heavy meal at night. William Windham thought French meat very indifferent. Joseph Shaw complained from Paris, 'most of the meat being rotton [sic] before they eat it, which is very nauseous to strangers'.[31]

However, the dominant impression is one of satisfaction. The fictional squire of *Mist's Weekly Journal* who complained because he could not get 'a Buttock of salt beef and carrots for supper' in Paris was not much in evidence. Though dissatisfied with the way in which it was prepared John Boteler found the meat in Rheims 'tollerable' in 1722. Six years later Robert Trevor's complaints were limited to the fact that the figs, melons, plums, summer pears, peaches and nectarines which he tasted in Paris were below expectation, being no better than British fruit, and that as the French neither hunted fallow deer nor thought it worth eating 'an haunch of venison is a dish unknown here'.[32] Charles Thompson was delighted by the food at Lyons, Valence and Montélimar. At Avignon he, 'found all sorts of fish, flesh, fruit, and wines in the greatest plenty . . . and at the most reasonable rates'. His discussion of French dietary habits was not unfavourable.

The French are more extravagant in their dress than in their diet. It is certain they eat not near the quantity of flesh that the English do, nor do they often dress it in the same manner. Soups, fricassees, ragouts and hashes, season'd with onions, spices, and herbs, are generally preferred before whole joints of meat boiled or roasted; and what they do boil or roast has scarce a drop of gravy left in it. They often keep their meat so long before they dress it, that an Englishman would think it fit for nothing but the dunghill; and: indeed were it not for their herbs and high seasoning, it would scarce be eatable. But if they eat less meat than we do, they eat twice the quantity of bread, which in France is generally very light and good. In Lent the common people feed much on white kidney-beans and white lentils, which is a sort of pulse not known in England. The French are great lovers of salads, roots, etc. and particularly are very fond of sorrel . . . But they seem to delight in nothing more than mushrooms . . . Their pears, apples, plums, peaches, and other fruits are admirable . . .

Thompson even went so far as to compare the French and the British diet to the favour of the former: 'The French are remarkable for their sprightliness and vivacity, to which the air of their country, their wines and diet, must very much contribute; for those who drink malt-liquors, and eat great quantities of flesh, may well be supposed to be heavier and slower of apprehension.'[33]

Smollett's comments from Paris were reasonably favourable: 'All manner of butcher's meat and poultry are extremely good in this place. The beef is excellent . . . I can by no means relish their cookery; but one breakfasts deliciously upon their *petit pains* and their *patés* of butter, which last is exquisite.' William Windham, writing in 1769, thought the food in Paris good apart from the fish. Fruit was cheap and plentiful, better than in England because of the climate, though he claimed that the English took care to select the best fruit. Windham was particularly struck by the French peaches which had a finer flavour than their British counterparts. A tourist's account published three years later gave a very favourable impression of the meals available in Paris: 'We generally dine at a Table d'Hote, where we find genteel people, and good dinners, the price is different at different houses; but for forty sous a head, which is twenty-pence English, we dine most sumptiously on two courses of seven and five, with a dessert and a Burgundy; . . . We always sup at home. We buy our wine of the merchant, and our supper is sent from the neighbouring traiteurs.'[34]

That winter St Vincent praised the food at the inn he stayed in at

Amiens, whilst the following summer Essex had a good dinner at
Gravelines, and at Dunkirk a supper for four people at 15d a head:
'it consisted of two fowls boild, a duck roasted a very fine codling,
a dish of artichokes and a fine salad, these were replaced by a dish
of tarts, a plate of apricots, 2 plates of maccaroons with other
confectionarys.'

Wharton was pleased with French food. On his way from Calais
to Paris he found 'the victuals very eatable'. In Paris he discovered
'that a French dinner is of 2 courses the first Boulli, of soups boiled
meats hashes etc. the next Roti, of roast meats pies and the Desert'.
Lent did not disturb him. He informed his uncle Thomas Lloyd
that it was not necessary to fast: 'I dined today at a Table d'Hote
on soups, beef, roast mutton, fowls, pigeons, besides made dishes,
nor have I seen a maigre table since I have been here except one and
that was in the midst of four gras ones. Either dispensations are
very cheap or consciences very easy here. I rather think the latter.'
His other Parisian meals were lighter: 'my breakfast is excellent,
tea (at 10 liv. a pound) good cream, good butter and French rolls.
My supper is a little bread and (English cheese), and a glass of
burgundy and water.' From Paris he travelled to Dijon and on the
way at Moret 'breakfasted on wine of the country, small, but well
tasted enough, like small Burgundy; Radishes, and bread and
butter'. At Dijon he discovered new dishes: 'Among the strange
dishes we had were artichokes unboiled, and just cut out of the
garden. They eat the bottoms of them cold with pepper and salt.
When I eat my salad with mustard they stared at me and still more
so when I eat it with the roast meat. They eat it only with a bit of
bread.' The habit of comparing British and French food was a
common one among tourists. From Marseilles he wrote: 'the fruit
was better at Lyons than it is here except the melons. I had as leave
eat an Old Park fig as a Marseilles one. The peaches of Lyons are
the best fruit I have yet met with. They have few nectarines and
those not so good as ours.' Wharton also commented on the contrast between British and French table manners,

> . . . it is rude to eat with your fork in the left hand. It is also rude
> to put the side spoon into your mouth, to put a knife in is
> shocking. Yet it is polite to lick up the sauce with your bread, to
> take a fowl by the leg to carve it, to lay hold of the shank of a leg
> (gigot) of mutton which indeed is wrapped in a clean paper, hold
> it up and slice it, to pick your teeth with your knife etc. etc.[35]

The following year Lady Knight, who had found the food at Paris 'admirable good', gave a dinner for three at Toulouse: 'We had a soup, and a dish of the stewed beef, a very fine large eel, mutton chops, a brace of the red partridge, an omelet with peaches in it, grapes, peaches, pears, and savoy biscuits; a bottle of Bordeaux — sixteen-pence — bottle of our own wine, value three-halfpennys. The whole expense amounted to ten shillings, wine included and a very fine cauliflower.' Thomas Brand, who disliked the vegetable diet he was given in lodgings near Geneva, found that it was difficult to obtain meat when he visited the Perte du Rhône in 1780, 'It was maigre day and as I was taken for a cure or some limb of the church we found it difficult to get meat for our supper'. Five years later Lady Craven tasted the best crawfish and trout she had ever eaten in the Sorgue and purchased 'very excellent melons out of the fields for five sols a piece' in Provence. In 1786 Lord Gardenstone observed that 'Most kinds of provisions are good and plentiful in this country' and at the La Rape restaurant in Paris had a dish called Matelot: 'It is a kind of fish Olio, composed of eels, carp, etc. with a high season and savoury sauce. I own I have a vulgar taste.' Arthur Young had a fine taste for regional varieties of French cooking. Between Toulouse and the Mediterranean he noted: 'immense quantities of poultry in all this country; most of it the people salt and keep in grease. We tasted a soup made of the leg of a goose thus kept, and it was not nearly so bad as I expected.' Near Strasbourg he commented on the German style cookery and singled out schnitz, 'a dish of bacon and fried pears; has the appearance of an infamous mess; but I was surprised, on tasting, to find it better than passable'.[36]

Variety, good value, plenty and interest was what many tourists recorded of the food they found in France. Edward Mellish wrote of 'my good living at Blois, where with a good Bottle of wine, a soupe a joint of mutton; and a fowl I used to regale myself with much pleasure'. It was pleasant for tourists to have the opportunity to enjoy French food, to spend time as Garrick did in Paris: 'did very little this day but idle and eat and drink.'[37] And yet some British writers, including several who had been to France, continued to print denunciations of French food and cooking. In 1788 James St John printed the letters he had written the previous year:

the French peasants eat great quantities of salad; which I am inclined to think, can never afford anything but an acid and unwholesome chyle; for a raw, watery vegetable, with an incongruous of oil, salt, vinegar, and spice, can never be agreeable to the nature of man; and a continued use of such a composition must be highly detrimental . . . the French stew their meat to an excess, that renders it sapless and dry, and very indigestible; though perhaps nature never intended that we should dress our meat at all; and therefore we hear the French continually complaining of indigestions . . . The quantity of spices which the French take in their ragouts and fricassees, must be unnecessary in a temperate climate, and injure the constitution . . . the French would be much superior to what they are in arts and sciences, if they nourished themselves as nature intended and requires

St John went on to suggest that a banning of soup would be in the French interest.[38] It is often difficult to take this writer seriously, and possibly his comment on the banning of soup was meant facetiously. However there is no doubt of his vigorous attack on French salad and spices, views not shared by most tourists, though his views on the manner in which the French cooked meat were widely shared. There were dangers in French cooking but they were not those that St John decried. Instead they were dangers common throughout Europe: unhygienic cooking utensils and inadequate and unhygienic cooking methods such as those that killed thirty students in a Caen seminary in 1769.[39]

No other country aroused anything like the interest and criticism that French cooking received in Britain. As far as British tourists were concerned the general picture was the same as that with French food: enjoyment, or at least acceptance, of the food although they were often critical of the cooking. Germany was not regarded as a culinary paradise, though complaints about German food tended to relate to the difficulty of securing it rather than to questions of quality. Boswell complained in Westphalia that he could get nothing for dinner but eggs, and that he had had to eat bread that was black and sour. Travelling from Donauwörth to Nürnberg, Stevens observed 'the provisions on the road are but indifferent'. Brand complained of the lack of food when he had dinner in the palace gardens at Potsdam: 'I could get little else to eat than sour crout [sic] and sausages and my napkin had served some greasy whiskered Hussar the day before.' Walker noted that when he stopped at Montebauer on his trip through the Rhineland:

'At the post-house we were regaled with wild-boar ham, a kind of savage food.'[40] Clearly part of the problem was that German food — black bread, sausages and sauerkraut and many game products — was new to many British tourists, whereas many who had had experience of London society were no strangers to French cooking. Many tourists liked what they found in Germany. Stevens found an inn 20 miles from Hanover where there was no bed but 'the provisions and wine were extremely good'. Lady Craven was delighted by the large crawfish and the delicious flavour of the Bohemian pheasants that she found in Vienna, and by the availability there of peas, artichokes and asparagus in December. Robert Arbuthnot and Lord Ancram had 'an excellent supper' at an inn in Rheinfels in 1787. Garrick praised Bavarian food. German meat could be acclaimed as the best in the world.[41] Further east tourists had to accept what they could find and much of that was certainly very different to that available in Britain. Lady Craven found excellent dried fish in the Balkans and in the Crimea fresh butter made of buffalo milk, which she liked, wild asparagus, a wild kind of delicious enormous horse radish and 'sherbert, an indifferent kind of lemonade'. She noted that 'Tartarian cookery consists in much grease and honey' neither widely used in British cooking, and largely lived upon new milk in which she melted a little chocolate.[42] In Iberia the food was not so unusual. Some of the inns offered unsatisfactory cooking, but there was a profusion of fresh fruit and Arthur Young, a stern critic, was satisfied in Barcelona: 'A good supper, with some excellent Mediterranean fish; ripe peaches; good wine; the most delicious lemonade in the world . . .' As with Germany the essential problem in Iberia was to find sufficient, rather than satisfactory, food. There was a generally favourable view of Spanish food,

> . . . such variety of delicious fruit, that I must confess I never saw any place comparable to it . . . Their rabbits are not so good as ours in England; they have great plenty of partridges, which are larger and finer feathered than ours. They have but little beef in Spain, because there is no grass, but they have plenty of mutton, and exceeding good, because their sheep feed only upon wild potherbs; their pork is delicious, their hogs feeding only upon chestnuts and acorns.

Thomas Pelham supped every night in Madrid on roasted apples. He was conscious of the difficulties of obtaining food outside the major cities, and made preparations accordingly. Before his trip into southern Spain he wrote: 'a Boiler is making that may hang under my chaise to boil my dinner, for there are as many precautions to be taken for travelling in this Country as if I were going into Arabia: my journey from Lisbon (to Madrid) has taught me all the desagremens and how many of them are only imaginary ones for after two or three days travelling you fancy your boiled chicken or rabbit better than all the blankets [sic] or ragouts from a French kitchen, . . .' For the first three days of his journey from Madrid to Cordoba he 'lived upon Madrid provisions'.[43]

The availability of food in Italy varied greatly. Martyn's guidebook provided information on the food in the markets. Of Nice he wrote,

> The market is tolerably well supplied with fish, beef, pork, mutton, and veal; the lamb is small and often poor; poultry is very indifferent and dear; butter is good and rather cheap; bread very indifferent indeed . . . rabbits are rare, and geese scarcely to be seen. All winter they have green pease, asparagus, artichokes, cauliflowers, beans, kidney beans, endive, cabbage, radishes, lettuce, etc. Potatoes from the mountains, mushrooms, and the finest truffles in the world. Winter fruits are olives, oranges, lemons, citrons, dried figs, grapes, apples, pears, almonds, chestnuts, walnuts, filberts, medlars, pomegranates . . . and the berries of the laurel . . . The grapes are large and luscious. Musk-melons are very cheap, . . .

In an age when food was difficult to preserve and transport poor, and when, in consequence, such fruit were rarities in Britain, Nice was indeed a terrestrial paradise. Rome offered porcupine and small birds,

> Provisions are plentiful and good; their *Vitella mongana* particularly excellent, as is also their swine's flesh; the worst meat is mutton: they have *capretti* or kid, and the venison of wild deer or *capreole*, but very lean: porcupine is also sometimes sold in the markets. Poultry and wild fowl are fine and plentiful. They eat all sorts of small birds, down to the wren; and several birds which we never touch; as hawks, jays, magpies, and woodpeckers. They have a good variety of fish, both of the fresh waters, and of the sea.

In Naples, 'Provisions are plentiful and cheap: poultry, game, and fish are abundant; fruits and garden-stuff are to be had all winter in so favourable a climate.'[44]

Tourists' experiences were more varied. Swinton complained of the food and wine at Lerici, where the food was ruined by too much oil, but he was generally impressed by Italian food. He thought the beef and veal in Genoa the best in the world, the beef being very sweet and tender, and was pleased that meat cost less than in Britain. After describing delicious broccoli, and ravioli, he went on to praise the large pigs and pigeons in Livorno, where he thought the meat was very good, and the superb pigeons and good large carp in Pisa. He was also very impressed by the peas. Mitchell praised the mutton in Spoleto and Pococke the cherries in Bologna. Pococke was generally satisfied with what he ate. In April 1734 he encountered the problem of meatless Fridays: 'dined at a small inn called Postificiciola 5 miles from Rome; the woman told me none but Jews eat meat on Fridays, I told her travellers might, she said it was excommunication to eat it, I had a good dish of fascoli dryed, kidney beans broth, all beans almost, eggs and a good sallade and a pint of wine for 6½d.' Four weeks later he breakfasted at Albano on eggs he boiled in the sulphur baths, whilst at Venice he was able to 'eat very well in the English way, have 6 or 7 dishes'. Whilst waiting to cross the Tessino on the ferry he 'breakfasted on the bank on Bologna sausages, and drank the clear river water'. Crossing the Alps back to France he praised the butter and 'bought a salted Marmot which they say eats like ham and costs 1s 6d'.

William Drake 'Paid exorbitantly' at Radicofani in 1769 for a 'supper, which consisted of some broth, a boiled fowl a roast fowl and a fricassee of chickens'. Viscount Perceval, who had visited Italy, wrote to the younger Edward Southwell who planned to travel there: 'I wish health, safety and pleasure may attend you, but the most substantial good of an Englishman three meals a day I cannot pray for, because it is impossible to find it of a constancy in Italian journeys without a special miracle . . .' Joshua Pickersgill and two friends became very ill at Turin as a result of bad food. Mrs Flaxman had her first Italian dinner at Chivesco,

> . . . and being Saturday we found a meagre fare; being the first real Italian dinner I shall enumerate the dishes — a macaroni soup with cheese, some nasty rice fritters with cheese, salt fish, pickled fish, and a plate of little fried things that were tolerably

palatable but as I fancied they were snails I could not be prevailed on to eat any; the Dr. was the only one among us who relished it, insisting all the while that it was little fish. It might have been, but I am sure I saw one or two long snails if not more among them — any kind of flesh could not be got for love or money. We . . . entered our carriage hungry and discontented . . . We from this day carefully charged the landlords of all inns to omit cheese in our soup and garlick in our meat — the supper turned out tolerable, a weak broth with the liquor of a tough wild fowl; a ditto roasted dry as a stick, the two principal dishes.

Stevens complained in Ferrara of 'provisions excessive dear, and what is still worse very bad' but praised the 'very reasonable' provisions in Verona. Philip Francis dined well in Siena and at Livorno had 'an incomparable dory' for dinner, but he had to put up with 'the vilest of all cookery' at his Turin lodgings. Crossing the Cenis he had an excellent meal — 'a black cock for dinner. Here they call it Pheasant — exquisite, as I hope to be saved; . . . a slice from the breast would bring Apicius to life again.' At Capua he dined upon provisions he had brought with him. Robson had 'an excellent supper' 15 years later. Richard Garmston had 'a bad supper' at Tolentino on his way from Loretto to Rome: Brand and his pupil dined in Turin at the British and French Ambassadors on 'wild boar and truffles, aspicks and pasticietti . . .'; and Walker's arrival in Italy was marked by his enjoyment of 'ripe and delicious grapes'. On the boat on the Brenta, Walker dined 'on fish fried in oil, for the first time, and I cannot say but I liked it much better than I expected'. As with so many other British tourists, Walker was impressed by the Italian fruit. 'I never saw such large and beautiful apples, melons, pompions, nor such quantities and variety of fine grapes' he recorded at Venice. Walker's travels revealed how the difficulties of moving fresh food ensured regional variety in the availability of food. On his return from Venice he travelled in a boat up the Po, where 'Mereschino, grapes, and brown bread are our victuals and drink, the wine on the banks of this river is so sour we cannot drink it'. He crossed the Appenines near Narni: 'a country without corn, grapes, grass, or almost any food for man or beast; we could get neither tea, coffee, chocolate, butter, or cheese; we got a few eggs, and roasted them in the ashes of a wood fire, while our horses were changing; and these are all we have eaten for the last twenty-four hours.' At Radicofani he dined in a room full of pigeons: 'we are now waiting for a dinner made up of fowls killed since our arrival — the very idea of which has spoiled my appetite several times since we arrived in this ill-accommodated country . . . our dinner has roasted pigeons in it . . . something cannibal in the idea.' At the Albergo Reale in Milan, Walker

> . . . had an excellent dinner of plump fowls, tolerable boiled beef, and the delicious small birds called Bechia Fecchi; and for the first time since we entered Italy, had a boat of melted butter to our greens. This was a great treat, though at the better inns we seldom sit down to less than a dozen dishes, (half of which we cannot eat) and a dessert of peaches, pears, and delicious grapes. Every kind of provision in this rich vale must be better than in the other parts of Italy — for Lombardy is certainly the garden of it.

Walker's general reflection on Italian food was not very encouraging,

> . . . the soil bears no grass, and of course their beef, mutton, etc. is wretched. Venison they have little or none, and what they have we should esteem carrion in England. Their fowls are a nuisance in the streets of Rome — yet I have never seen a large or a fat fowl since I entered Italy. The fish from the Mediterranean are very good — fine lobsters, plaice, sardines, mullets, etc. The bread is chiefly of Indian corn, dark coloured, and tough. Butter they have none an Englishman can eat. The pork they brag much of, but I have seen none yet I could eat — and the wild boars I have had no opportunity of tasting.

Clearly there was less good meat in Italy than British tourists were accustomed to at home. Particularly outside the big towns they found themselves eating eggs, beans and cheese rather than meat. Travelling from Rome to Naples in 1769 William Drake dined on 'red eggs, anchovies, bread and cheese' and local wine. When comparing Italian and British food, tourists, such as Walker, drew attention to the poor meat, but the usual Italian substitutes do not appear to have upset many tourists.[45]

Though the tables of all orders of people are covered with a variety of dishes, which may catch the eye, or provoke the appetite, an Englishman whose stomach is not depraved, will soon wish to see a plain wholesome dish or two of meat a la mode d'Angleterre set before him.

Thicknesse.[46]

The overwhelming impression gained from reading tourist accounts is that British travellers accepted the food they were offered, and were reasonably adventurous in their eating habits abroad. There were complaints naturally enough, but many of these related to issues that would have produced complaint at home: the difficulty of obtaining food, particularly meat, in poor areas, the absence of variety in some areas, the difficulty of keeping food fresh in a society with primitive facilities for refrigeration.

William Bennett and the Rolles were dissatisfied with the food on their journey from Brives to Orléans in October 1785. Bennett noted in his journal, 'eat a very scanty dinner of stale meat (which we could not get without difficulty)'. Their dinner at Rouen was a scandal: 'a pye had been bought and we eat some of it, but differing about the meat . . . tore off the crust, and discovered by indubitable signs that we had been devouring a cat. It is needless to say that we could eat no more, and I shall remember a Norman dinner as long as I live.'

Reading journals or correspondence in order to spot references to food and meals is possibly not the best guide to the experiences of tourists. One would expect them to stress the exceptional: a very good or very bad, very expensive, very cheap or novel meal. Many references are unhelpful: 'a good supper' being a typical one. Typical of their experiences were the following items from the journal of the 1766–7 trip of Messrs Tracy and Dentand to France and Italy,

We lay at Cambeau Fontaine, where we could get nothing but most dreadful bread and stinking cheese — in short worse accommodation than at the most wretched alehouse in England . . . [Pontarlier:] unfortunately for us it was a fast day, so that we could get no meat, but however got a tolerable supper of fish, vegetables, etc. . . . [At Pipernon on the road from Rome to Gaeta they stopped at an inn,] the victuals so filthy and so bad we could not eat them . . . [However at Naples they noted,] Green peas and Cauliflowers all the year and in short meat,

Poultry, fish, game, garden stuff, fruits, of all kinds etc. at the cheapest rate.

An anonymous tourist who travelled in 1783 noted of his supper in Arras, 'though a maigre day consisted of mackrel, cotelet and chickens, part good and part bad'. Next day he dined at Breteuil on 'fried mackerel and an omelette (being maigre day again there was nothing else to be had) and a bottle of bad wine' for all of which he was overcharged. At Chantilly he supped on a 'cold fricassee of chickens with a good dessert of strawberries'. At Châlons-sur-Marne supper was 'an omelette, a roasted fowl and part of a boiled trout'. Dining in Schwetzingen he did 'not much like the German dishes of which there was an immense variety, but were greatly pleased with the German Girl who waited on us, attempted to teach us the name of everything in German and seemed in her turn highly entertained'. At Cologne he had 'a wretched breakfast — bad tea and bad butter for the first time'.

An anonymous tourist of 1721 was displeased to find that on entering the United Provinces: 'we were now come into a new way of living. Our Burgundy wine was transformed into Dutch stum and our well served tables after the French fashion into Dutch stews.' Lady Polwarth, who was later to 'feast upon' vegetables at Nice, suffered more sickness as a result of eating greasy spinach at Péronne than on her first Channel crossing. Viscount Perceval, visiting Vincennes in 1726, 'made an excellent dinner on cold pidgeon pye and mutton loaves' which he had brought with him from Paris. He took 'cold loaves' similarly to Meudon. Zachary Grey was so interested by the cabbage salad he was given in a village near Antwerp that he recorded the method of preparation.

British dishes, particularly dishes prepared in a manner to which British tourists were accustomed, could not be obtained readily over most of Europe, and most tourists accepted this with few grumbles. Naturally many compared their food with what they were accustomed to at home, and most preferred the latter. Such patriotism was understandable, but it did not lead to a generally critical attitude to European food. Watkins wrote from Corfu in July 1788: 'you will read it over a comfortable English breakfast, which is not however preferable to ours in the Greek Islands, of rich fruits, good bread, and excellent coffee.' Tourists were pleased to find abroad excellent food similar to that which they remembered from Britain, such as trout from Lake Geneva, or the tench and perch Philip Francis enjoyed at Strasbourg and also to discover dishes that were new — the enormous Portuguese cucumbers noted by Swinton, or the plate of shrimps washed down by a glass of milk and gin enjoyed by Pratt in Holland. Charles Drake Garrard was delighted to be invited to an al fresco meal in a meadow to celebrate the Burgundian wine harvest in 1778. Tolerance to European food and cooking customs was further increased by the lengthy nature of tourist trips. Robert Poole's initial impressions of French food in 1741 were particularly bad,

> The meat in this country . . . is far less agreeable than that in London. The salt is of a very black, disagreeable colour . . . I dined this day, upon a Veal Ragoo'd; but I did not like their Ragooes, nor method of cookery, in these parts. Their soups, to me, are very indifferent. Their roast meat is not well order'd. Their boil'd is done to rags, in order to make good their soup. Their bread, for common use, is generally made into long rolls, of 2 or 3 foot long; it is sometimes pretty good, at other times hardly eatable, and often but very indifferent.

Poole was forced by hunger to try new dishes, and some he found passable, such as 'an Emmulet, vis. Eggs fry'd with herbs, which looked very black, but to hungry stomachs, tasted pretty well'. After several months abroad tourists became accustomed to different food and, in particular, to different methods of preparation. Furthermore, the fashion for French cooking in Britain led to a willingness among many to accept foreign customs. Swinton noted in Italy that British aristocrats and gentry who travelled liked their dishes dressed after the French fashion.[47]

Drink

> Of young men here is a vast abundance . . . most of them who are meer casks of *British Oak* imported hither to be filled and emptied daily with the delicious wines of the Vaux and the Côte.
>   Brand, Lausanne, 1790.[48]

Massive wine imports ensured that wine was no novelty in eighteenth-century Britain, but nevertheless the difficulties of transporting wine long distances and the limited range of wine available in Britain, ensured that many tourists were able to discover wines that they did not know before. Many were very pleased with the wine they drank. John Boteler visited Rheims in 1722 for the coronation of Louis XV and drank 'excellent champagne'. Twelve years later Richard Pococke travelled from Dijon to Calais via Rheims. At Thil he drank red champagne, and at Joinville 'we were so extravagant as to give 18d for a bottle of white champain, and have come to a resolution now we are going into the part of the country where it grows, to drink no other wine till we come into the Isle of France'. In 1730 in Vienne, Edward Mellish 'drunk some excellent wine called Cotarote' and wrote 'we stayed a day extraordinary only to regale our palates with this delicious liquor'. Gardenstone in France in 1786 noted, 'the wine better and cheaper; — good burgundy for the price of adulterated port in the English inns'. Thompson praised burgundy and champagne, and Richard Garmston, touring France in 1787, was very pleased with the wine. In Chantilly in the Auberge de Poste he 'had good Burgundy and Vin de Grave'. Travelling by diligence from Paris to Lyons he found the 'wine plenty and tolerably good'. At Montros he 'had good Burgundy and Champaign' at dinner; at Mâcon 'most excellent wine' at supper; and at Lyons excellent wine. Outside France the wine could also be good. Garmston found 'very good wine' at Otricoli, Martyn praised the quality and price of the wine at Nice, and Stevens that at Verona, whilst Walker was delighted by the excellent wine of Montefaiscone; Harry Digby had 'fine Hungary wine' at Vienna; Rhenish wine also pleased travellers such as Walker, Francis and Stevens. An anonymous tourist of 1720, on his way to the Academy at Lunéville, could obtain no wine at a 'very poor village' in the war-wasted region near Mons, but had a good burgundy to accompany his satisfactory fish at Gravelines, and drank 'incomparably good' cheap wine near Rheims and 'very good', though more expensive, wine at Châlons.[49]

However there were also complaints and criticisms. Edward Mellish, who liked the wine in Blois, complained of the wine he was given at Tours, writing to his father: 'you seem to talk of my drinking Bourdeaux Claret, alas I have never drunk a drop of good wine since I came here; which makes me often think of the last bottle of strong beer which we used to brag of at Cambridge. In this country one may buy the best wines for three pence english a bottle; notwithstanding that they give one wine at our meals which is almost sour.' An anonymous tourist noted in Rotterdam, in 1721, that the most commonly drunk wines in Rotterdam were very adulterated particularly with brimstone. William Drake found the water 'preferable to the wine' at Ravenna. Lord Leven complained about French wine in 1749. He wrote from Péronne: 'This night I have got wine I was forced to warm with sugar before I could drink it, . . . The Windmiln twopenny is better than any wine I have yet seen, except at Lille, and it not very good.' At Bernay, in 1787, Arthur Young 'met with that wine of whose ill fame I had heard so much in England, that of being worse than small beer'. St Vincent was very disappointed by the Hermitage wine he drank at Thienne,

> . . . having talked over the excellence of this wine, guess at our disappointment after tasting four or five bottles of red and white, we fixed upon one for four livres, which we were not able to drink, not the first instance of the disappointment of our expectations of drinking wine in perfection upon the spot where it grows.

James Hume could find no good brandy at Nantes, and complained that all the good brandy was exported, and Thompson made a similar allegation in the case of champagne. Thicknesse, who praised German and Hungarian wines, claimed that the Brussels wine merchants added pigeon dung and brimstone to their wine, whilst Stevens found German beer 'excessive bad'. As with food much was a matter of expectations. Wine drunk abroad was supposed to be better. Thus St Vincent was disappointed at Thienne, while Thicknesse observed, 'even the Bath road to London is not so dear as on the great roads in France, or Flanders, with this difference only, that the traveller *thinks* he drinks better wine'. Many appreciated the quantity of inexpensive wine available, and the drunkenness of British tourists was a major issue in the press discussion of tourism. Some simply disliked what they were not used to. Arriving in Paris in 1714 James Hume went to 'a cabaret where we drunk excellent English beer, I mean brewed after the English manner, which was very acceptable to us who had been reduced for some time to the necessity of drinking nothing but wine'.[50]

The poor quality of drinking water available was commented on by many tourists. This was a particular problem in coastal areas. Few shared Lady Craven's fear of being poisoned by the waters of Tartary, but many experienced discomfort, usually in the form of diarrhoea, from drinking water in Europe. Lockhart Muirhead commented on the lack of good drinking water in Ostend in 1787, Alexander Thomson the lack of 'fresh wholesome' water in Amsterdam, and Richard Pococke, the same problem in Ferrara. Tracy and Dentand complained that 'the water tasted of nothing but sulphur at Piperno'. The result was all too often illness. Smollett noted that the water in Boulogne, 'when drank by strangers, never fails to occasion pains in the stomach and bowels; nay, sometimes produces dysentries'. Carpenter thought that the water in Bruges and Dunkirk would cause a fever; Poole warned that the water in Paris caused diarrhoea; Crewe suggested that it should be drunk with lemon peel; and Sacheverell Stevens wrote of the Seine water: 'I would advise every stranger to be very cautious how he drinks too freely of it at first; since, for the generality, it occasions the flux, as much as drinking their new wines.'[51]

Soft drinks were popular with some tourists, particularly the lemonades and iced drinks of Italy. Tea, coffee and chocolate could be readily obtained in western European towns, though for Watkins the Balkans offered a discovery in this respect. At Sir Robert Ainslie's in Constantinople he obtained 'what I never tasted before I came here, *good* coffee, for you have it not in England, as it loses so much of its flavour upon the sea'.[52]

Notes

1. Stanhope to his mother, 11 July 1769, Bradford, Spencer Stanhope.

2. Pelham to Lord Pelham, 4 Nov. 1775; 12 Dec. 1776, BL, Add. 33126–7; Carleton, pp. 300, 326; Young, I, 31–4, 38.

3. Craven, *Journey*, 368, 381; *Memoirs*, I, 163.

4. Gordon to Keith, 8 Sep. 1787, BL, Add. 35539; Ogilvie, Aberdeen, 26 Jan. 1779.

5. Pococke, BL, Add. 22978, fo. 90; Mitchell, BL, Add. 58320, fo. 16; Stevens, pp. 277, 325; G. W. Stone (ed.), *The Journal of David Garrick describing his visit to France and Italy in 1763* (New York, 1939), p. 60; Brand to Wharton, Walker, p. 330.

6. Walker, p. 381; Pococke, BL, Add. 22978, fo. 82; Pomfret to Countess of Hartford, 13 March 1741, Leic., DG7 Finch D5; Stevens, pp. 281–2; Nuneham to his grandmother, Mrs Harcourt, 8 Nov. 1755, *Harcourt Papers*, III, 161; Bulkeley to Keith, 12 Oct. 1785, BL, Add. 35535.

7. *Weekly Journal, or Saturday's Post*, 15 Dec. (os) 1722; Haggerston to mother, 13 July 1711, Haggerston; Molesworth to Stanyan, 27 Nov. 1720, PRO 92/30; Pollnitz, letters of 10 Oct.; 30 Aug. 1729; Stevens, pp. 372, 375–6, 381, 383–4.

8. Walker, p. 92; Wharton to his mother, 18 Feb. 1775, Durham, Wharton; Aberdeen, University Library, MSS 206, MacLaurin jnl., fo. 202.

9. Petty to Keith, 15 Nov. 1785, BL, Add. 35535.

10. Stanhope to mother, 25 Nov. 1769, Bradford, Spencer-Stanhope; Edward Mellish to John Gore, 17 Nov. 1730, Mellish to father, 22 Jan., 1731, Nottingham, University Library, Mellish.

11. Essex, p. 25; L. Aikin, *Aikin*, I, 81, 43; Cradock, pp. 255, 258.

12. Tilson to Delafaye, 29 June 1723, PRO 43/4.

13. Arbuthnot to Keith, BL, Add. 35539, fo. 242.

14. *Tour of Holland* (1772), pp. 131–2.

15. O.J. Reichel (ed.), 'Extracts from a Devonshire Lady's Notes of Travel in France in the Eighteenth Century', *Transactions of the Devonshire Association for the Advancement of Science, Literature and Art*, V (1902), p. 268; Knight, p. 6; Devonshire Lady, p. 273; Montagu, I, 320, 328.

16. Stevens, pp. 7–9; *Tour of Holland* (1772), p. 130; Garrick, 1751; Smollett, pp. 42–3; Montagu, I, 315–16.

17. Smollett, p. 42; Young, I, 87.

18. Essex, p. 8; Young, I, 88, 92, 49, 61–2, 14, 53, 58, 98.

19. Montagu, II, 127; Devonshire Lady, pp. 273–4; St Vincent, BL, Add. 31192, fo. 19; Charles Stanhope to Essex, 18 Oct. 1732, BL, Add. 27732; Tempest, 1, 2, 3, 4 April 1769.

20. Brand to Wharton, 7 April 1780, Durham, Wharton.

21. Wharton to his mother, 1 May 1775, Durham, Wharton. He also compared the taste to chicken, Wharton to Thomas Lloyd, 2 May 1775, Durham, Wharton.

22. Anon., *The Norfolk Congress* (1728); Orrery, I, 77–8; *Worcester Journal*, 13 July 1749.

23. Orrery, I, 48; Anon., *A Trip through London* (8th edn., 1728), p. 54.

24. Wharton to Thomas Lloyd, 4 April 1775, Durham, Wharton.

25. Wharton to Miss Lloyd, 29 Feb. 1775, Durham, Wharton.

26. St John, *Letters from France to a Gentleman in the South of Ireland* (2 vols., Dublin, 1788), II, 207–8.

27. Brand to Wharton, 1 Dec. 1792, Durham, Wharton.

28. Shaw, p. 18; Grey, BL, Add. 5957, fo. 63–4; Essex, pp. 10, 23, 24–5.

29. Cradock, pp. 262–3, 271.

30. Queensberry to Mrs Herbert, 4 Aug. 1734, BL, Add. 22626; Wharton to his mother, 2 Oct. 1775, Durham, Wharton; MacLaurin, Aberdeen, Mss. 206, fo. 198; Young, I, 5.

31. *Boswell in Holland*, p. 185; Windham, 7 July, 1769; Shaw, p. 118.

32. *Mist's Weekly Journal*, 18 Sep. 1725; John Boteler to first Earl Cowper, 28 Sep. 1722, Herts, D/EP F53; Robert Trevor to Thomas Trevor, 27 Aug., 3 July 1728, BL, Add. 61684.

33. Thompson, I, 63, 34–5, 31.

34. Smollett, p. 44; Windham, 10 July 1769; *Tour of Holland* (1722), p. 132.

35. St Vincent, BL, Add. 31192, fo. 3; Essex, pp. 6, 8; Wharton to mother, 26 Feb., Wharton to Thomas Lloyd, 4 April, Wharton to Thomas Wharton, 21 March, 10 May; Wharton to mother, 18 July; Wharton to Thomas Wharton, 7 Oct., Wharton to Thomas Lloyd, 24 March 1775, Durham, Wharton.

36. Knight, pp. 6, 19; Brand to Wharton, 14 Dec. 1779, 7 April, 1780, Durham, Wharton; Craven, *Journey*, p. 44; Gardenstone, I, 15–16, 21–2; Young, I, 23, 156–7.

37. Edward Mellish to father, 25 Jan. 1731, Nottingham, Mellish; Garrick, 1751, p. 34.

38. St John I, 75–7, 81; Foote, *An Englishman in Paris* (1753), I, i.

39. *St. James' Chronicle; or British Evening Post*, 20 May 1769.

40. *Boswell in Holland*, p. 309; Stevens, p. 373; Brand to Wharton, Oct. 1787, Durham, Wharton; Walker, p. 63.

41. Stevens, p. 381; Craven, *Journey*, p. 149; Arbuthnot to Keith, 30 April 1787, BL, Add. 35538; Stone (ed.), *Journal of David Garrick*, p. 60; *Present State of*

Germany, II, 388.

42. Craven, *Journey*, pp. 376, 213, 238−9, 241, 217.

43. Young, I, pp. 32, 41, 38; Carleton, *True and genuine History*, p. 309; Thomas Pelham, 18 Dec. 1775, BL, Add. 33126; Thomas to Lady Pelham, 27 Sep. 1776, BL, Add. 33127.

44. Martyn, pp. 19−20, 234−5, 264.

45. Swinton, 5, 6 June (os), 30 Jan. (os); 4, 23, 27 Feb. (os), 20 March (os), 14 April (os), 16 June (os) 1731; Mitchell, BL, Add. 58320, fo. 60; Pococke, BL, Add. 22978, fo. 80, 74, 79, 82, 90; Stevens, pp. 332, 363; Francis, 23, 25 Oct., 14, 16 Nov., 4 Oct. 1772, BL, Add. 40759; Robson, BL, Add. 38837, fo. 46; Brand to Wharton, 18 Feb. 1787, Durham, Wharton; Walker, pp. 126, 142, 145, 182, 215, 332−3, 373−4, 299−300; Drake to father, 10 April 1769, Aylesbury D/DR/8/2/11; Perceval to Southwell, 16 Aug. (os) 1728, BL, Add. 47032; Pickersgill to sister, Sally Saunders, no date (1760s), Aylesbury, Saunders temp. deposit; Journal of Mrs Flaxman, BL, Add. 39787, fo. 23.

46. Thicknesse, *Pais Bas*, p. 177.

47. Watkins, II, 158; Robson, BL, Add. 38837, fo. 13; Swinton, 19 Oct. (os) 1730; Pratt, *Gleanings*, II, 96; Poole, I, 27, 32, 24; Swinton, 30 May (os) 1731; Garrard to father William Drake, 19 Oct. 1778, Aylesbury D/DR/8/10/7; Francis, 23 July 1772, BL, Add. 40759; Bennett, 10, 23 Oct. 1785; Tracy and Dentand, Bodl. Ms. Add. A. 366, fo. 9−19, 10, 52, 63; anon., Bodl. Ms. Eng. misc. e 250, fo. 4, 5, 27, 39, 57; anon., BL, Stowe 790, fo. 160; Polwarth, 23 Nov., 20 Dec. 1777; Perceval to Daniel Dering, 2 April; 18 March 1726, BL, Add. 47031; Grey, BL, Add. 5957, fo. 63−4.

48. Brand to Wharton, 2 Oct. 1790, Durham, Wharton.

49. Boteler to Lord Cowper, 28 Sep. 1722, D/EP F53; Pococke, BL, Add. 22978, fo. 92; Mellish, Oct. 1730; Gardenstone, I, 16; Thompson, I, 35; Garmston, BL, Add. 30271, fo. 3, 9, 10, 29; Martyn, p. 20; Stevens, p. 363; Walker, pp. 327, 45; Stevens, p. 373; anon., BL, Add. 60522; Digby to Hanbury Williams, 25 Dec. 1751, BL, Add. 51393.

50. Mellish, 25 Jan. 1731; Leven, I, 326; Young, I, 5; St Vincent, BL, Add. 31192, fo. 18; Hume, BL, Add. 29477; 17 April 1714; Thompson, I, 44; Thicknesse, *Pais Bas*, pp. 195−9; Stevens, p. 373; Thicknesse, *Pais Bas*, p. 6; Hume, BL, Add. 29477, 25 April 1714; Drake to father, 21 June 1769, Aylesbury D/DR/8/2/16; Anon., BL, Stowe, 790, fo. 163.

51. Muirhead, p. 1; Thomson, p. 146; Pococke, BL, Add. 22978, fo. 79; Smollett, p. 22; Poole, I, 40; Crewe, BL, Add. 37926, fo. 32; Stevens, p. 22; Tracy and Dentand, Bodl. Ms. Add. A. 366, fo. 52; Starke, 92, 193, 203; *Harcourt*, III, 6; Carpenter, p. 8.

52. Watkins, II, 218.

4   WAR, DISPUTES, ACCIDENTS AND CRIME

War

> The Cloud which seems to threaten Italy, makes it a very
> improper place, to reside in, at present . . . Nobody can tell,
> what may be the consequences of a General War in Italy; and
> how improper in every respect, it may be, for an English noble-
> man to be there, at that time.
>
> Duke of Newcastle, 1741.[1]

International and civil wars affected British tourism to a varying
extent. The circumstances in each conflict were different and much
depended on the attitudes and positions of the individual tourist.
For Horace Walpole, son of the first minister, or the Earl of
Lincoln, nephew and heir of the Duke of Newcastle, Secretary of
State for the Southern Department, the situation was different to
that for a tourist without sensitive political connections. Both were
in Italy in early 1741 and both were ordered home before they could
be cut off by the Spanish forces which invaded Italy that year.
Spain was then at war with Britain, partly over the matter of an ear
removed without medical assistance in the Caribbean. However
this war, which broadened into the War of the Austrian Succession
and entailed hostilities until 1748, did not prevent other British
tourists from visiting Italy. The relationship between war and
tourism was a complex and ambivalent one.

Travel required permission — though the degree of stringency
varied greatly. It was easy to leave Britain, though those holding
commissions were expected to stay in the country in times of war
and international crisis. On the continent British tourists, in
common with other travellers, were examined at many control
points. Most towns were still walled with military posts at the gates
at which travellers had to stop, identify themselves, declare the
purpose of their travel and often where they were going to spend
the night in the town. Guards often accompanied them to the hotel
to check on the latter. When James Hume arrived in Dieppe in 1714
he was taken to see the Governor, 'who examined us whence we

came, what our profession was, and what business we had in France'.[2] In 1772, Philip Francis was delayed leaving Paris by the difficulty of obtaining a passport: 'Impossible to get the passport in time to set out this evening, as I wished and intended. Everything in this country is calculated for check and controul.'[3] Within Europe the need for passports and for specific permission to enter a country, varied. Some countries were very strict. The Kingdom of Naples was an example. On arrival it was necessary to show a passport that had been obtained from the Neapolitan Ambassador in Rome.[4] Difficulties were created over passports in the later years of the Walpole ministry, when Naples clearly supported the Jacobites. In eastern Europe passports were particularly important. Lansdowne's bastard, Mr Petty, wrote to Keith from Schemnitz in 1785 of 'the passport which you was so good as to procure me when I went into Transilvania and which on several occasions I found *absolutely necessary*', and asked for a new one. Quarantine regulations were a variant on passport controls and Mediterranean tourists who visited North Africa or the Turkish Empire had to undergo lengthy quarantine. Thomas Glynn underwent one such in Marseilles in 1784, and four years later John Hawkins had a thirty day quarantine in Messina.[6]

In wartime the need for passports increased, whether Britain was a participant in the conflict or not. They were however readily granted. Britain, despite being an ally of Austria, was neutral in the War of the Polish Succession of 1733–5, a war which, despite its title, involved major hostilities in the Rhineland and in Italy. Some tourists were affected by the hostilities. Three English gentlemen found themselves in Italy late in 1733 when the French, Sardinians and Spaniards attacked the Austrian possessions in the peninsula. 'We took it for granted, that the Maritime Powers could not avoid concerning themselves in that Quarrel', and therefore they decided to return to Britain via Germany rather than France. Two years later the Duke of Grafton's wishes for his son's — Lord Euston — Grand Tour were guided by the war, 'considering ye situation the country is in at present and ye armys in ye field without a preparation he cannot goe there'.[7] However most tourists were not affected by the conflict and the participants made no effort to limit British tourism despite the widely held assumption that Britain would enter the war on the Austrian side. 'M. Chavigny has acquainted the Court, that the king of France hath sent orders to all his generals in Italy, to take care that none of the English noblemen and gentlemen, that are upon their travels, receive any molestation or injury whatever, but that they upon all occassions do pay them all the respect imaginable,' announced one London newspaper soon after the start of the war.[8] British tourists found no difficulty in obtaining passports and touring the field of conflict. In 1734, Philip Kinsky gave Walter Molesworth, his wife and son, a passport to go to Spa. Viscount Harcourt viewed the battle of Parma from the ramparts of the town; Sir Hugh Smithson and Sir Harry Lyddel visited the French army near Mantua in 1734; and Richard Pococke was allowed by the French to visit the castle in Milan where they were constructing new fortifications. Though he informed his mother that he would return to England 'at some distance from the Rhine' he changed his mind and went home through France. Euston was received by Charles Emmanuel III of Savoy and discussed the war with him, whilst Henry Fox used his wartime stay in Turin as the basis for parliamentary comments in a 1740 debate in the House of Commons on the augmentation of the army by the creation of new regiments. Andrew Mitchell was annoyed to find that the war led to the inaccessibility of the picture collections at Modena and Parma (the latter was moved to Genoa). He toured the battlefield of Parma soon after the battle with a French officer with whom he discussed it, and also discussed the battle of Guastella with participants. He found many of the churches and monasteries in Parma full of wounded and found the 'cart loads of wounded and sick sent in everyday from the camp to the hospitals . . . a miserable spectacle'. However, bar the removal of the paintings, he suffered no inconvenience from the hostilities. Tourism in France continued throughout the war though the Rhineland seems to have been avoided.[9]

Britain was not a participant in the War of the Polish Succession, but in the following war, that of the Austrian Succession, when she was involved, tourism did not cease. The legal situation during the war was fairly complex. Britain was at war with Spain 1739–48, but war with France was not declared until spring of 1744 even though Dettingen had been fought the previous year. War disrupted routes of communication, the seizure of horses harmed the posting system and, whatever their legal status, tourists could be ill-used. The Elbe causeway between Saxony and Bohemia was broken up in 1744 and the Earl of Holderness, a British diplomat on his way to Venice, was ill-used by the hussars of Britain's ally Austria near Nürnberg that autumn. In 1739 Francis Hare, the

Bishop of Chichester, wrote to his son, then in Italy: 'I had a letter from Mr. Spateman in which he says . . . if a war should break out, passports may protect you from public seizures of either your person or goods, yet private violence is always more busy in such times of commotions, and one travels with less safety, which no doubt is true, but I should hope with proper precautions there would be no great danger from thence. I have told him I believed you would govern your motions by what you saw other English gentlemen do, . . .'[10]

In general 'other English gentlemen' did not panic. The newspapers printed occasional atrocity stories, such as one in August 1742 of a British woman being raped on the Dutch crossing when her ship was captured by a Spanish privateer. There was also a press item at the beginning of the war that: 'The several British Noblemen and Gentlemen abroad on their travels have been wrote to by their relations and friends to return home.'[11] However the reality was otherwise. British tourism continued. It was often best to leave the scene of conflict — Lady Mary Wortley Montagu left Chambéry in early 1742 because of the approach of Bourbon troops — but tourists in Italy in the early 1740s crossed between armies with little difficulty. There was a somewhat facetious attitude by some towards the dangers posed by war.[12] The Channel crossings were generally safe at least in the early stages of the war where Spanish privateering was not much of a threat.[13] The situation changed with the French invasion of the Austrian Netherlands. Ostend, the principal tourist port on that coast, fell to the French in August 1745. Two years later a French conquest of the United Provinces appeared a real threat. However ugly these developments might be for the British, tourism continued. Sacheverell Stevens in his trip down the Main had to go to the Austrian camp to obtain a passport from Marshal Traun 'which he readily granted us'. He took a boat from Wertheim 'in order to avoid the trouble of passing thro' the army'. The Austrian piquets 'all examined our passports'. As he had a French passport he 'passed in our boat down the river Main with little trouble, except that once a party of them (the French army being encamped on the side of a hill) descry'd us sailing down the Main, numbers of them came running to the river side, and forced us to come on shore to the commanding officer, to whom we produced our passport, notwithstanding which, with all their authority, they could not without great difficulty hinder the common soldiers from plundering us'.[14]

Woodhouse suggested from her sample of tourists that the wars of the 1690s and 1750s discouraged all but diplomatic travellers to Paris.[15] However true this may have been for Paris (and it was certainly not true of the War of American Independence) it was not true for Europe as a whole. Many travelled during the War of the Spanish Succession (1702–13). Samuel Tufnell toured the United Provinces, Germany, Italy and Switzerland in 1703–5; Edward Montagu Italy in 1708; David Papillon Germany the following year; Uvedale Price France and Italy in 1709–12; and John Wallop Italy and Germany in 1710. Sir Carnaby Haggerston's 1711 journey to a Lorraine school was affected by the war. At Antwerp he was advised to go via Cologne as the safest route but at Cologne he was forced to renew his pass as Trier was in French hands. Several years earlier Joseph Shaw was warned not to travel late as he might be plundered by soldiers. However, what is interesting is that Shaw and Haggerston should have been travelling at all, particularly the latter whose school lay very near to the zone of hostilities.[16]

The Seven Years War (1756–63) had an effect on tourism. The Earl of Orrery returned from Italy in the winter of 1755–6 through Germany and the United Provinces, not France, because of the poor state of Anglo-French relations. In 1759, Charles Selwin, an English banker at Paris, advised David Garrick against a return trip to Paris during the war. In February 1762, Mrs Montagu wrote to her sister-in-law, Mrs William Robinson, at Rome: 'I am under some anxiety least our rupture with Spain should occasion you any inconvenience.'[17] Despite this situation many still went on the Grand Tour. Sir Wyndham Knatchbull-Wyndham went on one in 1757–60 and spent a long time in Italy. James Ferguson and Sir Adam Fergusson were on the Grand Tour in 1757–8, and James Grant in 1758–60. Sir Humphry Morice went to Italy for his health in 1760 returning to Britain for the autumn Parliament in 1762. Francis Russell, Marquess of Tavistock, was abroad in 1761–2, and at Rome met John, later first Lord, Crewe, Dr Hinchcliffe, his tutor, later Master of Trinity and Bishop of Peterborough, Augustus, third Duke of Grafton, 'Crauford, James and others'. Whereas most British tourists during the Seven Years War travelled in Italy, where conflict was small-scale during this war, Grafton was able to visit France. 'Through the interest of the Marquis Du Quesne, a Prisoner on his parole at Northampton, I obtained a passport, which for years past had been refused to every Englishman. We received particular civilities from various quarters during our short stay at Paris. At the old and respectable Duke of Biron's I dined with a numerous set of officers; and his reception of me was flattering.' In Geneva Grafton met the Duc de la Rochequin and his mother: 'We had the pleasure of meeting them frequently in different houses, for a foolish etiquette prevented us from visiting directly each other, while our countries were at war; but we were not prevented from interchanging every possible attention. With Voltaire there was not the same scruple; . . .'[18]

Good social relations were not unknown during the War of American Independence. This was aided by the ambivalent attitude of many of the British social elite to the war, and by the fact that there were no hostilities on the continent. Lady Knight left Toulouse, where she had been staying, for Rome in 1778, 'for though I shall ever esteem the French I know, yet I could not have stayed contentedly in the country, if at war with England'. Two years later she observed, 'Travelling in time of war is not convenient'. Madame du Deffand, whose letters to Horace Walpole, are an interesting source for British tourists in Paris, wrote to him in July 1778: 'Les Anglais qui sont en France y resteront tant qu'ils voudront, ceux qui n'y sont pas n'y viendront point parcequ'ils n'y voudront pas venir.' The British response to war with France varied greatly as the following extract from Brand in 1779 reveals, 'am just come from dinner after laughing very heartily at a very absurd Frenchman and as absurd (or more so I think) Englishman who have been abusing each other country and gasconading most delightfully'. Keith, as a British envoy, could describe Bourbon celebrations in Vienna as 'poison to English lips' but not all shared his opinion. However, as with Henrietta Pomfret who had felt in August 1738 that she would have to leave Paris if there were Anglo-Bourbon hostilities, so in the later conflict many felt uncomfortable at the idea of visiting a state with which Britain was at war. The French were, however, prepared to give passports. Frank Hale, wishing to return from Lausanne to London in 1779, determined to go to Brussels 'from whence I shall have a pass to carry me to Calais'.[19]

The explosion in numbers of tourists to France from 1782 would suggest that the war had restricted the numbers of those travelling. The tourists in the 1780s were not, however, to be free from the threat of war. Tourists to the Low Countries in 1784–5 noted military preparations linked to the apparent imminence of Austro-Dutch conflict. In 1785, an Austro-Prussian war was feared. In

March 1785, Sir Grey Cooper wrote to Keith about his son's return route from Vienna via Berlin and Hanover: 'Perhaps from some intelligence I have received since I wrote my last letter, the route by Berlin will not be so proper at the time of his return: There are I fear appearances which portend a storm: . . .'[20]

In 1787 a major European war appeared likely. Britain and Prussia supported the Orangist faction in the United Provinces whilst France supported the 'Patriots'. A Prussian invasion in September, supported by a British naval demonstration, tipped the balance in favour of the former. The threat of war affected tourists. Brand, then accompanying Duncombe, wrote from Vienna in August: 'We are in great uncertainty about our motions. The disturbances in Holland and rebellion in Flanders have so far alarmed us as to make us hesitate whether to go to our intended circuit by Dresden Berlin and The Hague or straight to Paris.' The following month he wrote from Berlin: 'I know nothing of our future destination. If the P. of Orange is victorious we may perhaps go to the Hague.' In the end he reached The Hague. 'The only marks of war which we saw were the destruction of a number of trees by the roadside to make batteries.' Lord Charles Fitzroy, who had spent his time in Vienna playing cricket, riding in horseraces and brawling, returned through the United Provinces that autumn but found nothing particularly interesting. At Turin, Walker, returning from Italy, was filled with foreboding by the prospect of war: 'Here are near a dozen English in our inn, the Albergo Reale, who have given us the first intimation that England is likely to be engaged in a war. This unhappy news will imbitter the rest of our journey home! We have got from our Ambassador here credentials, that "We are good men, and true" — in case we should be molested in our passage through France.'[21]

In the 1780s, civil conflict in various European states became a major problem. Geneva was followed by the Austrian Netherlands and United Provinces and then by France and the bishopric of Liege. By 1792–3 even the faintest disturbance in Italy could be seen as the harbinger of revolution. These civil disturbances were more serious for tourists than the state wars earlier in the century. When countries had been at war they had been internally peaceful, and passports had been respected. Civil violence conjured up for many the fears of mob-rule and of the destruction of civil government. Furthermore internal war, such as the conflict in the Austrian Netherlands in the late 1780s, disrupted communications and currencies. Towns were besieged, the roads full of threatening soldiers. British residents in Switzerland, such as Robert Ellison, were worried by the Genevan troubles in the early 1780s but these appeared minor when compared with the civil war in the Austrian Netherlands. The French Revolution, therefore, was not a new development as far as tourism was concerned and it did not lead to the immediate ending of tourism to France. Some, such as Dr John Moore, rushed to Paris filled with enthusiasm and interest. A correspondent of James Bland Burges wrote in October 1789 that he was off to Paris and Versailles 'for a very few days. . . . The very extraordinary scenes which have arisen in France present an object of curiosity so irresistible'.[22] Others, such as Brand, found France a more inconvenient country to travel in — carriages were stopped by the National Guard and there was increasing antagonism towards foreigners. Arthur Young, who had been to hear a debate at the Estates General in June 1789, was in trouble the following month in Alsace for not having a cockade of the tiers état, and he was further worried because he could not obtain a passport. That autumn Mrs Montagu urged her nephew Matthew not to visit France, 'I hope future opportunities will present themselves in which Mr Wilberforce and you may indulge your benevolent intentions, and enjoy any scheme of pleasure, but to go into a country to partake of the horrors of a famine or mix in the confusion of civil war would be very unbecoming your prudence'.[23] In December 1789 Robert Arbuthnot could still consider taking a pupil 'to Paris, where if we find things tolerably quiet, we shall remain some months', but by the following May Lord Auckland, the envoy at The Hague, could write, 'our countrymen are flocking much to this place, instead of going to Paris'.[24]

There was considerable ambivalence about the Revolution. Brand wrote to Wharton in May 1791: 'I too have had the news of Sr. Jemmy's trip to France. He wrote me a very long letter full of nonsense and mistaken zeal about the "mighty Revolution" which I answered immediately in two sheets labouring hard to correct certain republican and philosophical ideas which however I am afraid are incorrigible.' Two years later he wrote from Naples to complain of the activities of the Dowager Countess Spencer: 'Our countrywomen at Naples under the auspices of a great Lady who I in my private opinion look upon as but little better than a female Tartuffe have subscribed and (which I feel more) made the men subscribe . . . for flannel waistcoats to be sent to . . . Toulon!'

Brand's letters are a good source for the varied response of the British tourist community in Italy to the Revolution.[25]

The year 1792 brought war to the Rhineland and the Austrian Netherlands; and the following spring saw Britain enter the Revolutionary Wars. In one sense these wars were not a new departure. Tourists had become used in the 1780s to the problems posed by revolutionary governments and still travelled widely in the 1790s. Tourism had been affected by the threat of war for years. Sir John Macpherson's travel plans in 1790 were affected not by the progress of the French Revolution, but by the prospect of war in Germany between Austria and Prussia.[26] In another sense the revolutionary wars were dramatically different. The bloodier acts of the Revolution aroused in most a sense of horror that meant that many not only did not wish to visit France but that they did not consider it safe. As French armies spread across Europe new-modelling states, redistributing art treasures and defeating Britain's allies, Europe became an alien entity. Contacts were executed or forced to flee, British diplomatic representation withdrawn, old activities such as visiting nunneries, attending academies, being presented at court, and watching the ceremonies of court and religious society, ceased. Europe became less accessible, less comprehensible, and hostile, and the old-fashioned Grand Tour was a victim of this change. Tourism continued, but it followed a different course.

Disputes

Some English gentlemen went in a yacht to visit some of the English students there; among the company was a painter, who innocently making a drawing of some part of the town which was grotesque, they were all apprehended and detained some days till they could send to Paris and get their liberty.

> Item about Caen, *The Gazetteer and New Daily Advertiser*, 30 August 1770.

They look upon strangers as a prey, and squeeze from them what they can: this we found almost everywhere, but especially where we lodged this night; for we having anticipated our supper by an afternoon's repast, and our host thinking himself thereby baulked of some part of his expected profit, charged us no less than 10 sols for one candle.

> James Hume, Brittany, 1714.[27]

As was to be expected tourists were involved in a number of disputes. Most involved money. Throughout most of Europe there were no set prices for the accommodation and food that tourists used, although there were usually set prices for transport charges: the cost of posting, bridge and ferry tolls, barge charges. Guidebooks and published travel accounts frequently warned against fraud. Pratt made the obvious point that it was easy to be defrauded if a tourist did not know the language. Walker encountered difficulties with his postillions in the Austrian Netherlands and at Reggio and Loretto. He wrote of the Italians: 'As to the lower orders of men, they seem what we call blackguards, in the most savage sense of the word . . . ever on the watch to cheat or impose upon strangers; . . .' Northall wrote of young English aristocrats in Rome being deceived by antiquarian guides into buying copies thinking they were originals by Raphael, Titian and Michelangelo. Sacheverell Stevens wrote of Amsterdam,

> the precaution before given in regard to the French inns, is equal, if not more necessary here, that is to make a bargain for everything you want beforehand, when you will be well used, otherwise you must pay whatever exorbitant bill they are pleased to bring in, for they are the most imposing people in the world, if you dispute it you can get no redress, will be abused into the bargain, which is somewhat strange in so large a trading and flourishing city.

Thicknesse repeatedly warned against fraud. In Paris the postillions were bribed to take tourists to particular hotels; there were sharpers and the town was not safe for young British tourists. The Austrian Netherlands were also dangerous,

> To the younger part of my countrymen who are constantly making excursions to the continent, these letters may prove useful, for I have met with none who have escaped the impositions of the lower order of the people, and but few who have been wise enough even to perceive the artifices of the UPPER; an order, by much the most dangerous, in general, for a young Englishman of fortune to be connected or acquainted with. I must observe therefore, that strangers, who are permitted to the *honour* of eating, and conversing with the high and mighty people of the *Pais-bas*, should avoid playing with them; first, because they

understand play; and secondly, because they do not *always*, as Englishmen do, *pay when they lose* . . . Never trust to the word of a tradesman in this country, nor buy anything without paying the price and taking a receipt; there is no dependence on any man in business, nor that he will send you home the *same* goods you have bought.[28]

The press fortified this impression of deceitfuil foreigners. The *Newcastle Journal* carried a London item in 1752 of 'an Insult of the grossest kind' to 'an English Lady of the first Quality' in Paris. In 1786 another newspaper reported difficulties in the United Provinces,

. . . the English who happen to be in the country, even on business or amusement, with difficulty escape insult from their supposed adherence to the Stadtholder. We found this temper very unpleasant in travelling; exorbitant charges were often made with wanton insolence, and we were obliged to submit in silence.[29]

The press did however also mention British tourists who caused a nuisance, often by drunken brawling. On Christmas night 1727, visiting English gentry blocked the passage to the Cordeliers' church in Paris and abused those who attempted to pass. Some tourists brawled easily. John Lindesay, Earl of Crawfurd, threw a French marquis who was rude to him into a pond at Versailles in 1723. Lord Leven's son beat up a troublesome postillion at Lille. The future General Sir John Moore was taken to Paris, aged eleven in 1772, by his father who was acting as Bearleader to Douglas, Duke of Hamilton. The young Moore, on a walk in the Tuileries, disliked the French children's fashion of dressing like adults. He 'could only express his dipleasure by gestures. Mutual offence was taken, and the parties proceeded to hostilities; but as French boys know nothing of boxing, they were thrown to the ground one across the other'. Fifteen years later Brand referred to the British youth in Vienna, principally Charles Lennox and Lord Charles Fitzroy: 'the Rhein wine sometimes evaporates so strongly at their fingers ends that it knocks down every Austrian within its reach.'[30]

The conduct of tourists varied. Some might urinate on the Senate of Lucca from a balcony or excrete in Italian churches, but most behaved in an acceptable fashion. Townshend claimed that the reports of English conduct in Vienna were 'in general totally invented or aggravated'.[31] Disputes were not always the fault of British tourists and many did what they could to avoid them. In 1741 Poole ran away to avoid having to kneel to the host in the street, as he feared he would otherwise be compelled to do so. Mrs Crewe encountered the noisy disapprobation of the pit when she went to see the burlesque play *Le Roi de Cocagne* in Paris because she hung her cloak over the front of the box: 'I have since thought their Etiquettes are cruel in the case of strangers who can never learn them but by such experiences as mine!' Thicknesse gave an account of a disturbance in Liège occasioned unintentionally by a short-sighted English lady tourist looking at the altar through an opera glass.[32]

Most tourists did not seek trouble and most of the disputes they became involved in related to difficulties over alleged frauds. In 1725 Francis Colman, envoy in Florence, had a tailor and an attorney who had quarrelled with two British tourists, sent to prison. Travelling from Rome to the Tuscan frontier, Philip Francis was: 'cheated regularly at every post, in the very teeth of the tariff. There is no remedy, for if you refuse to pay, they take away the horses. At least we are clear of the Romans, and here I most devoutly pray that both they and their neighbours the Neopolitans may be everlastingly cursed. Sooner than live with such villains, I would renounce society.' Francis's views of the Italians were echoed by Manners — 'I think even in the very beggars I see falsity wrote on their countenances' — and Garmston —

> I do not approve of the people in the Venetian state, they impose upon strangers, more than any other people I ever met with, and you pay more for going, upon very bad roads, than in any other part of Italy, for the postillions and ostlers, are never satisfied. The post horses are very indifferent, and the master of the post too proud to be spoken to, but he leaves all to the conduct of an impertinent staliere, who always takes part with the postillioni.

Brand was falsely accused in Venice of stealing a diamond, an attempt at extortion. He observed that Italy was the only country where rascals were not ashamed to have their rascality discovered.[33]

Difficulties were not restricted to Italy. Disputes over posting — the availability of horses and the speed or pay of the postillions — were common all over Europe.[34] Disputes over the price of food and accommodation were frequent. Pratt complained that in Holland he was made to pay for a plate of shrimps and a glass of milk and geneva four-and-a-half times what he had seen a Dutchman pay.[35] Wharton, travelling down the Rhône by water, was affected by a dispute between officers and the master of the boat, that led to them all being put ashore at 'a wretched place where we could neither get victuals, drink, nor beds'. Bennett was involved in similar difficulties on the same journey a decade later.[36]

Many disputes reflected the absence of fixed prices, but, as several commentators pointed out, the extravagent conduct of many British tourists made life more difficult for their compatriots. Tourists found they could place little reliance on local judicial institutions. Most of those who presented complaints did not receive redress. However, the ability to appeal to British envoys ensured that in the event of serious difficulties assistance could be obtained. Diplomats, such as Colman and Keith, often complained of the cost and time involved in entertaining tourists. They were expected to entertain them, present them at court, introduce them into local society and fulfill a number of miscellaneous requests. Waldegrave was asked in 1733 to look after Sir John Shadwell, a relation of Charles Delafaye's wife, and ensure that medicines, chocolate and snuff for his use were not seized by the Boulogne customs. Well-connected tourists could be sure of letters of recommendation from ministers to envoys. Robert Carteret, the son of Lord Carteret, one of the leaders of the opposition, obtained recommendatory letters to the envoys at Copenhagen, Dresden, St Petersburg and Vienna. Thicknesse recommended tourists to wait on the envoy in order to ensure protection, and noted the Earl of Rochford's defence at Paris of tourists, including one defrauded by sharpers. Waldegrave was involved in lengthy representations on behalf of a Scottish visitor involved in a duel in the Loire valley. The protection provided by the diplomatic service was an indication of the relatively small-scale nature of tourism and the role of personal connections in what was still essentially an aristocratic milieu.[37]

Accidents

In turning upon one of the Bridges this morning about a post from our inn, my friend Edward and I had the misfortune to be overturned, and if it had not been for the railing of the Bridge the Chaise might have gone compleate into the river.

Robson, Savoy Alps, 1787.[38]

Carriages were very susceptible to accidents, particularly given the often poor nature of the road surface. Many tourists were halted as a result of such accidents, usually broken axletrees. Lady Exeter's axletree broke near Loretto in 1699. George Woodward was delayed on the way to Paris in December 1726,

> . . . having had the misfortune of the axle tree of my chaise breaking in the night at above a league's distance from Montreuil. The getting it to the town and the time in mending of it detained me more than a whole day. Just before the accident, I was overturned into a hollow way, and was so lucky as to escape with a little bruise only, tho' Mr. Smith fell upon me; he was so much hurt that he is still lame. Such is so often the fate of travellers . . .

William Bentinck's 'hind axel-tree' broke and was badly mended. At Vercelli in 1772, Philip Francis found 'the axle tree has again given way: a cursed plague, and loss of five hours'. Hale had a terrible journey from St Petersburg to Warsaw in January 1779, 'loosing our way, falling into rivers, breaking an axle-tree, a spring, a wheel etc. by which means I was upwards of three weeks upon the road from Petersburg'. Brand found the roads so bad from Orléans to Toulouse in 1783 'that at last our Axletree broke near Montauban in a dark night when it rained as if it was a prelude to an universal deluge'. Nine years later his axletree broke on the way from Leghorn to Rome though fortunately 'it was within a mile of the only place in a whole day's journey where it could have been well mended'.[39]

Overturning could be unpleasant. Shaw was overturned near Leyden, though without hurt, 'thro' an excess of complaisance in giving the way to a cart'. Lady Craven was twice overturned on the way from St Petersburg to Moscow and noted that the postillions treated it as a common occurrence. Mrs Crewe was overturned between Amiens and Breteuil in 1786. She received no hurt but was: 'full of tremors ever since. For several stages after our accident I hardly could bear the appearance of a hill, or the sensation which the chaise gave me when inclined at all on one side.' She blamed the accident on the absence of a drag chain: when the heavy carriage went downhill the horses could not bear the weight of the carriage.

The following year Richard Garmston was nearly overturned passing another chaise on the Padua-Ferrara road, which was too narrow for two carriages to pass without great difficulty. That year Brand, on the way from Dresden to Berlin, was 'overturned upon the road so gently that not even the glass was broke', but the following year Payne had 'a compleat overset of our coach between Zurich and Berne, which fractured all our glasses but spar'd our Bones'.[40]

Wheels breaking were another problem. Lady Craven had to stay four days in Hermanstadt in 1786 to have a new set made. Conway's carriage wheel disintegrated in Upper Silesia in 1774; and two years earlier Philip Francis, on the way from Paris to Calais, 'lost a wheel, which broke to pieces. Yet I paid a villain 3 Louis for a carriage from Paris to Calais'.[41] Carriages were vulnerable to accidents. The leathers supporting Walker's carriage broke, and later near Roanne in France, the broken road surface, 'broke one of our spring stays . . . and we were obliged to walk back three miles, and to lose three hours in the mending it'.[42] Horses could also be a problem. Stevens had to stay two days at Viterbo in 1739 because of lame horses. In 1786 Mrs Crewe was stopped on the way to Versailles: 'one of the Horses tumbling down, and my maid and I being detained upon the bridge of Sèvres three quarters of an hour, — both terrified to death, because we were on so narrow a part of it that every carriage which came by gave us a shock, as if it meant to tip us over into the Seine —' The following year, on the way from Worms to Manheim, one of Walker's horses fell down asleep and threw him amongst the feet of another horse.[43] For many coach accidents no details were given, but their numbers suggest that travel was more hazardous than has usually been realised. The Duke of Kent's eldest son was involved in a coach accident on the side of the Rhône in early 1716; Lord Leven's carriage broke down three miles from Paris in 1749; Sir James Porter's at Breslau in 1762; and the Duchess of Ancaster's near Florence in 1785. Lord Ancram was delayed for twelve hours in 1787 when his carriage broke down at St Tron in the Rhineland.[44]

Aside from vehicle breakdown, travellers faced a variety of hazards. Trunks could be lost,[45] litters break,[46] ships run aground and sink,[47] coaches become stuck in the snow,[48] crushed by falling customs barriers[49] or nearly fall in the river when postillions lost their way.[50] Travellers fell down stairs,[51] had accidents with guns,[52] and ran the risk of being knocked over in Paris, where there was an absence of pavements.[53] Hume's horse was trapped in the bridge at Angers in 1714 when it was being repaired. The curtains of Cradock's carriage were forced open by the wind on the way from Amsterdam to Saardam in 1786, and his 'hat, with some other articles, was carried quite away'.[54]

Getting lost was a major hazard, particularly for those who travelled by night or in the snow. There were few road signs, and most roads were poorly marked. Joseph Shaw became lost on the road from Amersford to Dieren,

> . . . on the fine heath . . . about nine of the clock, after having been for some hours alone in the endless desert, not able to speak one word of the language of the country, we found the road split into two; and absolute darkness had now rendered our eyes of so little use, that we were all forced to alight, and for about half an hour with our hands grope, and by the largeness of the tracks to discover the most probable way. In this condition we were reduced to such a perplexed uncertainty, that the Doctor was for taking up his quarters there all night, and I had much ado (tho' backed both by the coachman and footman) to persuade him to pursue that way that seem'd probable, and which, how probable soever it seem'd, in about an hour grew so very narrow, as to admit one coach abrest, and brought us at last into a wood, so thick, that the trees hindered us from advancing any faster than an insensible pace, and gave me some slight apprehensions of mischief; augmented by the Doctor's representations of our wickedness in travelling on the Sabbath and of the probability of a conspiracy between the coachman and footman in their language, . . . to decoy us into a place so horrid, on some bloody design . . . on a sudden, in the middle of this dark wood, some men cry'd out aloud *Hold — stand!* . . . I thought I heard the signal for an attack that would probably put an end to my travels with my life, and immediately cocked my pistols . . .

Happily for Shaw the mysterious callers were other travellers. Sacheverell Stevens on the way from Rome in 1739 became lost on a snowy heath near Siena.[55] The weather was a major hazard to tourists. Snow could make roads dangerous, rain make them difficult and thaw make them impassable. Storms prevented sea and lake travel, high winds river travel, and floods ferry passages.

Travel was not easy, and it was rarely pleasant to spend days on end in coaches. This was another reason for the zeal with which tourists raced from town to town. However, travel in Britain was not trouble free. Coaches overturned and travellers were killed, horses fell because of bad roads and accidents were common. The American preacher Samuel Davies encountered difficulties in 1754 on the way from London to Edinburgh and noted: 'Providence, no doubt, has some important design in these alarming Trials.'[56] Others were less phlegmatic, but for all tourists travel was a hazardous pastime.

Crime

> The people here are half starved, and are ready to devour you for money. Indeed they are all beggars. Wherever you stop to change horses they swarm about you like bees, I believe some of them would be wasps if they durst but they are generally cowards if spoken sharply to.
>
> Richard Garmston, Spoleto, 1787.[57]

Crime was a threat tourists had to face continually. A few tourists were murdered, though this was a rare occurrence. In September 1723, Messrs Davis, Locke, Mompesson and Sebright were robbed and murdered seven miles from Calais. They had exchanged their money at Calais too publicly and their carriages were stopped soon after they left the town. The murders caused a sensation. They were reported extensively in the British press and led the French chargé in London, Chammorel, to bring the matter to the attention of the foreign minister, Morville. Morville replied: 'Je ne suis point étonné que le menu peuple de Londres ait tenu les discours que vous marqués par rapport au meurtre commis aux environs de Calais, mais je n'aurois pas crû que des personnes de distinction, et des gens sensés eussent pû les adopter.' Morville promised that he would do everything possible to preserve the safety of the roads. The murders continued to attract attention. A monumental cone was erected at the site of the murders and, when it was defaced in 1724, an engraving of the cone and its inscription was printed. The following year the press reported that: 'Charles Evelyn, Esq. and some other English gentlemen, were lately robbed between Calais and Lyons, by several highwaymen, and were afraid of being killed as the Gentlemen near Calais were; but however, they had the good fortune to escape.'[58] These murders created such a sensation because they were such a rare event. There are records of very few other tourists being murdered. In 1735, William Yates, 'a young gentleman who set out for his travels to Italy', was found murdered near Ghent.[59] As it was usual for robbers to attack their victims,[60] tourists had much to fear. Boswell feared attack in the United Provinces and Craven in the Balkans. As Horace Walpole had his trunk stolen at Chantilly, William Cole determined not to go there; Henry of Nassau and a friend were robbed in Venice; James Walker was badly beaten and robbed when the Würzburg-Frankfurt diligence was attacked by ten highwaymen in 1787. In the same year, Adam Walker was attacked by highwaymen between Spa and Aachen. In 1749, Lord Leven had a frightening trip from Calais to Paris — between St Omer and Béthune 'ruffians' abounded and Leven 'saw many that day who would have attacked us if they durst, but the gun frightened them; . . . the apprehension of being robbed took off some of the pleasure' of the trip; St Vincent feared having his throat cut by the rowers on the boat he hired on the Rhône; Arthur Young feared attack at Montadier; Brand was robbed at Virterbo; and Stevens threatened near Bolsena.[61]

Tourists showed an understandable interest in the quality of the police. The situation in both France and the Austrian Netherlands was praised,[62] though Joseph Shaw warned of the dangers of Paris, 'there being nightly Robberies, and often Murders committed'; and noted that he witnessed a violent robbery from his window.[63] The majority of tourists encountered no difficulties. One may doubt James Essex's claim on behalf of the roads in the Austrian Netherlands: 'these roads are so safe in the day, that a child might travel with a purse of gold and not be robbed of it . . .' However, Wharton was well-satisfied with his experience of Paris in 1775: 'Nor are the people here such rogues as we imagine. I have twice left my knife at the Auberge, where however there are knives . . . laid at dinner, and it has been restored to me safe and sound, so that I do not think I shall be pillaged at least in this place.' Twelve years later Adam Walker wrote: 'It is a compliment . . . to Italy, that we neither were robbed, attempted to be robbed, or heard of a robbery, the time we travelled through it, and we travelled early and late.'[64]

Possibly the hazards of travel can be exaggerated, but when ill-health, crime and accidents are considered it is clear that tourists faced many dangers. It is important to place them in perspective. Coach accidents were frequent but usually not serious; most of those who died from diseases were already ill when they left Britain; one was more likely to suffer from food-poisoning than from a stiletto. Accidents were common in Britain and some European states, particularly France, as travellers such as Mildmay noted, were better policed than Britain was. It was nevertheless true that tourism entailed hazards that are too easily forgotten and that the fact that these proved serious or fatal in only a few cases, was scant consolation to tourists wondering whether they would be robbed, involved in a major accident or afflicted by a serious illness.

Notes

1. Newcastle to Lord Lincoln, then in Italy, 16 March (os) 1741, BL, Add. 33065.
2. Hume, 29 March, 1714, BL, Add. 29477.
3. Francis, 9 Dec. 1772, BL, Add. 40759.
4. Northall, p. 177; Garmston, 1 Nov. 1787, BL, Add. 30271.
5. Petty to Keith, 10 June 1785, BL, Add. 35534.
6. Glynn to Keith, 11 July 1784; Hawkins to Keith, 26 Feb. 1788, BL, Add. 35532, 35540.
7. 'The Travels of three English Gentlemen, from Venice to Hamburgh, being the grand tour of Germany in the Year 1734', *Harleian Miscellany* IV (1745), p. 348; Grafton to Essex, 2 May (os) 1735, BL, Add. 27733.
8. *Universal Spectator*, 29 Dec. (os) 1733.
9. Kinsky to ———, 13 May 1734, PRO 100/11; *St. James Evening Post* 28 Nov. (os) 1734; Pococke, BL, Add. 22978, fo. 87, 89, 80; Villettes to Newcastle, 25 Dec. 1734, PRO 92/37; W. Cobbett, *Parliamentary History*, XI, 977; Mitchell, BL, Add. 58319, fo. 39–43.
10. HMC., *Hare*, p. 250.
11. *Cirencester Flying-Post, and Weekly Miscellany*, 9 Aug. (os) 1742; *Northampton Mercury*, 16 July (os) 1739.
12. John Sturrock to Richard Neville Aldworth, 19 Dec. 1740, Essex D/D By Cl.
13. HMC, *Hare*, p. 255.
14. Stevens, pp. 376–8.
15. Woodhouse, p. 48.
16. Haggerston to mother, 13 July 1711; Shaw, *Letters*, p. 7.
17. Garrick. 1751, p. 113.
18. W. Anson, *Autobiography . . . Third Duke of Grafton* (1898), pp. 16–19.
19. Knight, pp. 47, 83; *Deffand-Walpole*, V, 60; Brand to Wharton, 30 July 1779, Durham, Wharton; Keith to Lord North, 21 July; Hale to Keith, 27 April 1779, BL, Add. 35517, 35516.
20. Cooper to Keith, 17 March 1785, BL, Add. 35534.
21. Brand to Wharton, 4 Aug.; 10 Sep., 18 Oct. 1787, Durham, Wharton; Fitzroy to Keith, 14 Nov. 1787, BL, Add. 35539; Walker, p. 390.

22. Piggott to Burges, 8 Oct. 1789, Bodl., Dep. Bland Burges, 18.

23. Young, I, 124–6, 159, 162.

24. Arbuthnot to Keith, 28 Dec. 1789; Auckland to Keith, 7 May 1790, BL, Add. 35541–2.

25. Brand to Wharton, 30 May 1791; 14 Dec. 1793; 26 Jan 1793; 1 Feb. 1794.

26. Macpherson to Keith, 19 June 1790, BL, Add. 35542.

27. Hume, BL, Add. 29477, fo. 14.

28. Pratt, II, 48–9; Walker, pp. 9, 266–7, 203, 157, 307; Northall, p. 127; Stevens, p. 388; Thicknesse, 1768, pp. 134–5, 160–2; Thicknesse, *Pais Bas*, 3–4, 49, 6.

29. *Newcastle Journal*, 29 Aug. 1752; *Daily Universal Register*, 22 July 1786.

30. *Evening Journal*, 26 Dec. (os) 1727; *London Evening Post*, 21 May (os) 1730; J. C. Moore, *Life of Lieutenant General Sir John Moore* (2 vols., 1833), I, 5; Brand to Wharton, 4 Aug. 1787, Durham, Wharton.

31. Townshend to Keith, 12 March; Bulkeley to Keith, 13 March 1787, BL, Add. 35538.

32. Poole, I, 56; Crewe, BL, Add. 37926, fo. 96; Thicknesse, *Pais Bas*, pp. 178–9.

33. Colman to Delafaye, 18 Aug. 1725, PRO 98/25; Francis, 22 Oct. 1772, BL, Add. 40759; Manners to Keith, 24 April 1779, BL, Add. 35516; Garmston, BL, Add. 30271, fo. 24; Brand to Wharton, June 1784, Durham, Wharton.

34. Craven, *Memoirs*, I, 137.

35. Pratt, II, 96–9.

36. Wharton to mother, 2 Oct. 1775, Durham, Wharton.

37. Delafaye to Waldegrave, 25 July (os) 1733; Chewton, BL, Add. 32693, fo. 401–2; Thicknesse, 1768, pp. 158–60.

38. Robson, 5 Aug. 1787, BL, Add. 38837.

39. Creed; Woodward to ———, 30 Dec. 1726, PRO 80/60; Bentinck to mother, 18 Jan. 1727, BL, Eg. 1711; Hale to Keith, 28 Jan. 1779, BL, Add. 35515; Brand to Wharton, 12 March 1783; 13 Nov. 1792, Durham, Wharton.

40. Shaw, *Letters*, p. 28; Craven, *Memoirs*, I, 162; Crewe, BL, Add. 37926, fo. 120–2; Garmston, 18 Oct. 1787, BL, Add. 30271; Brand to Wharton, 10 Sep. 1787, Durham, Wharton; Payne to Keith, 1 Nov. 1788, BL, Add. 35541.

41. Conway to Keith, 11 Sep. 1774; *Keith . . . correspondence,* II, 24; Francis, 10 Dec. 1772, BL, Add. 40759.

42. Walker, pp. 96, 424.

43. Stevens, p. 162; Crewe, BL, Add. 37926, fo. 70; Walker, pp. 71–2.

44. Earl of Harrold to Lord Henry Grey, no date, Beds. L 30/5; Leven, p. 328; Davies to Keith, 30 Dec. 1785, Arbuthnot to Keith, 6 May 1787, BL, Add. 35535, 35538.

45. Young, I, 8.

46. Stevens, p. 325.

47. Grey Journal, BL, Add. 5957, fo. 62–3.

48. Giffard to Keith, 9 April 1785, BL, Add. 35534.

49. Cottrell in Riga, 1741.

50. Sutton to Townshend, 1 May 1727, PRO 81/122.

51. Essex, p. 65.

52. *Loyal Observator*, 31 Aug. (os) 1723; Moore, p. 3.

53. Stevens, pp. 63–4.

54. Cradock, p. 269.

55. Shaw, *Letters*, pp. 7–9; Stevens, pp. 156–7, 158.

56. G. W. Pilcher, *The Reverend Samuel Davies Abroad* (Urbana, 1967), p. 87; Cradock, *Memoirs*, p. 17.

57. Garmston, 23 Oct. 1787, BL, Add. 30271.

58. *Reading Mercury*, 16 Sep. (os), *Post Boy*, 17 Sep. (os), *Flying Post and Post Master*, 17 Sep. (os), *Northampton Mercury*, 23 Sep. (os) 1723; Morville to Chammorel, Oct. 1723, AE CP Angleterre, sup. 7, fo. 94; *Applebee's original Weekly Journal*, 27 June (os) 1724; *Wye's Letter*, 16 Sep. (os) 1725.

59. *General Evening Post*, 29 May (os) 1735.

60. *Tour of Holland*, p. 229.

61. Pottle, *Boswell*, pp. 230–54; *Cole-Walpole correspondence*, I, 98; F. G. Stokes (ed.), *William Cole, A Journal of my Journey to Paris in the year, 1765*, p. 328; Henry of Nassau to William of Nassau, 30 March 1732, Herts D/ENa F57; Walker to Keith, 20 Nov. 1787, BL, Add. 35539; Walker, p. 38; Leven, pp. 326–7; St Vincent, BL, Add. 31192, fo. 19–20; Young, I, 51; Brand to Wharton, 13 Nov. 1792, Durham, Wharton; Stevens, p. 160; Mitchell, BL, Add. 58314, fo. 46; *Worcester Post-Man*, 13 Dec. (os) 1723; anon., *Present State of Germany* (2 vols., 1738), II, 366; Carleton, pp. 271–2.

62. *Tour of Holland*, pp. 229–30; Thicknesse, *Pais Bas*, p. 17.

63. Shaw, *Letters*, p. 119.

64. Essex, p. 38; Wharton to mother, 5 March 1775, Durham, Wharton; Walker, p. 414.

LOVE, SEX, GAMBLING AND DRINKING

I saw Spencer at Brussels, he is at present in England, where his
father will insist upon his remaining; for when at Brussels he was
so exceedingly smitten with a Miss Rockford that many of his
friends were afraid he might be imprudent enough to marry her.
It is certain that he left Oxfordshire very suddenly in order to go
there, was overtaken by his father at Dover, and with some difficulty brought back to town.

Lord Dungarvan, 1787.[1]

Love and Sex

. . . afterwards to the Thuillerie Gardens and walked by moonlight, which would have been extremely agreeable, but for the
interruption of too many of the votaries of Venus for the most
part of the lowest class.

St Vincent, 1772.[2]

Travel abroad provided a great opportunity for sexual adventure.
Tourists were generally young, healthy, wealthy and poorly, if at
all, supervised. Many enjoyed sexual adventures whilst abroad, but
it is difficult to obtain information on the subject. To a great extent
it was the 'good-boys' such as Wharton, well-behaved young prigs
such as Thomas Pelham, and the scholars, such as Pococke, who
wrote lengthy letters home to their relatives. There is very little
personal correspondence, other than demands for money, from
those whose conduct was castigated by their contemporaries. The
vast majority of the journals that have been preserved relate to
blameless tourists. Philip Francis might speculate on whether he
would prefer relations with the Venus de Medici or Titian's Venus,[3]
but such daydreaming was banished from the accounts of his more
respectable contemporaries. It is also possible that journals and
correspondence may have been tampered with by descendants.
There is evidence of this in several cases.
   The public attitude to sexual adventure abroad was generally

unfavourable. It was heavily influenced by the prevalence of venereal disease for which there was no cure and whose consequence could be serious not only from the point of individual health, but also because it harmed the chances of securing heirs to an estate. In 1725 *Mist's Weekly Journal*, the leading Tory London newspaper, attacked the conduct of British tourists abroad. On 14 August (os) the paper printed a letter from 'Tibullus', who had been sent on his travels when 17 'and spent betwixt three or four years abroad, during which time I worship'd the merry Deities, and only acquired the languages necessary for entertaining the fair'. On 18 September (os) the paper printed an account of British tourists in Paris who went drinking until 2 or 3 am and 'then return home, unless they chance to stumble into a Bordel by the way; a misfortune which has often happen'd . . . the whole account of their travels is generally no more than a journal of how many bottles they have drunk, and what loose amours they have had'. On 9 July (os) 1731, the *Daily Post Boy* claimed that British gentlemen travellers spent all their time drinking and whoring; whilst on 7 August (os) 1731 'Civicus', in an anti-travel piece in the *London Journal*, stressed the sexual risks presented by women travelling: 'it is highly probable, that by means of our ladies travelling, some of our noble families may be honoured with a French Dancing Master's son for their heirs.' There was a clear sexual allusion in a newspaper comment of 1739: 'I look upon France as the Hot-bed to our English Youth, where they are immaturely ripened, and therefore soon become rotten and corrupt at home.' A guidebook for tourists warned of the prevalence of veneral disease in the south of France, and of the expense that it entailed and stated,

> You will, no doubt, be frequently accosted in the streets, by fellows who are lookers-out to bawdy-houses; asking you, if you want a jolie fille; and happy are they when they can lay hold of an Englishman, as the girls say they bleed freely: the reward on those occasions, is to break your cane over their shoulders; for many unguarded foreigners have been seduced by those notorious villains, into places from whence they have never more made their appearance.[4]

Venereal disease was indeed a problem. In 1734, Lord Rockingham was upset by claims that he had it; Charles Howard, Viscount Morpeth, died in 1741 of venereal disease contracted in

Italy; and a long series of distinguished tourists remembered their travels for years afterwards for reasons that bore little relation to the restrained portraits by Batoni that decorated their libraries. Joseph Shaw attacked the preference of the English gentry for French surgeons: 'having travelled into France, and brought home French vices and diseases, to the disgrace of the nation, they are glad to make use of those surgeons who best understand their distempers.'[5]

Paris was the great centre of sexual activity, partly because it was the city in which tourists tended to spend most time, and partly because access to local society was relatively easy. Paris, according to one London newspaper, was 'a city the most noted for Intrigues of any in Europe';[6] and French women had a reputation for flexibility: 'It is observable, that the French allow their women all imaginable freedoms, and are seldom troubled with jealousy; nay, a Frenchman will almost suffer you to court his wife before his face, and is even angry if you do not admire her person: And, indeed, by the liberties I have often seen a married lady use, I have been at a loss to distinguish her husband from the rest of the Company'. Lord Glenorchy wrote of the Danish court: 'The Ladies are much in the French way extremely free.'[7]

The picture painted in Britain was one of British sexual conquests,

> Our Gentry will make themselves as famous in making conquests among the French women, as their brave ancestors have been heretofore in subduing the French men . . . We hear from Paris, that one of the dancers at the opera, called La Salle, so remarkable for her chastity, as to have obtained the name of Vestal, has at last surrendered to a young English nobleman, who was introduced to her at an Assembly in woman's apparel, and so far insinuated himself into her favour, as to be permitted to take part of her bed.

Thicknesse stated,

> It is certain that men of large fortunes can in no city in the world indulge their passions in every respect more amply than in Paris; and that is the lure which decoys such numbers, and in particular Englishmen, to this city of *love* and folly; and occasion such immense sums to be drained from other countries, and lavished

away in debauchery of every kind, in a town infinitely inferior to London. I verily believe Paris to be the theatre of more vice than any city in the world, drunkenness excepted.

He claimed that Parisian wives, including those who were religious, were generous with their sexual favours. Thicknesse was sardonic about the sexual adventures of British tourists. Commenting on the donation of £1,000 by the son of an English Duke to 'one little piece of readymade love' he wrote:

This is one instance, and I could give you a thousand, of the great influence of novelty, change of country, and of manners; for in London the same woman, and consequently the *same charms*, would not have produced a tythe of such liberality. But it was Paris, a Paris opera girl, and an Englishman at Paris, who is nobody without he cuts a figure, . . .

A Bristol newspaper reported that 'the English when at Paris, make Opera girls and actresses objects of idolatry'.[8] There was a certain basis to these reports. John Lindesay, Earl of Crawford, had an intrigue with a French noblewoman 'of the greatest quality' in 1723. When Lord Clinton left Paris in 1725 he left 'behind him a fine lady'. Viscount Weymouth caused diplomatic complications when he took his mistress, Mlle Petit Pas, back to Britain in 1732. She was one of the leading dancers of the Opéra and 'being of the French King's musick, and consequently a menial servant of His Majesty's she ought to be sent back'. She returned to Paris in May 1733 'avec quarante mille livres, beaucoup de joie, et un petit milord dans le ventre'. In 1736, the Duke of Kingston brought his Parisian mistress, Madame de la Touche, back to Britain. Her husband, a royal official, wrote to Lord Hardwicke to complain.[9]

The well-informed Philip Francis observed: 'In England the commerce between the sexes is either passion or pleasure; In France it is gallantry, sentiment or intrigue: In Italy it is a dull, insipid *Business.*'[10] Many British tourists found their time in Italy far from dull. Italy, and, in particular, Venice, was notorious for prostitution,[11] and some British tourists became heavily involved with mistresses. Pococke wrote from Venice in June 1734, 'Mr Wynn . . . has been 2 or 3 years at Venice, enchanted with a Mistress'. Three years later the Earl of Radnor's dominance by a Venetian mistress attracted comment. The engagement of Lord Lyttleton's son was broken off in late 1764 because he was 'detained by Circes and Syrens of the coast about Genoa'. One of the fourth Earl of Chesterfield's brothers 'spent a great deal of money on a Venetian woman, whom he thought in love with him'. In 1785 the British envoy in Turin, Trevor, had to intervene in the case of 'a silly young countryman of our's Mr. Fox Lane, a man of fashion and great fortune having, from an infatuated complaisance to the Lady he was in love with, changed his Religion, or rather for the first time adopted one, which unluckily for him, is the Roman Catholic . . . I cannot but look upon this step as an act of Infatuation and childishness'. George Lyttleton set off for Italy in 1729 with a warning from his father against 'grapes, new wine, and pretty women'. David Mallet bragged of having 'lain with a Sovereign Princess in Italy'. Horace Mann commented on how 'An English traveller frequently deranges the whole harmony of "cicisbeship" '.[12]

Foreign travel also provided an opportunity for people to live together unconstrained by the pressures of British life. Consequently there were many elopements to Europe. Lord Euston, the son of the second Duke of Grafton, eloped to Italy in 1744 with a Miss Nevill 'of a very ancient family in Lincolnshire, with eleven thousand pounds for her fortune, and a celebrated beauty' giving her a promise of marriage which he never fulfilled. In December 1778, Amelia D'Arcy, Lady Carmarthen, ran away to Europe with John Byron, the father of the poet, and married him when Lord Carmathen obtained a divorce. In 1785, Miss Murray, Keith's source of British gossip, wrote to him: 'Mr. M: is I am told gone to France with Miss Johnson and left Lady Catherine to pray for his soul.'[13] Free from prying eyes Henry Fox could live with Mrs Strangeways Horner in Europe in the early 1730s. In 1730 Viscount Harcourt met a former MP, Richard Cresswell, living with his mistress in a way that would have been more difficult in Britain. Lord Craven took his mistress on a trip to the continent.

Living with another's spouse was also easier abroad,

The Florentine minister [William Wyndham] is parted in due form from his wife. She returned with Lord Wycombe to England. At present they halt to Bologna, in company with Lady Webster and Lord Holland. They talk and act as their convenience directs. I am told laws civil and divine are not any guide to their words or actions. Lady Plymouth was there with her husband, at least he was in the same house. Mr. Amherst does all the leading honours to the Lady, . . . our present travelling ladies out-Herod Herod, or to speak more modernly, live with more effrontery than even their teachers, the French ladies.[14]

There is little evidence of homosexual activity. Swinton was accosted by a pimp in Lisbon in 1730 who offered him men or women; and male prostitutes were noted in Paris in the late 1710s, but if tourists did take advantage of these facilities they were careful to conceal their activities. Sodomy was regarded in Britain as a foreign vice of Mediterranean origins. It was particularly associated with Italy, and in some writings linked to Catholicism. In Protestant Europe homosexuals were often treated savagely. The brutal punishments that followed the major sodomy trials in Holland in 1730 (which were reported fully in the British press), indicated the official response in northern Europe to homosexual activity. There tended to be more tolerance in the Mediterranean countries. This did not prevent Cresswell from getting into trouble in Genoa in 1716. The British envoy Davenant informed his counterpart in Paris,

I met with a very dirty piece of business upon my arrival here. The 4th instant Mr. Cresswell was arrested by an order of a Deputation of the Senate, which has the inspection on cases of Sodomy, they call em here *il Magistrato dei Virtuosi*. He was immediately carried to the prison of the Palace, with a young Genoese boy he had lately drest up, and nobody is admitted to see him. He has been so publick in his discourse and actions that they can fix on him the fact above 38 times, in his own house, the streets, in porches of Churches and Palaces, in short I never heard of so flagrant a Delinquent, however I have some hopes of stifling the process, in regard of the nation's honour, and of the circumstances of my being here at this time to make em a compliment from His Majesty. They have been encouraged to this proceeding, by my not permitting him to visit me, but it is my opinion they would have shown more respect to His Majesty and the nation, if they had traced out one of their people for an example of severity, without fixing it on an Englishman, . . .[15]

The sexual activities of most tourists caused few problems. General Dalrymple could run after 'the filles de l'opéra' in Paris; Lord Pembroke could appear in Florence 'with a Brunette en homme';

and an Irish peer could live in Pisa with both wife and an Italian Comtessa as mistress.[16] The activities of adults gave little concern. In addition in Italy the cicesbo system, by which Italian married women were escorted by a man other than their husband, provided opportunities for a relationship that was in accordance with local customs. In the spring of 1791 Brand took Lord Bruce to Siena 'to see an old Lady to whom Ld Ailesbury was Cavalier Servente *Thirty nine* years ago! She gave us many anecdotes of Ld. A.'s Sienna life which perhaps had better been concealed'. The lady urged Bruce to live like his father; Brand commented: 'It was the very reflexion I wished to avoid. But Pazienza! If he imitates his fathers youthful faults I hope at least he will equally imitate the virtues of his maturity'.[17]

Problems were created when impressionable young men fell in love. Venereal disease was bad, but a mésalliance was far worse. Brand, who served as a 'bearleader' for over a decade, found himself forced to consult the parents of his charges on several occasions. In 1783, his pupil fell for the elder Miss Berry in Boulogne; in 1793, Lord Bruce fell for a slightly older English tourist in Rome. The latter episode led to a marriage in Italy, but with the blessing of the Earl of Ailesbury.[18]

Wharton met some very attractive French women in 1775, and had to reassure his relations about his intentions: 'You have no occasion to fear my being in danger of captivity from any French Beauties. I see nothing in them capable of touching an Englishman like his own countrywomen'.[19] Forceful intervention was necessary in other cases. George Viscount Parker's involvement with an Italian woman, and his failure to heed the instructions of his father, Lord Chancellor Macclesfield, led Macclesfield to mobilise the resources of British diplomacy to regain his son. The nineteen-year-old James Stuart Mackenzie fell for the famous opera-dancer Barberini and arranged to marry her in Venice. This was prevented by Archibald, Duke of Argyll, who used his friend Lord Hyndford, British envoy in Berlin, to have Barberini brought to Berlin and Mackenzie banned from Prussia.[20]

It is not surprising that impressionable young men, poorly, if at all, supervised, sometimes fell for local women. Very few went as far as one of Sarah Marlborough's grandsons, William Godolphin, Marquess of Blandford, and married a local woman whom they had met abroad. Brief affairs or visits to brothels were more common, though it is impossible to assess the extent to which tourists took advantage of the possibilities. Harcourt's tutor, Bowman, might write of 'the low vices of our countrymen in Italy', but some tourists were uninterested in or contemptuous of such activities. William Bentinck smugly informed his mother from Paris: 'All the young men here are petit Maitres, and there is no conversing with them without falling into their way and being debauched with them, which I do not design to begin now for myself . . . whereas among people of a certain age, and character, there is here all the good breeding and politeness, and sense and knowledge of the world that one can desire'. William Windham found French women unattractive and claimed that licentiousness was more gross and common in London than in Paris.[21] If one is to judge from correspondence and journals 'low vices' were of less interest than accommodation and food, paintings and statuary. However, contemporary printed criticism of tourism would suggest the contrary. Clearly interests varied by individual. There was no common response to the opportunities of travel, and there was no reason why there should be one.

Gambling

> The French only regard strangers according to the money they spend and figure they make with their equipages, and provided you game and play you will be well received in the best company at Paris; where one risques losing five ten or fifteen pounds sterling in two hours time, besides at games of hazard the French of the very best fashion, make no scruple of cheating you, for they will do it to one another, therefore I can . . . compare seeing (what is styled) the very best company of Paris to nothing else but a company of sharpers, and pickpokkits, and at all their great assemblys the conversation consists of cards, and trifles, which will by no means contribute to the improvement of young people and moreover every stranger that runs into this fashion-able way of life, ought to have about two or three thousand pound a year to support this figure, which is not to be done by people of moderate circumstances'.
>
> Edward Mellish.[22]

Gambling played a major role in polite society in eighteenth-century Europe. The British gambled a lot at home, to the despair of contemporary moralists, and it was not surprising that when they went abroad many gambled heavily. Gambling was an integral part of eighteenth-century life and people gambled on everything — political, social and economic news as well as sports such as horseracing, boxing, billiards and cards. The same happened abroad. Charles James Fox won a bet with Lord Kildare in Florence in 1767 on how many sheets of paper the latter had with him.[23] Most tourists however gambled on cards and this was the activity on which some lost heavily, and which earned the denunciation of commentators.

Gambling was of great importance in France: 'An itch for gaming has infected the generality of French, and may be deemed one of the plagues of the nation: and yet one would think it impossible for people who seem naturally restless, and desirous of moving from place to place, to sit cutting and shuffling the cards for five or six hours together'.[24] Andrew Mitchell wrote,

> It is a great misfortune for a stranger not to be able to play but yet a greater to love it. Without gaming one can't enter into that sort of company that usurps the name of *Beau Monde*, and no other qualification but that and money are requisite to recommend to the first company in France, for this reason several sharpers, whose characters obliged them to leave the country, are here well received and caressed only because they play and are rich.

He commented on the Parisian custom of gambling in respectable houses on the footing of an assembly, where the banker paid the lady of the house for the privilege of fleecing her guests: 'I knew several gentlemen drawn in unwarily to such company, which obliged them to leave the place sooner than they otherways would have done'.[25] In 1727, Sarah Marlborough instructed Humphrey Fish not to let her grandsons gamble in France. She noted the cost involved and added: 'I know, in France they will all be wonderful civil, in hopes of cheating you: and when they find people won't play, they grow very cool . . . it is better to be without such civilities'. Three years later Edward Mellish wrote to his uncle from Blois that he had been 'lately informed by an English Gentleman who was sometime at Tours . . . that if one expected to be well received by persons of the best fashion, one must be obliged to play deep and game sometimes which would have been very inconsistent with the money I proposed to have spent at Tours'. The following February he wrote to his father from Saumur, 'I avoid gaming as much as is possible, which is a most pernicious entertainment, and there is no country in the world free from it except England' — a surprising statement. Having arrived in Paris he reported that he would 'avoid all play as much as possible; tho it is very difficult even in the best companys to avoid it at Paris'. He added that it was necessary to gamble if one wished to see women of quality and the sons of the aristocracy. Richard Lyttleton, who was sent to the academy in Besançon in 1737, informed his father, ''Tis impossible to avoid play and keep any company'. He was soon in debt as a result.[26]

Some British tourists lost heavily. Robert, fourth Earl of Sunderland, who died in Paris in 1729, 'had lost a considerable sum at play at Versailles'. The previous year George Lyttleton, who claimed that Parisian society necessitated gambling, wrote to his father 'I am weary of losing money at cards'. Harry Pelham, studying at the Caen academy, ran up a debt of 50 guineas as a result of gambling on backgammon games at Harcourt. The *Daily Universal Register* claimed that English tourists were defrauded regularly by Parisian card sharps.[27]

Andrew Mitchell, Edward Mellish, Richard and George Lyttleton were correct in noting the pressures to gamble, but it is clear that some British tourists enjoyed gambling and that some of the sharps were British. George James Cholmondeley ran a public gaming table in Paris and a faro bank at Brooks Club. Edward Wortley Montagu and Theobald Taaffe, both then MPs, were arrested in Paris in 1751 accused of cheating a Jew at cards and robbing him when he refused to pay. Both were imprisoned. They were cleared in the first court hearing, but this favourable verdict was overturned by the Parlement of Paris and they were fined 300 livres each with costs. Taaffe, who acted as a faro banker, continued his Parisian acitivities. In 1755 he won a large sum of money from Sir John Bland MP, who committed suicide after being arrested (at Taaffe's instigation) because of the dishonouring of the bills he had given for the debt. Thus, France provided opportunities for both the professional gamester and for the simply enthusiastic gambler, such as those (including women) whom Lady Knight noticed in Toulouse in 1776—7.[28]

Paris was not the only centre of gambling. There was a lot of gambling in the Austrian Netherlands, and, in particular, in the nearby watering places of Spa and Aachen. Walker, who visited Spa in 1787, noted the dominance of gambling and wrote that the town was becoming 'a den of thieves . . . I recognised more of my countrymen than that of any other nation'. Thicknesse warned against gambling in the Austrian Netherlands and of the particular need to avoid Spa and Aachen where he claimed a lot of British money was lost to sharps who congregated there specifically in order to defraud young British tourists.[29] The United Provinces were not noted as a centre for gambling, but John Stanhope managed to lose £450 there; Edward Coke gambled heavily in 1737; Oliver Goldsmith characterised the English on the Dutch passenger-barges as playing cards; and Boswell gambled.[30] In Italy many of the British tourists gambled on cards, though usually with each other. Cunningham reported them doing so in Venice in 1717; Charles Stanhope gambled heavily in the same city in 1732; the Duke of Gloucester 'played at cards with a few English Gentlemen' at the masked ball held in his honour in Leghorn in 1771; and both Thomas Brand and Lady Knight commented on British gamblers in Italy in the early 1790s.

Losses could be serious. The Jacobite Catholic baronet, Sir Carnaby Haggerston, who visited Italy in 1718, showed a great facility for losing money that made his frequent requests for more funds less acceptable. In 1717, he wrote from France to his mother's Jesuit counsellor, Francis Anderton, that he had lost nearly £200: 'what wonder that young people who stay so long without exercises and without change fall in to some change of fortune desiring to try at game since he cannot in battles . . . I've taken a resolution never to playe more except to oblige companie and that only at small games.' His resolution was unsuccessful. The following September his Jesuit Bearleader, John Thornton, informed Anderton that Haggerston had lost £150 lately, though he consoled himself by writing: 'He has indeed avoided all gaming for some time and I both hope and suppose he will fall no more into it finding the inconveniencys must necessarily attend it.'[31] Gambling could be disastrous and the frequent denunciations of the habit arouse no surprise. Gambling losses, like venereal disease, often left scars that never healed. They could wreck family fortunes and represented the threat posed by whim and passion to the attempt to safeguard order and stability in the fortunes of Georgian families. Tourism accentuated the risks in both cases.

Drinking

> Strangers and especially the English are more in danger than the
> people of the country, only because they will drink foreign wines,
> which do not agree with the air of the country, and will not be
> moderate upon eating, but sup and sit up late.
>
> William Bentinck, 1727.[32]

Many British tourists drank heavily. Alcohol was inexpensive and
easy to obtain. There were few barriers to alcoholism and little condemnation of heavy social drinking. In 1722 Colin MacLaurin met,
in the suite of Lord Polwarth at the Congress of Cambrai, 'a young
Gentleman unhappily addicted to drinking to the highest degree;
who was kept abroad on purpose lest his grandfather should find
out his follies and disinherit him'. Eight years later a drunken brawl
involving young Englishmen in Paris was reported in the London
press. The following March, Edward Mellish reported from Blois:
'Sr. Thomas Twisden asked the Dr. [King] to drink a bottle Extraordinary, upon which the Dr. replyed if you insist upon it, I shall
make you repent of it upon which there was a trial of skill; and Sr.
Thomas was wursted, and was obliged to quit the field of battle and
retired to bed.' In August 1734, the Duke of Queensberry's party
'went drunk to bed' at Brussels. Nine years later Horace Walpole
directed his acid at the pretensions of 'the Dilettanti, a club, for
which the nominal qualification is having been in Italy, and the real
one, being drunk: the two chiefs are Lord Middlesex and Sir
Francis Dashwood, who were seldom sober the whole time they
were in Italy'. The *Gentleman's Guide* noted: 'There is a famous
tavern or wine-cellar, where all sorts of good wines may be had, on
the road to Seves. The English are so accustomed to resort thither,
that it will not be difficult for any stranger to find it out.' Walker
spent a sleepless night at Milan because of the antics of a group of
drunken English: 'last night a party of them, about a dozen, drank
thirty-six bottles of burgundy, claret, and champaign, (as our landlord showed us in his book) and made such a noise till six in the
morning we could not sleep'. In 1792, Brand complained of the
'bad sort' of English at Vienna: 'They are of the two-idea sort —
The Bottle is one.'[33]

Critics were correct in claiming that some tourists were more interested in sex, gambling and drink than improving themselves. However, many of them would probably have acted in the same fashion at home. The Grand Tour served the useful purpose of letting people sow their wild oats abroad. Some commentators suggested that many tourists were too young: 'Of old, not boys, but men, were sent to travel for the views of men in leaving their own country was not to see fashions, to examine how periwigs or coats were made, but to inquire into the excellency of the laws of other nations, and, by comparing them with their own supply their defects . . .' Andrews was firm on the point,

> Until we are five-and-twenty, little or no benefit results to the far greater part of those who make what is called the grand tour. Nature has given to few men such talents as will enable them to travel at an earlier period. A Bacon, a Wotton, and a few others, are exceptions which will not justify the sending abroad mere youths, unacquainted with their own country, and totally unfit therefore to draw those comparisons between it and others, which are the very intent of travelling . . . I remember to have heard a Swiss gentleman of excellent capacity remark, that most of our English travellers were sent abroad much too young and inexperienced in the affairs of their country. Without a competent knowledge of which, he was positive in his conviction, that travelling became no better than a mere amusement. No man, till he had attained his four or five-and-twentieth year, was fit to judge with solidity concerning the transactions and business of his own country, much less of another, to which he was an utter stranger. The only reasonable expectation to be formed in regard to a travelling youth, was the acquisition of foreign languages. Were it not to this intent, he would often say, that no people could betray more thoughtlessness and imprudence than the English, in suffering, or rather indeed encouraging their young gentlemen to make such long and expensive excursions.

Brand, who had considerable personal experience of the difficulties presented by young charges, wrote from Dresden in 1791,

> I am very much concerned at a practice which gains ground every day, that of sending, not young men, but *boys* to travel thro Europe when they ought to be learning logic and mathematics in some sound seminary at home. They are launched into vicious

society before they know even any theory of virtue and morality and being too childish for the company they are introduced to they lose the consideration which an Englishman has hitherto had on the Continent and they become a more easy prey to the villainous and interested of both sexes.[34]

Possibly these commentators were correct. The most perceptive and best-informed accounts of Europe written by those who travelled for pleasure, tend to have been written by older travellers such as Gardenstone, Holroyd, Mitchell and Walker. The correspondence of young tourists, and of their Bearleaders, is often about debts, gambling and the purchase of clothes. On the other hand some young tourists, such as William Bentinck and Thomas Pelham, sent informed and intelligent letters. Given the length of time that a major tour entailed it was understandable that most tourists were young. Older men had their careers to pursue, their estates to manage; not that either of these precluded many from foreign trips, albeit often short ones to Paris, such as those Lord Fife took in the 1760s or that Lord Cassillis made in 1788. Older men who travelled for a long time tended to have a specific reason: health and/or retirement as with Gardenstone, Sir Richard Lyttleton and Sir Humphrey Morice; the death of a spouse as with Mitchell and Lord Stormont; or a need, often fiscal or political, to be out of Britain. Thomas Barrett-Lennard (1717–86) went to Italy in 1750 with his wife Anne following the death of his child. However some older men did take long trips for pleasure. The very wealthy Joseph Leeson, later first Earl of Milltown (1701–83), visited Rome in 1744–5 and also 1750. Sir Matthew Fetherston-haugh (1714?–74) travelled in France, Italy and Austria with his wife and several relations in 1749–52. James Alexander (1730–1802), a very wealthy Ulster landowner who had made a fortune in the East India Company, visited Rome with his wife in 1777.

These were exceptions however. Most older men could not spare several years for a foreign tour and the Grand Tour in the strict sense, the protracted trip to France and Italy, tended to remain the prerogative of youth. As such it fulfilled a major social need, namely the necessity of finding young men, who were not obliged to work and for whom work would often be a derogation, something to do between school and the inheritance of family wealth. University could only be a temporary stopgap as few scions of the aristocracy stayed for three years or read for a degree. Foreign travel filled the gap. It was expensive, but less expensive than many parliamentary contests or than setting a son up with his own British establishment. It allowed the young to sow their wild oats abroad and it kept them out of trouble, including disputes with their family, at home. A certain amount of drinking, gaming and wenching was an acceptable cost of the system.

Notes

1. Dungarvon to Keith, 9 Feb. 1787, BL, Add. 35538.
2. St Vincent, BL, Add. 31192, fo. 12.
3. Francis, BL, Add. 40759, fo. 20.
4. *Craftsman*, 21 July (os) 1739; *Gentleman's Guide*, pp. 124–5.
5. Rockingham to Essex, 2 Feb. 1734, BL, Add. 27733; Shaw, *Letters to a Nobleman* (1709), xx.
6. *General Evening Post*, 12 Sep. (os) 1734.
7. Thompson, I, 31; Glenorchy to Duke of Kent, 13 Jan. 1721, Beds. L30/8/10/8.
8. *London Evening Post*, 27 Jan. (os); *Daily Advertiser*, 27 Jan. (os) 1737; Thicknesse, 1768, pp. 169–70, 179–80; Lord Hervey to Richmond, 27 Dec. (os) 1733, Bury St Edmunds RO 941/47/25; *Newcastle Courant*, 18 Dec. 1784; *Felix Farley's Bristol Journal*, 5 Jan. 1788; Pottle (ed.), *Boswell*, p. 250.
9. Rolt, *Crawfurd*, pp. 52, 55; Waldegrave to Delafaye, 30 Nov. 1732, PRO 78/201; H. Duranton (ed.), *Journal de la Cour et de Paris* (St Etienne, 1981), 28 Nov. 1732, 1 June 1733; Hervey to Stephen Fox, 4 Dec. (os) 1736; M. Vallet de la touch to Hardwicke, 4 Jan. 1737, BL, Add. 51345, 35586.
10. Francis, BL, Add. 40759, fo. 20.
11. Stevens, p. 360.
12. Pococke, BL, Add. 22978, fo. 84; HMC, *Denbigh*, V, 221; *Queen of the Blues*, I, 121; Horace Walpole, *Commonplace Book*, p. 29; Trevor to Keith, 15 Dec. 1785, BL, Add. 35535; M. Wyndham, *Chronicles of the Eighteenth Century*, I, 21; J.P. Shipley, *James Ralph: Pretender to Genius* (Columbia, PhD, 1963), p. 380; *Mann-Walpole correspondence*, IV, 284.
13. HP, II, 37; Murray to Keith, 11 Nov. 1785, BL, Add. 35535.
14. *Harcourt Papers*, III, 3; Craven *Memoirs*, I, 71; Knight, pp. 210–11.
15. Swinton, 2 Nov. (os) 1730; Davenant to Stair, 8 Dec. 1716, SRO GD135/141/6.
16. *Auckland Correspondence*, I, 399; Riddell to Keith, 6 July 1784, BL, Add. 35532; Brand to Wharton, 3 Jan. 1791, Durham, Wharton.
17. Brand to Wharton, undated, Durham, Wharton.
18. Brand to Wharton, 17 Nov. 1783; 26 March 1793, Durham, Wharton.
19. Wharton to his mother, 18 May; Wharton to Thomas Lloyd, 21 Sep.; Wharton to Miss Raine, 7 Oct. 1775, Durham, Wharton.
20. Memoir by Lady Louisa Stuart as introduction to *Letters and Journals of Lady Mary Coke* (4 vols., 1889–96), I, lii–liv.
21. *Harcourt Papers*, III, 13; Bentinck, BL, Eg. 1711, fo. 610; Windham, p. 4.
22. Mellish to father, 25 April 1731.
23. Fox to Lord Fitzwilliam, 27 Oct. 1767, BL, Add. 47576.

24. Thompson, I, 32.

25. Mitchell, BL, Add. 58314, fo. 8, 27.

26. Sarah Marlborough to Fish, 12 Oct. (os) 1727, BL, Add. 61444; Mellish to John Gore, 17 Nov. 1730; Mellish to father, 25 Feb.; 18 April 1731; Wyndham, *Chronicles*, I, 115–16.

27. Charles Stanhope to third Duke of Marlborough, 30 Sep. 1729, BL, Add. 61667; Wyndham, *Chronicles*, I, 10, 16; Harry to Thomas Pelham, 6 Nov. 1776, BL, Add. 33127; *Daily Universal Register*, 5 Sep. 1786.

28. Montagu to Earl of Albemarle, Ambassador in Paris, 24 Dec. 1751; judgement of court, 21 Aug.; J. Jeffreys to second Earl Hardwicke, 23 Aug.; Albemarle to Newcastle, 31 Aug. 1752, BL, Add. 32832; 35630, fo. 49, 48; 32839; HP, II, 461; Knight, pp. 10, 31; *Deffand-Walpole correspondence*, V, 6.

29. Walker, p. 36; Thicknesse, 1786, pp. 4, 102–10, 126–45.

30. Stanhope to third Duke of Marlborough, undated, BL, Add. 61667, fo. 86; Horatio Walpole to Robert Trevor, 5 April (os); 3 May (os) 1737, Trevor Mss., vols. 7, 8; Balderston (ed.), p. 24; Pottle (ed.), *Boswell*, pp. 176, 200, 238, 261.

31. *St James's Chronicle*. 28 Dec. 1771; Brand to Wharton, 3 Jan. 1791; 26 Jan. 1793, Durham, Wharton; Knight, pp. 176, 179; Haggerston to Anderton, 1717; 20 Dec. 1717; Thornton to Anderton, 31 Sep. 1718.

32. Bentinck to mother, 14 June 1727, BL, Eg. 1711.

33. MacLaurin, fo. 200; *London Evening Post*, 21 May (os) 1730; Edward Mellish to father, 12 March 1731; Duchess of Queensberry to Mrs Herbert, 4 Aug. 1734, BL, Add. 22626, fo. 69; *Walpole-Mann correspondence*, II, 211; *Gentleman's Guide*, p. 231; Walker, p. 381; Brand to Wharton, 30 June 1792, Durham, Wharton.

34. *Mist's Weekly Journal*, 18 Sep. (os) 1725; Andrews, 1–2, 18–19; Brand to Wharton, 20 Aug. 1791, Durham, Wharton.

6 HEALTH AND DEATH

The second day after my arrival at this place the gnats stung my legs so bad I was obliged to lie in bed a week and the bugs bit my face so much in the night that I was swelled prodigiously, that I did not leave my chamber for a fortnight, but by taking Physic and the use of the vegito mineral water and the pomatum of goulard I got well.

> Richard Garmston, Geneva, 1787.[1]

Travel for Health

Frederick Ashfield, Esq; one of the Decypherers belonging to the Secretary's Office, died lately in his way to Italy, whither he was going for the recovery of his health.

> *Craftsman*, 4 January (os) 1729.

One of the most important motives for travel to Europe was health, although this was less true for the younger age group. The idea of travelling for health became well-established in eighteenth-century Britain as large numbers travelled to the developing spas such as Bath, Buxton, Scarborough and Tunbridge Wells. To travel *abroad* for health represented a fusion of two of the more important developments in upper-class activities in this period: tourism and travelling for health. It did not need to involve much time, for the leading continental watering place visited by British tourists, Spa, was a relatively easy journey from London. Those who travelled for health did not share the same itinerary as those on the classical Grand Tour. Italy (apart from the Bay of Naples), Paris, Vienna and the United Provinces were replaced by watering places, principally Spa and Aachen, by Portugal and Montpellier and later by the Provençal coast and Nice. Travel for health was restricted to Europe, though John Macdonald, who visited St Helena in 1773, praised its virtues: 'St Helena is a wholesome, pleasant place, and a fine keen searching air. If noblemen and gentlemen of Great

Britain and Ireland would go to Madeira and St Helena for their health, instead of going to France and Portugal, they would be sure to reestablish their health.'[2]

In the early decades of the century most went to Spa and Aachen. Lady Glenorchy went there in 1725; Sir Robert Sutton, his wife Lady Sunderland, and her sister following three years later; Colonel Pulteney went to Aachen in 1730; the Duchess of Newcastle to Spa in 1731; Walter Molesworth, his wife and son to Spa four years later.[3] However other areas were visited too. George Berkeley on his second European tour acted as companion and tutor to St George Ashe, the son of the Bishop of Clogher, who travelled for health and education. Ashe visited Italy, including Apulia, and in early 1718 Sicily, before dying in Brussels in 1721. In the mid-1720s Dr Josiah Hort, Bishop of Ferns, visited Montpellier and Marseilles, but doubted if his health was better as a result of 'his long and expensive journey'. In 1731, Dr King, the Master of the Charterhouse, went to Blois. Edward Mellish, who was there, was clearly impressed by King whom he wrote, 'is seventy years old, and is come here upon the account of his health, having been troubled with an asthma; however he has found so much benefit by this air, that he is become younger than any of us; and has a much better appetite for eating, and drinking'. Lord Berkeley went with his wife to the Loire in 1735 for his health, and stayed with Bolingbroke. The following year William Pulteney went to the United Provinces to take medical advice; and Sir William Wyndham went to France in 1737 for his health; two years later Spark Molesworth died at Naples, whither he had gone for his health; Erasmus Philipps MP survived a similar trip the same year; in 1742, the Earl of Essex, accompanied by his wife, went to France to see if a change of air would lead to his cure, but the trip was unsuccessful.[4]

Despite this variety the majority of health-seekers continued to go to Spa and Aachen (Spa being the more popular). Francis Head reported to Archbishop Wake, in August 1725, that nearly a hundred British travellers were at Spa for their health. In 1743 Cuthbert Ellison wrote to his brother Henry that, as he had received benefit 'by the last season at Spa', he should try another. Spa had many attractions. Being small it could be dominated by the tourists, and their money brought them great power. They could act as though they were in Britain. Spa's popularity, unlike that of Montpellier, remained strong throughout the century. In 1731 the

Earl of Portmore and Lord James Cavendish visited it and Edward Mellish found a large company in July including the Duchess of Newcastle: 'Sr. Thomas Littleton Bart. his two sons, my Lady Jersey Mr. Webb and his Lady, My Lord Marr [the Prominent Jacobite] Sir Robert Long Bart; Mr. Holbitch, Sr. James Folbin, Mr. Warburton, Captain Halked, Mr. Price and his Lady, Sir Alexander Macdonnal Bart. Mr. Forringal, . . .' The following August 'near 100 English gentlemen and ladies' were there. In 1734 it was visited by the Queensberrys, the following summer by Colonel Martin Bladen. When the Earl of Bath was ill in 1763, a journey to the Spa waters was prescribed for him, and thither he went with Dr Douglas, later Bishop of Salisbury, and Mrs Montagu, the 'Queen of the Blues'. In 1768 Henry Ellison went to Spa with the Ryders because of concern about the health of Mrs Ryder. The following year Lord and Lady Marchmont, Sir Charles Bunbury and Colonel and Lady Gore went in a group. Thus travelling to Spa was often not a matter of solitary invalids, but groups of travellers not all of whom were ill. The invalid's need for the waters provided the excuse for a group trip that was further facilitated by proximity to London, the good roads from the Channel to Liège, Spa's reputation for a good social life in the summer season, and the British love of travelling with and finding compatriots, that was commented on by many.[5] Montpellier lacked these advantages, and suffered accordingly, and it was only in the 1780s, when Spa was affected by the civil wars in the Austrian Netherlands and the Bishopric of Liège, that there was a discernible shift towards the distant sun of the riviera.

The waters of Spa seem to have been fairly efficacious, though it is equally likely that regular hours, fresh air and the relative sobriety of Spa activities had a beneficial effect. Mrs Ryder 'received benefit from the waters' and Henry Ellison was pleased by his trip there: 'As far as I can yet judge the society seems to be on an agreable and easy footing arising from the concourse of people from all nations. The English are by much the most numerous, and among them we have . . . Lord Northington and Lord Clive. The former has already received benefit here, if I may judge from his countenance, and the latter has profited still more by having wintered in France.'[6]

Travelling for health lost none of its popularity as the century advanced. Lord Cornbury went abroad in 1748 to seek a better climate for the recovery of his health; the Graftons travelled for the

Duchess's health in 1761; Lord and Lady Fife went to Spa in 1765 for Lady Fife's health. Patrick Moran died on the way to Lisbon in 1769; and William Montagu MP died in Lisbon itself in 1775; both had gone for their health. John Armstrong went to the Mediterranean for his health in the early 1770s; and the Gloucesters there in 1771 for the health of the Duchess. William Dowdeswell MP was ordered abroad in 1774 and died in Nice the following February; Lord John Pelham Clinton MP had no better luck in Lisbon in 1781; nor Sir Thomas Wroughton in 1787 — he died in Maastricht — whilst Lord Heathfield died at Aachen in 1790 where he had gone for his health. Philip Yorke went to Switzerland for health reasons; and Lady Craven was visited in Paris in the early 1780s by her sister-in-law, Lady Emily Berkeley, and the latter's mother, Lady Louisa Lennox, who were going to the south of France for Lady Emily's health, and by her brother the Earl of Berkeley who was going to Florence for his gout.[7]

Travelling abroad for health remained the prerogative of a small group. Whereas it was possible for the 'middling orders' to take a 'mini-Grand Tour', a brief tour to Paris and possibly the Low Countries, such as that outlined in William Lucas's 1750 guidebook, *A Five Weeks Tour to Paris, Versailles, Marli*, it was not so easy to take a quick trip to a health resort, other than Spa. Furthermore the cures were lengthy: a prolonged course of taking the waters or a long period in the warm air of Portugal, the Riviera or Naples. Thus most who needed to travel for health went to British spas. This partly accounts for the customary picture of eighteenth-century British tourism: travel for health or for health-related purposes was usually within Britain, but travel for education and pleasure was generally abroad.

Loss of Health

Thank God I keep my health, which is a great happiness in travelling.

Charles Cadogan.[8]

Lanced the swelling in my throat myself with a penknife, and find great relief.

Philip Francis, Florence.[9]

Ill health whilst travelling could be a major problem. To fall ill in the major cities, as Henry Ellison did in Paris in 1765, at least ensured medical attention, a mixed blessing in this period, but in much of Europe it was difficult to obtain such attention. Sir Henry Lyddel became 'exceedingly ill' in Savoy in 1733 and Shallett Turner had to ask the Earl of Essex to persuade the royal physician at Turin to send advice. Travellers who had accidents crossing the Cenis generally had to send to Turin for assistance.[10] When, in 1783, Sir James Graham became ill in Paris, his Bearleader Brand was 'thankful that we had got no further and that we were not stopped in a village or country town where we could not have had proper advice or attendance'. Yet even in the towns the situation was far from perfect and British travellers had little confidence in the attention that they could expect. In Hamburg there was a hospital staffed by 'a Physician and Surgeon, with necessary medicines for poor strangers and travellers, that fall sick or lame'. Whatever the charitable provision for poor travellers, British tourists in Europe tended to rely on local doctors. This did not always have beneficial results. The death of the fourth Earl of Sunderland was blamed, albeit by a rival doctor, on bad medical advice. In 1785 the Consul in Venice, John Strange, blamed his wife's death on the unparalleled 'Treachery and Malversation' of a local doctor: 'I ever must look upon [him] as her deliberate Murderer . . .' Six years later Brand, who had 'a vile scorbutic humour', wrote that he had 'no confidence in the medical people of this country if I should find it necessary to employ them'. There was a general preference for British doctors. When Mrs. Crewe was in Paris her mother became ill. She sent for Dr Lee:

. . . an English physician, who has resided here since he left off practice, and is good enough to give assistance to people of our own country when they stand in need of it . . . a plain good sort of regular physician . . . But, had he been the lowest in our school he would have been worth fifty of the French practitioners who talk such old fashioned nonsense, even the best of them, about bleeding in the foot, a seventh day crisis, and a thousand other long exploded notions, as prove them to be very far behind us in this science. It is not likely indeed the case should be otherwise for the profession is treated in so humiliating a way that no Gentleman can enter into it . . . in general they are certainly bunglers.

However, a preference for British doctors was not always best. In February 1784, Brand wrote from Italy that Sir James Graham had had: 'a very violent fever . . . His partiality to everything English made him consult a Physician [Metcalfe] whose skill I hold in sovereign contempt for I found he had no confidence in himself and would have prescribed anything that I proposed. He would have given him Madeira and roast veal when his pulse beat 120 in a minute. Lady Warren's maid died under his care.' Fortunately Metcalfe fell ill and Brand was able to persuade Graham to consult the well-regarded Neapolitan doctor, Cyrillo, who had studied in London, and who cured him. The following October Lord Bulkeley became ill with 'a bilious fever' because of the heat and fatigue of a journey from Vienna to Venice. At Trieste the British Consul recommended 'an excellent Physician'. Lady Granard found very good doctors at Linz in 1787.[11]

Much of the ill health suffered was intestinal, due to bad water and poorly-prepared food. Shaw had the flux almost all the time he was in Paris; Lady Derby had the gripe at Munich in 1782; the Duke of Gloucester the flux in Tuscany in 1771; and Dawkins had a 24 yard tapeworm removed in Dresden in 1785.[12] Coughs and colds were another problem. Francis had a violently sore throat in Tuscany in 1772; Richard Garmston caught a bad cold twice in 1787. On the Paris-Lyons diligence 'it was exceeding hot in the day six passengers on the inside, I caught cold the first night by sleeping with the windows open'. At Naples he suffered as a result of watching an eruption of Vesuvius from his balcony for three hours. Despite a very bad cold Lord Bruce wanted to go to The Hague fair in 1790.[13]

Malaria was a fear in the Campagna;[14] Lord Balgonie was nearly bitten by a scorpion which had crept into his bed at Padua in 1775; James Coutts died at Gibraltar in 1778, possibly of a respiratory illness (he was travelling home from Turin, where his unstable mental condition had led to his being confined); Lord Wycombe had a very bad inflamation in Paris in 1787.[15] For most tourists there is however no indication of what they were suffering from. They were simply reported as ill, as Charles Dering was in Amiens in 1730, Mr Heneage in Venice in 1787, and Lord Downe, Lady Ann Wellsley and Miss Payne in Paris in 1786.

Illness clearly affected travel plans. The return home of the second Earl Cowper was strongly pressed on the grounds of health by a British doctor, Hollings, who was consulted by post. William

Coxe had to cut short his Swiss trip in 1779 due to ill health.[16] The difficulties of being ill abroad underlined the degree of bravery shown by many on the Grand Tour. Despite their wealth and connections and the knowledge that they could rely on the British diplomatic service, tourists faced an alien and to some extent dangerous environment. This was more striking as it contrasted so sharply with their experience of life in Britain. Aside from the dangers presented by crime and the ever-present threat of vehicle accidents, tourists faced a situation in which illnesses, that by modern standards would rank as holiday mishaps, could well be fatal. Limited medical knowledge could turn minor ailments into killers.

Death

> In our last we gave an account that one Charles Cotton, was killed at Paris for drowning a priest in a butt of wine; but we have since been informed by some of the Deceased's friends, that he having been carousing with some of his acquaintance at Versailles . . . and going hot into the water, it threw him into a violent feaver, of which he died.
> *The Weekly Journal*, 18 October 1718.

A large number of British travellers died abroad. Many would have been travelling for their health and, in particular, a certain number died of tuberculosis in Naples or Portugal. As death is not usually seen as part of the Grand Tour it might be helpful to mention just a few deaths selected at random from the files. In January 1716 Mr St John, Viscount Bolingbroke's brother, died on his Italian travels. Three years later Henry Vincent MP died of a fever at Aachen, aged 33. In 1731 Lady Garrard died at Joppa on her way to Jerusalem. The following year Charles Hamilton died of consumption at Naples; and the following January the same illness claimed Sir Thomas Grosvenor at Naples. In October 1735 Edmund Duke of Buckingham died at Rome; and in September 1738 Lewis Langton died 'of a fever' in the same city. George Dashwood died in the same city the following spring; and Lord Charles Fitzroy died in Naples that summer. According to Sacheverell Stevens he had danced 'the major part of the night at one of these assemblies, where he overheated himself, and travelling early the next morning over some terrible cold mountains, got an illness, which soon occasioned his death'. Stevens's book was a warning of the dangers of travel. Whilst he was at Bologna, Viscount Beauchamp, the only son of Algernon Duke of Somerset, died. In 1740 William Cecil, son of the fifth Earl of Salisbury, died at Montpellier; and four years later William Bateman died at Paris. The same city claimed Sir John Swinburne in 1763; and the Duke of Buccleugh's brother Campbell Scott died there of a fever in 1766. Sir James Macdonald died in Rome in 1766; and George III's brother, Edward Duke of York, died in Monaco the following year en route for Rome. Lady Tavistock died of consumption in Lisbon in 1768 — the same illness that had recently killed Charles Compton, seventh Earl of Northampton, in Italy. Lord Baltimore died in Naples in 1771; Lawrence Sterne's wife Lydia in Albi in 1773; Smollett in Leghorn in 1771; and Gilbert Elliot MP in France in 1777. Sir Humphry Morice died at Naples in 1785; Lord Dalhousie at Abbeville in 1787; and Lord Craven in Lausanne in 1791.

Tourists were often reminded of the risk of mortality. In 1787 Walker saw in Rome the gravestone of Mr James Six, a young fellow of Trinity, Cambridge, who had died in the city the previous December. Richard Garmston's passage along the dangerous Tolentino-Foligno road, where there was no barrier between the road and its neighbouring precipice, was not eased by the knowledge that several years earlier a British traveller had been killed and his carriage dashed to pieces by the carelessness of the driver. Readers of Philip Thicknesse's tour of the Austrian Netherlands could have taken little comfort from his mention of the recent loss of the Dover packet with all its passengers on the Margate-Ostend crossing.[17]

Most references to deaths give few if any details. It is impossible usually to ascertain whether the traveller was ill before leaving Britain, or whether he died as a result of an accident or an illness. Furthermore most accounts, particularly the brief items printed in newpapers, do not distinguish between those who were travelling for pleasure, those who were travelling for health and those who were residing abroad. It is therefore difficult to suggest how many tourists died or how likely death was to end a Grand Tour. Possibly it is best simply to note the large number of deaths and suggest that this aspect of the Grand Tour, as much as the ill health that afflicted so many tourists, should not be forgotten when one sees the self-confident poses of aristocratic tourists in their portraits.

Notes

1. BL, Add. 30271, fo. 12.
2. Macdonald, *Memoirs of an Eighteenth-Century Footman*, p. 172.
3. L30/8/10/94−101; Chesterfield to Waldegrave, 23 July 1728, Chewton; *London Evening Post*, 17 Feb. (os) 1730; P. Kinsky to ———, 13 May 1734, PRO 100/11; Ailesbury, *Memoirs* (2 vols., cont. pag., 1890), II, 504.
4. Bishop Downes of Meath of Bishop Nicolson of Derry, 18 March (os) 1725, *Nicolson correspondence* (2 vols., cont. pag.), II, 599; Mellish to father, 12 March 1731; HP, II, 343; Ossorio, Sardinian envoy in London, to the Sardinian foreign minister, 6 Nov. 1742, Turin, Archivio di Stato, LM. Ing. 48.
5. Ellison, A19, no. 26; *Daily Post Boy*, 21 Sep. (os) 1731; Mellish to father, 2 July 1731; Dayrolle to Tilson, 9 Aug. 1732, PRO 84/319; *Daily Gazetteer*, 30 Aug. (os) 1735.
6. Ellison, A15, no. 24, 23.
7. Cornbury to George II, 6 June 1748, BL, Add. 32715; Ellison, A8, no. 26; *St. James Chronicle*, 1 April 1769; Cradock, *Memoirs*, p. 154; *Gentleman's Magazine* (1787), p. 838; Yorke to Keith, 12 May 1779, BL, Add. 35516; Craven, *Memoirs*, I, 121−2.
8. Cadogan to Sir Hans Sloane, 19 March 1720, BL, Add. 4045.
9. Francis, 1 Nov. 1772, BL, Add. 40759.
10. Turner to Essex, 12 Sep. 1733, BL, Add. 27732.
11. Brand to Wharton, 2 Feb. 1783, Durham, Wharton; anon., *Present State of Germany*, II, 416; Doctor De la Coste to ———, 8 Oct. 1729; Strange to Keith, 15 Sep. 1785, BL, Add. 61667, 35535; Brand to Wharton, 3 Jan. 1791, Durham, Wharton; Crewe, BL, Add. 37926, fo. 65, 76; Brand to Wharton, 18 Feb. 1784, Durham, Wharton; Fortescue to Keith, 7 Oct., Bulkeley to Keith, 12 Oct. 1785, BL, Add. 35535; Granard to Keith, 23 July 1737, BL, Add. 35538.
12. Shaw, *Letters*, p. 118; Wharton to Thomas Wharton, 21 March 1775, Durham, Wharton; Jane Campbell to Keith, 12 June 1782, BL, Add. 35525.
13. Garmston, BL, Add. 30271, fo. 8, 32; Brand to Wharton, 14 May, 4 June 1790, Brand, Wharton.
14. Sarah Marlborough to Fish, 15 May (os) 1727, BL, Add. 61444.
15. Memorandum on Coutts, BL, Add. 37848, fo. 11−12; Robert Arbuthnot to Keith, 16 Nov. 1787, BL, Add. 35539.
16. Hollings to Atwell, 23 Jan. (os) 1729/30, undated, Herts. D/EP F 55 fo. 31−4; Coxe to Keith, 26 Sep. 1779, BL, Add. 35517.
17. Stevens, p. 130, 327; Walker, p. 310; Garmston, 23 Oct. 1787, BL, Add. 30271; Thicknesse, *Pais Bas*, p. 13.

7 COST AND FINANCE

Eating, lodging, and chair hire are cheap enough here still, but as there is no manufacture in the country, and that everything must be imported that is necessary for cloaths, the carriage, duties, exchange and merchants advantage makes them very extravagant.

> Humphrey Fish, Bearleader of Charles Stanhope,
> Lunéville, 1726.[1]

In our *English* House at Rotterdam, for two wild ducks and two bottles of wine, we paid ten shillings *English Money*: and the Ducks (as we were credibly inform'd) cost but sixpence a piece, and the bottles of wine ninepence a bottle. This was a *Dutch Bill*.[2]

Cost was one of the principal planks of the attack on tourism, and it was possibly the major topic of the printed attack, particularly in the latter half of the century, when Jacobitism had ceased largely to be an issue and the sense of threat posed by Catholicism had receded to a considerable extent. The printed assult was constant,

> We expend more on travels than all Europe does besides . . . since Queen Anne's Peace, the Nation has thrown away near a Million of Species in foreign chaise-hire for our young quality . . . The meanest citizen would condemn a trade which carried out yearly upwards of 80,000 L. sterl. for outlandish commodities of real prejudice . . . all this national expence.[3]

On seeing a paragraph in the public papers, relating to the French prohibiting the English from travelling in France without passports, a gentleman declared, 'That it was too good news to be true; for he was much afraid the French would not, at their own cost, furnish a remedy to the most expensive of our national follies, which we passively suffer to run to an extravagant degree; nor hinder us from carrying them our cash, at a time when money is so scarce, and Provisions so dear in their country.'[4]

Newspapers produced estimates of expenditure by British
tourists; one such in 1786 claimed that over a million pounds was
annually spent in Paris by British tourists.[5] However, no official
statistics were kept and in assessing the cost of tourism it is best to
consider particular accounts, rather than general statements.
Finance and cost were issues that played a major role in the correspondence of most tourists. Either they were young and dependent
on relatives in Britain to arrange their finances and authorise their
expenditure, as was the case with travellers such as William Drake,
Thomas Pelham and Robert Carteret, or, as with Viscount
Perceval, they were adult and concerned to arrange their financial
affairs with British correspondents. Tourist correspondence and
journals provide a mass of information but it is often fragmentary.
Though many tourists kept accounts at some stage, few kept complete sets of accounts for their whole trip or, rather, relatively few
such sets have survived.

Finance

Cash (that has been lodged in Sir Robt: Harris's hands for our
use by Sir John Goodrick above ten weeks) has, either by mis-
carriage of letters, or the negligence of Sir Robt: Harris's office,
not yet come to hand: by which circumstance, we are at present
very low in pocket. Unknown as we are at Venice, I cannot hope
to obtain cash there for a bill of mine drawn upon Messrs. Hoar
[sic] and Co. for fifty pounds (my Banker in London) therefore
request that you will have the goodness to procure me credit
there to receive cash for a bill upon Hoar for that amount.

Major Gardner, 1787.[6]

There were several methods of financing a foreign trip. An
uncommon method was to take British money. This was current in
some towns in north-west Europe such as Rotterdam. In 1786 when
Gardenstone changed his money at the leading Calais hotel,
Dessein's, he was advised to keep his crowns and half crowns 'as
they have a profitable currency in all parts of France'.[7] Thicknesse
was ready to advise tourists to bring British cash with them: 'as
travelling in France is quite safe, . . . let your Agent get you good
bills at the Royal Exchange, or bring your cash with you. If a man
proposes to spend a thousand pound at Paris, he might get it

insured to Paris at one per cent; and if he draws for it upon his London banker, it will cost him five; nay more.'[8]

Carrying amounts of British money any further than Calais was unusual, however. Furthermore most tourists, probably unwilling to risk robbery, did not travel with large quantities of any currency. Insurance for Paris might be simple, but few seem to have considered it for further afield. Most tourists relied on paper instruments of credit. The most common arrangement was for a tourist to have an agreement by which he could draw on the foreign correspondents of his London banker for a certain sum. These correspondents were usually bankers themselves, though some were merchants. The tourist could also arrange to extend the geographical range of his borrowing beyond that of the correspondents of his London banker, by seeking credit from the correspondents of these correspondents. This system worked fairly well. It reflected the fact that most tourists spent much of their time in a small number of major towns.

James Compton drew on a Mr Knight in Venice in 1708. Ten years later the Northumberland tourist, Sir Carnaby Haggerston, profited from the connections of his Newcastle banker, Nicholas Fenwick. He drew £50 on him at Marseilles, £100 on his Leghorn correspondent, Mr Jackson, and had a £200 credit at Rome arranged for him by Fenwick's Italian correspondents. The same summer Perceval took up money at Calais and Bruges on the credit of the banker, Sir Alexander Cairns. Eight years later Perceval, planning a trip of the Low Countries, wrote from Paris to ask a London merchant to arrange credit at Antwerp and either The Hague or Delft. In 1728 Edward Carteret sent advice to J.C. Wetstein, Lord Dysart's Bearleader: 'Mr. Boeheme tells me that the Freres Aubert will give you credit anywhere in Italy, and when you leave Italy he will give you fresh credit in Germany.' Two years later Edward Mellish received money at Blois through the banker Alexander at Paris, paying £5 commission for drawing upon his, Mellish's, uncle, the London merchant John Gore, for £200. When Mellish planned to go on a tour of provincial France he received a letter of credit on a Lyons banker from Alexander, and a connection of his uncle's, the leading Paris financier Samuel Bernard, provided him with letters of credit for Lille and Antwerp. Pococke relied on the London banker Hoare, 'I desire the favour of you to order Mr. Hoare to send me a bill of £15 on Langres and a bill of £15 on Cambray, if he thinks it more proper he may only let me know where I may receive the money in these two cities'. The second Earl of Fife relied on another important London banking house, Drummonds. During the century the techniques and connections of these houses improved and they were able to offer a more comprehensive service to tourists. Alexander was instructed in 1736: 'This will be delivered you by the Right Honble. Earl of Salisbury who I desire you will furnish with what sums of money he shall require of you during his stay in your kingdom, taking his bills upon Matthew Lamb Esq., which shall be allowed you in account.' Hoares acted as bankers for William Drake, Thomas Pelham and Robert Wharton. Wharton's uncle, Thomas Lloyd, like John Gore and Perceval's cousin, Daniel Dering, had financial connections and arranged matters with the banker. In 1775 Wharton sought approval for an Italian trip and asked, if it was granted, for £100 more 'which you will desire Mr. Hoare to send me a letter of credit for on some banker at Lyons or Marseilles where I shall change my letters for others on the Italian banks'. At Livorno he exchanged his French money for Italian zecchines with Monsr. Berte and obtained bills on the latter's correspondents. Hoare's network served Pelham well on his Spanish trip: he was able to draw money at Madrid, Malaga, Lisbon and Cadiz. Planning his visit to Italy Pelham asked his father for letters of credit from Hoare to his correspondents at Turin, Rome and Naples, 'in case of accidents, a letter to a banker at any great town would gain me credit at smaller ones, where I might have no letter'. Hoare instructed his correspondents at Lyons, Turin, Milan, Rome and Naples to supply him with up to £200 each and Pelham took advantage of the facility. Drake was less satisfied with Hoare's correspondents. In November 1768 he wrote to his father: 'My letter of credit from Mr. Hoare is upon the Tassins at Paris, who could give no other than on their correspondent at Lyons, Mr. Auriol; from whom I received one upon Mr. Debernardy at Turin, and from him another upon ye Marquis Belloni at Rome, if these several bankers are to have each their profit upon the money I take up at Rome, as may possibly be the case, will it not be better to have a letter from Mr. Hoare immediately on his correspondent there?' Two months later Drake's Bearleader, Dr Townson, noted that the intermediary bankers were each charging 1 per cent commission. He complained bitterly of the Tassins' conduct,

We never took up more money at a time or oftener than was

necessary; and I was amazed to find the Tassins had drawn the whole sum, for which Mr. Hoare gave credit, out of your hands at one stroke: I believe no other bankers with whom English Gentlemen are concerned abroad, treat them in this manner; and in particular I believe you will find that the Panchauds, who are Mr. Maxwells bankers, have not used him thus. At Paris they gave him more livres than Mr. Drake received, for 100 £ sterling; and furnished him with letters of credit separately upon the bankers in the several towns thro' which we were to pass, so that he cou'd draw upon the Paris banker in any of them without reference to a middle man'.[9]

The principal alternative to an arrangement with the correspondents of a particular banker was to take bills of exchange that could be exchanged by any banker. A major problem with this method was that many European merchants and bankers were hesitant about paying money to someone they knew nothing about whose bill might subsequently prove to be worthless. This problem affected some British tourists in 1721. Running short of money at Bruges they 'apply'd to some Irish merchants to change our Bill but they were so little acquainted with things of that nature that they told us they should not know one if they saw it'. At Ghent they found they did not have enough money to take them to Brussels but they were fortunate in meeting 'an English Gentleman Captain of an Ostend East India man who with the loss of 25s gave us money for the 30 £ bill and which was yet more strange without anybody to vouch for us that the bill was good a circumstance severall before us have been at a loss in and for that reason wanted the money'.

To wait until confirmation could be received that a bill had been honoured was a time-consuming affair.[10] In the second half of the century several London bankers, such as Sir Robert Harris, offered bills accepted by a large number of foreign bankers. These were a very attractive proposition financially. William Blackett wrote to his father from Naples in 1785: 'with a letter of credit the bankers all over Italy and Germany take two per cent commission. If you have Morlands or Harris's bills you pay no commission at all . . .'[11]

In difficult circumstances tourists could usually obtain money. It was possible to borrow from British envoys. Francis Hale borrowed £590 from Keith in 1778; Sidney Clive borrowed money several years later. Large or small sums could be borrowed from other tourists or from fellow-countrymen resident abroad. This was also a useful method for obtaining and disposing of small change. Thomas Pelham took all Lord Dalrymple's Neapolitan money from him in Rome. Wharton drew on the guide James Byres in Rome. It was also possible to obtain money from well-intentioned local people. Francis's companion, Godfrey, did so in Lyons, 'having no letters of credit, borrows a hundred Louis dors of a good natured man'.[12]

Whatever the method used tourists usually complained about the commissions charged by bankers. Bankers were largely unregulated and free to charge what they chose. Many were British, such as Sir Thomas Foley in Paris and Mr Jenkins in Rome. They could be of considerable use to tourists, in particular in arranging accommodation and introductions. Jenkins's windows were used by tourists keen to get a good view of Roman processions. Peter Beckford recommended prospective tourists to Sicily to ask their banker to arrange accommodation. In many eyes these possibilities scarcely compensated for the commission that they charged. Henry Nassau, Viscount Boston, who visited Paris in 1716, forgot to allow for the cost of changing money and ended up with less money than he had anticipated. Francis complained of the exchange rate offered by the mint at Nancy: 'Mr. G. changed 20 guineas for Louis d'ors at the mint, with a loss of 15 sous upon each. In other places a guinea is worth more than a Louis d'or and confessedly weighs more.' Wharton complained about the rates offered by the bankers Sir John Lambert and Messrs Minet and Fectors. Thicknesse condemned the rate offered by Paris bankers, Dessein, and the bankers of Perpignan.[13]

Aside from the rate offered by bankers, another problem was to ensure that it was possible to obtain their services. If a tourist relied upon particular letters of credit from a London banker then a change of route or the non-arrival of these letters could create difficulties. Daniel Dering faced problems in Hanover in 1723, 'Mr. Schrader has not had any letter of credit which I assure you is a great disagreableness, for what we brought with us is much the greatest part spent'. John Clavering was worried in The Hague in 1717, 'I have no credit here upon any creature, and don't know who I shall draw upon in case of necessity'. Henry of Nassau's London banker could not give him letters of credit on Dresden or Vienna in 1732 as he had no correspondents there. Henry obtained a credit on Vienna from his Rome banker, but at Munich he found it difficult to obtain money without a letter from a banker at

Berlin. Bankers could also go bankrupt.[14]

Bankers apart, difficulties could be encountered from variable exchange rates, a shortage of coins and the wide variety of currencies. James Hay complained in 1708 that the wide variety of Italian currencies made it difficult to do his accounts. Sacheverell Stevens wrote of his journey from Donauwörth to Nürnberg, 'we passed this day thro' four different Princes dominions, which made it very troublesome, on account of the exchange of money, the coin of each state being likewise different'. John Richard noted at Hanover: 'Nothing is more troublesome to a traveller than the passing through different principalities in Germany, as there is continual objections to the money you have, nothing is generally current but ducats, but as they are weighed at every post you are continually losing. The Jews intermeddle in this business, and, as usual, are great usurers.' Walker's experience in Italy was similar: 'We find the exchange of money a troublesome business amongst these little states, they succeed one another so fast; for we have travelled the length of the Dukedom of Parma this day; and we came through part of the Pope's dominions, and the whole Dukedom of Modena yesterday . . . I can reckon ten potentates to whom we have been subjects in the course of two months.'[15]

The financial problems of France in the 1710s and 1720s, particularly during the Regency, were linked closely to problems with the currency that only ceased with the reforms of 1726. These difficulties affected tourists. In 1720 Joseph Burnet, finding Paris too crowded and expensive, resolved to tour southern France. However, he could get no further than Orléans, 'for want of currant spetie [sic] in the country and the country people would not take Bank-bills . . . obliged me to return to Paris'. The same year another tourist found an unwillingness 'to receive strangers for fear of Billets de Bancq which officers force upon 'em'. Perceval complained of the effects of attempts to reform the currency and claimed that they had led several tourists to abandon plans for visiting Paris'.[16] Poor coinages caused difficulties. Joseph Cradock was told in 1786 that it was best not to take 'the depreciated gold coin of France' into the United Provinces. Martyn noted that Genoese money would not be taken in any other state and advised tourists to Italy 'not to have more of the current coin of any state, than you are likely to dispose of before you quit it', with the exception of the sequins of Rome, Florence and Venice, on which there was the least loss elsewhere. Sir Richard Hoare 'found great difficulty in getting sequins at Turin, and Milan' and thought it best to take sufficient French Louis d'or to reach Florence, where sequins were not scarce. Bennett complained of heavy silver coins wearing out his pockets.[17]

How far financial problems affected the plans of tourists is unclear. In 1785 it definitely affected the plans of Mr and Mrs Rolle and William Bennett for their trip through southern France. They had failed to provide themselves with letters of credit, and were forced to cut short their journey and not to visit Bordeaux.[18] Probably potential problems with finance were but one of the factors dissuading tourists from travelling outside the usual range of tourist activity. Within this range, particularly in France, Italy and the Low Countries, financial facilities were well-developed and tourists could rely on a well-developed network of bankers. Horace Walpole visiting Paris in 1765 found that even small British bank-bills were accepted.[19] Further afield the situation was not so good, but it steadily improved during the century, and throughout most of Europe the far-flung nature of British commerce ensured that the connections of British banking were never too distant. In the last resort, well-connected tourists, who constituted the majority of those who went far afield, particularly to Vienna, could rely on the same sort of assistance that ensured them introductions at court, invitations to attend military manoeuvres and assistance in the event of legal difficulties. In 1778 Keith's bankers, Drummonds, wrote to inform him that the Earl of Bessborough wished him to procure credits for his son, Lord Duncannon, to the amount of £1,000 for his bills upon Drummonds. A man like Duncannon was rarely forced to rely on his own devices.[20]

Cost

. . . when our bill was produced were struck dumb with the impudent charge of £7 9s for a day and two nights. It is the misfortune indeed of all who travel in Switzerland to experience these impositions, which are made every day without a blush. The only way to prevent it is to make a bargain beforehand what to pay for beds, what for eating etc. This we have done in every place but the present, and we have sadly experienced the neglect of it. As a proof of the difference it makes I who arrived first, and made a bargain paid only 2s 6d for my room. Mr. R: whose apartment was hardly better, was charged 10s 6d for his. There is no redress, and we were forced to submit to the injury, which was attended indeed with no small degree of insult. R: could only revenge himself by swearing heartily at the man in English, who did not understand a word he said.

Bennett, Lucerne, 1785.[21]

The cost structure of an eighteenth-century tour was very different to that of a modern one, if only because it generally lasted for much longer. Allowances were often expressed in terms of so much per month or even year, and tourists, when they arrived at major towns, where they intended to stay for a while, such as Paris, Rome and Naples, tended to strike a bargain for a period of weeks or months for their accommodation and often for their food. There was therefore a clear difference in price often between, on the one hand, accommodation and food over a long period and, on the other, for only a night or for a short period. This was related to another clear difference, namely between prices agreed in advance, often by bargaining, and those which had not been. The latter were often substantially higher. Tourists who were travelling had less opportunity to strike bargains for a number of nights. Arriving late in small settlements they were often obliged to pay whatever was demanded. At times outrage led tourists to push on and travel by night, as William Drake did at Gaeta in 1769, but this was rarely comfortable or possible outside Italy in the summer, where it was common for those who wished to speed through the malaria-infested Roman Campagna. Guidebooks advised tourists on the need to bargain on arrival at inns and those who tried generally found bargaining effective. An anonymous tourist, probably Colonel James Riddell, noted in his journal at Novalese, near the Mt Cenis pass: 'We have agreed with our Landlady at this place for $3\frac{1}{2}$ livres a head for our dinner, wood or firing and wine, one livre a head for our coffee night and morning. The beds to be included. For the same fare yesterday we paid 23 livres owing to not having agreed.'[22] Charging bills in French livres was not uncommon in areas near France.

Travelling at speed, or in areas where there was little choice of accommodation, meant that tourists' costs rose. Areas that were popular and where demand exceeded supply by a large amount, became more expensive. This was true of the approaches to Mt Blanc in the 1780s and of Naples in the winters of the early 1790s.[23]

It was reckoned generally that tourists who spent most of their time in one or two large towns, even expensive towns such as Paris, would spend less than those who were constantly travelling. Edward Carteret suggested that this was a factor in Lord Dysart's expenses in 1728, 'frequent journeys from place to place, which I believe must be more expensive than to reside sometime in a place'. Thomas Pelham and James Hay complained of the same effect.[24] The distribution of costs varied by tourist. However much many tourists might follow the same route, see the same sights, and often stay in the same hotels, eighteenth-century tourists were not on a package holiday. No two tourists did exactly the same thing. In particular they stayed for differing lengths of time in the same places. They had to make their own arrangements and in both accommodation and food provision was very varied. There was no standardised hotel accommodation. The only sphere in which governmental regulation brought some degree of uniformity in pricing was transport. Most posting systems were governmental, essentially provided for couriers and others on government business, and the price of posting was fixed. However, as many tourists discovered, these prices bore little relation to what they were expected to pay, and disputes arose often over the cost of posting. Francis had a very bad dispute in the Papal States in 1772.[25] In so far as comparisons can be made, it could be suggested that as a proportion of their total expenditure eighteenth-century tourists probably spent less on food and accommodation and more on transport than their modern counterparts. Many purchased carriages, and though carriages were bought usually at the Channel ports on the understanding that they could be resold on return, the arrangement usually proved to be less attractive in practice than in theory. There were complaints about costs in every area. They were particularly marked in the case of Paris[26] and the United Provinces,[27] whilst there were comparatively few complaints about provincial France (particularly southern parts) and Germany.[28] In Italy there were many complaints about the cost of posting. In 1787 Walker claimed: 'Travelling in Italy is full dearer than in England, without a quarter the comfort, dispatch, or attendance. Our beds are, on an average, 2s 6d or 3s English, each per night; and nothing but a mattrass laid on a full bag of straw, coarse sheets, and no posts or curtains, dinners 5s and 6s a head, and travelling full 1s per mile. At Milan our charge was so extravagant, we resolved to leave the place as soon as possible . . .'[29]

Walker's comparison with British costs is interesting, because it is so unusual. Most British tourists had never toured for pleasure for any length of time within the British Isles. Aside from the Irish, Welsh and Scots, comparatively few had visited any part of the British Isles other than that portion of England that divided their county town or set from the 'great wen' London. These British trips were comparatively short, and consequently difficult to compare with travel in Europe. Comparisons between Britain and the continent were a common feature of tourist journals and correspondence, particularly comparisons between London and Paris, but also comparisons between most other facets of life, ranging from streetlighting and the length of women's petticoats to window casements, respect for old age, gardens, orphanages, churches and the width of the streets.[30] However, comparatively few comparisons were made between travelling in Britain and Europe. After exactions of the inns on the Dover road few tourists could have stated honestly that high charges and overcharging were a foreign monopoly. Gardenstone compared French and British travelling costs to the benefit of the former.

There is no shortage of information about the cost of food and meals in Europe. Prices could be cut either by purchasing food in the markets, or by making an agreement with a restaurant to supply meals on a daily basis at a set price. A tourist who paid four Louis d'or per week for a suite in the Hôtel de Moscovie in Paris 'settled with a traiteur for our dinner at 5 livres each and our supper, when we have any, 5 livres'. The Dowager Countess of Salisbury, widow of the fourth Earl, stayed in Paris in 1699 and 1702 during a lengthy continental tour. She had quite a large establishment and many of her bills have been preserved in the Cecil Papers at Hatfield. A sample bill, in livres and sols, from an undated bundle, 'Weekly expenses at Paris', includes the following items:

butcher	23	—	herbs and onions	1	12
fowls	18	6	10½ lb. sugar	7	8
bread and flour	11	17	fruit	9	11
2 tongues	1	4	vinegar	1	4
2 lb. bacon	1	4	oil	1	12
milk and cream	7	19	salads	3	4
11 lb. butter	5	10	beans	—	6
fish	1	1	peas	2	5
artichokes	—	16	eggs	2	12
melons	6	—	oranges		6

Perceval noted Paris market prices in British currency in 1725,

Hare	7 sh	Beef	8d a pound
Partridge	2 sh	Mutton	$5\frac{1}{2}$d a pound
Pigeon	1 sh	a sole 8 inches long	2 sh 9d
		egg	1d

The accounts of the sixth Earl of Salisbury only noted individual items of food when they were luxuries, three ortolans for 6 livres in June 1730, coffee and tea for 2 livres 18 at Blois in September 1730 and oysters for 7 livres in March 1730. 'Diet for a month' at Angers in 1731 came to 190 livres though it is not clear whether servants, and, if so, how many, were included. A tourist stayed a fortnight at Aachen in June 1720: 'at Florintin the Dragon D'Or a good house but at some distance from the fountain. Things are there tolerably cheap. Dinner 3 shillings and 2 at supper. Burgundy and Champagne 2 shillings a bottle. Moselle 3 shillings.'

Richard Pococke did not leave accounts but he included details of particular meals in his letters to his mother. At San Marino he 'demanded what I was to pay over night before I eat — they told me a penny my bed, I might have a pennyworth of soup, 1d meat and salad, to which at supper they added a 1d fricassee, and 1d cheese, and a large quart of wine 1d more; I had the best vermicelli soup I ever eat, all served very well, I paid 4d in the morning, 2d more than my reckoning came to'. At Bologna he noted: 'the common price of wine on the road was 1d a quart and once I had it for $\frac{1}{2}$ and good enough some of it; at Tolentino 4 pd. of cherries for $\frac{1}{2}$, and the common price everywhere is a half penny a pd the best sorts; we pay here 1s 6d for dinner each, eat very well, five dishes and a dessert by ourselves, 6d each for beds.'

At Venice and Milan however dinner cost three shillings each. A good dinner at Gravelines early the following decade cost 17d a head, whilst Martyn claimed that for four Venetian livres (about 20d) a good dinner could be had in Venice. When eating in their lodgings in Naples, Francis and his friend Godfrey paid three carlins each for breakfast, and, including wine, ten each for dinner and five for supper ($57\frac{1}{2}$ carlins then being worth a guinea). A guinea was considered too much to pay for 'some boiled perch and three bottles of Rhenish' in the Dutch village of Broek.

In Paris, in 1775, Robert Wharton regularly took a set-price dinner, generally agreed to be the best value. He had a good dinner and a pint of burgundy for two livres and left two sols for the waiter. Thicknesse was impressed by the good value of French meals. At Pont St Esprit he had a meal at three livres a head which he said would have cost a guinea each (25 livres) in Britain. He also praised the prices in the carriers' inns he stayed in on the Rheims-Dijon road. William Blackett, visiting Lausanne in 1784, where he found 'quite a little colony of English', complained that 'provisions are exactly doubled within this few years, . . . we cannot dine under six livres French a head, and for that a moderate dinner'. He wrote that if he stayed he proposed to hire a cook in order to save money. The following year Bennett was pleased to strike a bargain of three livres per head for supper at an inn on the Geneva-Lyons road and was scandalised by the minimum cost of five shillings for supper at Altdorf in Switzerland. In 1786 Gardenstone found French charges 'below the common rates in England'. In Boulogne he paid five livres for two bottles of very good burgundy, four livres for dinner for two and three for his lodgings. At Abbeville he dined very well, with a bottle of good burgundy, for six livres, and at Félixcourt he supped and stayed overnight at the post house, 'and fared well for seven livres'. In Paris he 'settled terms with a reputable traiteur, at the rate of five livres, when alone, and six livres a head, when I have company — I am very well served and so plentifully that the fragments are always sufficient for the use of my servants'.

Foreigners could not be sure that they paid the same as the locals. Francis and Walker complained of being charged more in Spa and Rome respectively; and Arthur Young, when he bought three large peaches for a penny in Barcelona, was told that he 'gave too much, and paid like a foreigner'. Young left some detailed accounts of the cost of meals. At an inn near the Pyrenees he noted:

A traiteur serves our table at 4 liv. a head for the two meals, two courses and a good dessert for dinner; for supper one course and a dessert: the whole very well served, with everything in good season: the wine separate, at 6s (3d) a bottle . . . As dearness is, in my opinion, the general feature of all money exchanges in France, it is but candid to note instances to the contrary. At Aire, they gave me, at the Croix d'Or, soup, eels, sweet-bread, and green-peas, a pigeon, a chicken, and veal-cutlets, with a dessert of biscuits, peaches, nectarines, plums, and a glass of *liqueur*, with a bottle of good wine, all for 40s (20d) oats for my mare 20s and hay 10s. At the same price at St. Severe, I had a supper last night not inferior to it . . . The landlord of the inn at Fontainbleau thinks that royal palaces should not be seen for nothing; he made me pay 10 liv. for a dinner, which would have cost me not more than half the money at the Star and Garter at Richmond . . . Dine . . . at the Palais Royal [Paris] at a coffee-house; well dressed people; everything clean, good, and well served: but here, as everywhere else, you pay a good price for good things; we ought never to forget that a low price for bad things is not cheapness . . . Rouen . . . At the table d'hôte, at the hotel *Pomme du Pin* we sat down, sixteen, to the following dinner, a soup, about 3 lb. of bouilli, one fowl, one duck, a small fricassee of chicken, a *roté* of veal, of about 2 lb. and two other small plates with a salad: the price 45s . . . at an ordinary of 20d a head in England there would be a piece of meat which would literally speaking outweigh this whole dinner! . . . Such tables d'hôtes are among the cheap things of France! . . . I find Rennes very cheap; and it appears the more so to me just come from Normandy, where everything is extravagantly dear. The table d'hôte, at the *grand maison*, is well served; they give two courses, containing plenty of good things, and a very ample regular dessert: the supper one good course with a large joint of mutton, and another good dessert; each meal, with the common wine, 40s . . . Musiliac [Brittany], if it can boast of nothing else may at least vaunt its cheapness. I had for dinner two good flat fish, a dish of oysters, soup, a fine duck roasted; with an ample dessert of grapes, pears, walnuts, biscuits, liqueur, and a pint of good Bordeaux wine: my mare besides hay, had three-fourths of a peck of corn, and the whole 56s. 2s to the fille and two to the garcon, in all 2s. 6d . . . Metz is, without exception, the cheapest town I have been in. The table d'hôte is 36s a head, plenty of good wine included. We were ten, and had two courses and a dessert of ten dishes each, and those courses plentiful. The supper is the same; I had mine, of a pint of wine and a large plate of chaudiés, in my chamber, for 10s. a horse, hay, and corn 25s. and nothing for the apartment; my expence was therefore 71s. a day, or 2s 11½d . . . In addition, much civility and good attendance. It is at the *Faisan*. Why are the cheapest inns in France the best? . . . [Nancy:] let me caution the unwary traveller, if he is not a great lord, with plenty of money that he does not know what to do with, against the *hotel d'Angleterre*;

a bad dinner 3 liv. and for the room as much more. A pint of wine, and a plate of chaudié 20s . . . I liked so little my treatment, that I changed my quarters to the *hotel de Halle*, where, at the table d'hôte, I had the company of some agreeable officers, two good courses, and a dessert for 36s with a bottle of wine. The chamber 20s; for building, however the hotel d'Angleterre is much superior, and is the first inn.[31]

Young's comments reveal what was only to be expected, namely that prices varied greatly, and that whereas some establishments aroused a sense of outrage, others were seen as being good value. There is no guide to the size of the portions: how ample was a good dessert, how much did a large eighteenth-century roast fowl weigh? Similar problems affect any discussion of the costs of accommodation. A 'large' or 'comfortable' room is difficult to compare with other such rooms. Furthermore there is very little information available about accommodation for other members of a party: the Bearleader and the servants. Best value was given usually if a guest ate where he stayed and many tourist costs are therefore expressed as board and lodging.

Perceval visited Paris in 1725 with his wife and two children. He paid 400 livres a month rent 'and a 100 more for the use of the kitchen, table linen and stables for 9 horses'. He subsequently moved to new lodgings — three apartments, two coach houses and stables for nine horses for 450 livres a month. Five years later the sixth Earl of Salisbury paid six livres for supper and lodging at the *Tapis Vert* in Montauban, though it is not clear how many servants were accommodated. Martyn claimed that in Venice, 'which however is not the cheapest place in Italy to live in', a stranger might rent a good room for 5–10d a day 'or he may provide himself with a genteel apartment and dinner for 4–4 sh 7d a day'. In 1734, Pococke stayed at 'Kennets a very good English publick house, but more like a lodging', in Venice for 1sh 6d a night, half the price of his dinner. At Milan he stayed in 'an excellent Inn' for 2sh. Samuel Smith stayed at the Hotel des Trois Villes in Paris in 1752 and 'agreed for 2 chambers one within another at a Louis per week'. The second Earl of Fife found accommodation very expensive in Spa in 1765, 'no less than 16 shillings a day'. Francis and Godfrey together paid 15 carlins (about 3s) a day for lodgings in Naples in 1772, less than the daily hire of their carriage (16 carlins) and less than they each paid for dinner (20 carlins). At the Hôtel de l'Impératrice in Paris three guineas a week were charged for 'an elegant dining-room, with two bed chambers on the first floor, and a bed chamber in the entresol, with an apartment for the servant'. This was considered expensive but there were compensations: magnificent furniture, a good situation, the ready availability of carriages for hire and the charms of 'Mademoiselle Brunett'. Lord Balgonie's lodgings in Orleans in 1772 were considered 'rather dear, but the object here is to have a house near to where you dine and sup, and mine is only across a square. I give a guinea a week, and for this I have a very good room without a bed, a nice little room to sleep in, Mr. Marshal [companion] has above an excellent bedchamber where he will sit often, and a clever place for Edward [servant].'

At first in Paris Robert Wharton lodged at the Hôtel de Luxembourg for half a guinea per week. He moved to lodgings costing '9 Louis a month, but then they were in the dearest place in Paris. I could have lodged well in several other places further from the spectacles and walks for 2 Louis'. William Blackett was very impressed by the low cost of accommodation in Lausanne in 1784. He looked round a house which was 'well furnished, four or five very good rooms which look to the lake, a pretty garden and terrace covered with vines from whence is a fine view of the lake and the mountains in Savoy, all for five Louis a month'. In 1785, Bennett and the Rolles paid 7s 6d per day for their small but convenient lodgings at Spa. They thought this reasonable for a dining room and four bedrooms on the second floor. In 1766, a very good double-bedded room in Lyons cost 2s 6d a day. Gardenstone stayed at the Hôtel de York in Paris in 1786 and had 'two handsome apartments for myself, and sufficient accommodation adjoining for my two servants at one Louis d'or and a half per week'. The following year Walker's party visited Venice: 'Our lodgings are elegant, and in the middle of the city, we pay about half-a-guinea per day for three bed chambers and a dining-room; . . .' Young was unimpressed by the charges at Cherbourg, but pleased at Nantes,

Cherbourg is not a place for a residence longer than necessary; I was here fleeced more infamously than at any other town in France; the two best inns were full; I was obliged to go to the *barque*, a vile hole, little better than a hog-sty; where, for a miserable dirty wretched chamber, two suppers composed chiefly of a plate of apples and some butter and cheese, with some trifle besides too bad to eat, and one miserable dinner, they brought us a bill of 31 liv. (£1 7s 1d) they not only charged the room 3 liv. a night, but even the very stable for my horse, after enormous items for oats, hay, and straw. This is a species of profligacy which debases the national character . . . Let no one go to Cherbourg without making a bargain for everything he has, even to the straw and stable; pepper, salt, and table-cloth'.[32]

There is plenty of information available concerning transport costs. They were a well-covered item, in both journals and guidebooks. In 1720, a tourist crossed in a yacht to Calais for three guineas. In 1722, Colin MacLaurain missed the packet at Dover and some seamen offered to carry him to Calais 'in an open boat of six oars for thirty shillings'. He noted that a sloop could be hired for the passage for 3½ guineas. Figures printed in 1772 suggested that it cost three gentlemen and one servant £8 on the Harwich-Helvoetsluys packet and £4 9s on the Calais-Dover packet. However for the actual trip discussed in the book the expenses proved greater: 'This expence was occasioned by the time of the tide and roughness of the weather, which prevented the vessel coming into the harbour: Boats therefore came off to us, and took advantage of our sickness and impatience, by extorting two guineas for putting eight of us on shore at the distance of half a mile.'

Regulated public transport was available on the rivers and canals of the United Provinces and on the Saône, Rhône and Canal du Midi in France. Tourists travelled in a boat on the Meuse from Liège to Huy in 1720 and 1721. The boats were towed and the charge was a shilling per person. Tourists who wanted to travel independently had to strike their own bargains. In 1776 a tourist 'embarked myself, servant, and cabriolet in a *bateau de poste* navigated by two men. I agreed to pay four Louis and six francs, for the voyage down the Rhône to Avignon stopping when and where I pleased, or proceeding all night if I chose it'. Tourists on the Rhine and Danube and in the Baltic and Mediterranean made their own bargains. Transport was cheaper by sea than land, but not if a boat had to be hired. Bennett paid a shilling to be carried from Altdorf to Lucerne in a merchantman. The best service was available in the United Provinces, where Ann Radcliffe noted that the price in 1794, including tax, was 1d per mile and a trifle more to hire the roof.[33]

Land travel was very expensive. A major cause of expense was accidents, which were very frequent.[34] Even if none occurred it was still necessary to bear the costs either of bringing a carriage from Britain or of hiring or purchasing one on the continent, which meant, in most cases, Calais. The Dowager Countess of Salisbury paid 260 livres for a month's hire of a coach and two horses in Lyons in 1699. In 1721, a postchaise and five horses cost 200 livres at Nancy; in 1777, a cabriolet and an English coach horse 17 guineas at Calais. MacLaurin noted that it cost two guineas to hire a coach with four horses and two postillions from Calais to St Omer. Drake hired a coach for the Calais-Paris trip in 1768 and paid six Louis d'or. The cost was similar in the opposite direction. Lord Leven paid three guineas at Lille in 1749 for the use of a chaise to Paris. Leven was delighted by the absence of turnpike charges in France, but appalled by the cost of transport,

The multitudes of English in this country has made travailing as dear as in England, the expence of horses for one chaise by the king's ordonnance comes to four shillings English every six miles, which is as much as we pay in England for both chaise and horses, except where they have close postchaises; for these we pay one shilling per mile . . . The guides [postillions], for I cannot call them boys, as they are generally old fellows, I have met with are allowed only threepence English per post, yet our countrymen have debauched them to such a degree that they grumble if they don't get double, and their post is generally but six miles.[35]

Posting charges varied by the number of people in, wheels on and horses before a carriage. It was less expensive to use public transport though this was not available over much of Europe. In the 1770s it cost 55 livres (£2 10s) for a place on the Lille-Paris diligence. The price included provisions and lodging on the way. On the Paris-Lyons diligence in 1739 'the fare for each passenger is 100 livres, and everything found you upon the road, or 70 livres without'.[36] The diligence system did not extend into Italy. Tourists seeking to travel between Lyons and Turin agreed often with a voiturier to take them and their carriage between the two cities for a price that included accommodation, food and posting. The Dowager Countess of Salisbury used such a service in 1699 and Walker paid thirteen Louis d'or for travelling in the opposite direction in 1787. Sir Richard Hoare paid more in 1785 as he had a larger party, and he went on to pay for the cambiatura, a payment which ensured free posting in Piedmont,

> We paid the voiturier from Lyons to Turin for taking our two postchaises with four horses to each, a bidet for my servant all our baggage etc. over Mount Cenis, and for *our* eating and lodging, forty six Louis d'ors, and we gave the drivers six Louis. They undertook the job somewhat cheaper, as they belonged to Turin, and had brought some gentlemen from thence to Lyons. From Turin you must procure the Cambiatura, which takes you near to Milan, viz to Buffalora: they made us pay in Octr. 1785 21 livres for 8 chaise and one small saddle horse, besides the postillions.[37]

In areas where there was no posting system it was necessary to make specific arrangements in order to travel. These could be expensive, as Thomas Pelham found with his mule-hire in Iberia, but they could also be reasonable: John Richard went on a 13-day coach journey from St Petersburg to Moscow, 'I engaged with a carrier for twelve roubles, which is about two pounds sterling, to drive me with three horses'.[38] In some areas it was more a problem of availability than money: shortages of horses were by no means unknown.

A separate transport cost was that within cities. It was usual in large cities to hire a carriage and this could be expensive. Perceval hired a carriage and two horses for 13 shillings a day in Paris in 1725. Francis and Godfrey hired a carriage and a coachman for 18 carlins (about 7 sh) a day in Naples in 1772. Half-a-guinea a day, and a shilling for the coachman, was one charge in Paris in the early 1770s.[39]

Food, accommodation and transport were the principal costs met by tourists. In addition there was a rich miscellany of expense. A major one was clothes, on which tourists tended to spend a lot of money. One reason for this was that, as they were abroad for a long time, they needed often to replace items of clothing. Compton had to replace his British shirts in the United Provinces. More significant was the social environment that many tourists spent some of their time in. To move freely in high society a gentleman was expected to dress well, and being a tourist did not alter this situation, although strangers were freed from some of the restrictions of European society: Joshua Pickersgill noted that strangers in the Turin carnival balls in 1761 were allowed to dance with whomsoever they wished, whilst the local citizens were not permitted to dance with noble women.[40] To appear in court society was expensive. Lord Nuneham bought new clothes for the celebrations in Hanover for the anniversary of George II's accession. Tourists in Paris tended to spend a lot on clothes and new tourists were beset often by tailors. Robert Wharton bought new silk stockings and a pair of shoes for himself in Paris in 1775, and was pleased at the low costs charged for washing clothes; Charles Spencer apologised to the Duchess of Marlborough for buying fine clothes in Paris in 1723; Spark Molesworth purchased clothes in Paris in 1739; George Lyttleton complained of the cost of clothes in 1728 and 1729. In Lorraine in 1728 he found that dress was a major item in his expenditure. Attending the court at Lunéville obliged him to wear fine clothes, and he found that all entertainments necessitated gambling. In Paris the following year he complained of the cost of clothes, coach hire, gambling, fencing and dancing lessons, and could only assure his father that improvement abroad was impossible without expenditure. His brother Richard, sent to the Academy at Besançon in 1737, was soon in debt as a result of clothes purchases and gambling. The accounts of Sir John Swinburne on his 1749–51 trip to France give some indication of the cost of clothes: 48 livres for a laced hat and feather bought at Lille, 216 for a waistcoat of rich Lyons stuff, 84 for six pairs of worked ruffles, 1,367 for 'my Taylor's bill', 299 for a lined crimson velvet coat and breeches, 848 for the embroidering of 'a sute of cloaths in Gold' — all paid in Paris between 20 December 1749 and 17 May 1750. At Aix-en-Provence in early 1751 he paid a tailor's bill of 45 livres, and bills for 'cloth, lace etc.' for making into clothes of 591 livres. In Toulouse he spent 135 livres on clothes for his servant John; and 34 on a plain hat and feather; later that year in Paris he paid 210 for embroidering 'a suit of cloaths'; 60 for a laced hat and feather; and 719 for his tailor's bill. The sixth Earl of Salisbury purchased in France in the early 1730s several pairs of shoes and gloves, as well as several hats. Items in his accounts included silk cloth and stockings, gold and silver lace, and tailor's bills.[41]

It was not very expensive to attend the theatre or musical entertainments. In the 1730s a place in the 'Concert spirituel . . . the finest musick at Paris' cost three livres, and in the Opéra the most expensive seats were just over seven livres. In 1775 Wharton paid four livres to go to the Opéra in Paris and six to go to the Comédie.

It helped, as so often with prices, if one paid oneself. William Drake was overcharged at the Siena theatre in 1769 because he entrusted his purchase to his guide.[42] Guides were a source of expense — it was usual to hire them in large cities, just as it was common to hire an extra servant (often the two were the same man). They were notorious for attempting to defraud tourists. As they were paid little, they sought to earn money by taking a commission from hotels, tailors etc. whose services they secured for their temporary master.[43] Hiring teachers could also be an expense. Perceval paid 100 livres a month for a French master in 1725, and 40 livres for 16 lessons from a drawing master.[44] Charles, later second Viscount, Fane paid his Bearleader, Chais, £100 per annum, and gave him his keep and a servant in all large towns, a cost of over £200.[45]

Presents, either for oneself or for others, could of course be a major item of expense. Visiting Rome in 1726, Edward Southwell junior 'spent 150 £ in 5 marble tables, 2 landscapes of ruins, a little suite of brass medals, more for use than show, 50 £ worth of prints of modern and antique Rome and of the chief paintings, 2 or 3 fans, 2 or 3 cameo's etc.'. Lord Nuneham sent melon and broccoli seeds home from Florence in 1756. The Dowager Countess of Salisbury paid 120 livres for a 'silver minute pendulum watch' in 1702. Perceval spent a lot of money in the Low Countries in 1718 buying lace for others. Richard Grenville bought his uncle four Italian paintings, costing £103 19s 2d in the early 1730s.[46] Not all were drawn in 'to make some expences more than I should have done' by women, as Henry Pelham was at Caen in 1775; nor did many spend what was probably over £600 on a sumptuous ball for 250 people, as Lord Duncannon did at Lausanne in 1785; but all had to spend, as Robert Wharton did, money on cosmetics at the barber — shaving soap, lavender water, powders, and tincture for the teeth — and on washing clothes.[47]

Tips were a constant drain. Tipping was widespread, whether to the sailors on the Channel packets or to the servants of houses that were open to visit, such as the Palais Royal in Paris. Thomas Brand complained of the cost at the Saxon fortress of Königstein,

It cost us a great deal of money at the different places we were taken to in making the round of the fortress — for the fat woman who shewed us the great *Tun* . . . for the perpendicular Engineer who shewed us the Arsenal . . . but I was really shocked where the *Parson* made a very servile bow for a florin for looking into his Church.[48]

'. . . certainly neither Mr. Drake nor Mr. Maxwell has shown the least disposition to extravagance, or, as far as I can judge, been guilty of any; but the very expences of travelling have been very great, and not the less so for our following the track of so many English as are now abroad.'

Dr Townson, Florence, 1769.[49]

Conclusions

The total costs of individual tourists were high by the standards of the annual costs of an artisan household, but, given the length of time they stayed abroad, the need to make independent arrangements and the distances many of them covered, they were not as high as might have been imagined, judging simply by press comment. Ashe Windham, who travelled in Europe in the 1690s, received an annual allowance of £600. Viscount Boston spent about £566 over a twelve-month period in 1715–16. Sir Carnaby Haggerston, his expenses increased by gambling losses, signed bills for £400 in a six-month period in Italy in 1718. Eight years later Charles Spencer rebutted complaints about his expenditure, 'it would be impossible for me to travel in any court of Europe with the least honour with £500 sterling a year'. His brother, the Earl of Sunderland, died in Paris in 1729 having drawn for all of the £1,000 credit he had there, and owing £300. From February 1730 to October 1732, the sixth Earl of Salisbury received £3,313 from his bankers. Robert Carteret aroused parental criticism spending over £1,850 in 1740–1. Sir John Swinburne spent £1,271 on his European trip from November 1749 to October 1751. The second Earl Fife spent over £1,700 in a few weeks in Paris in the winter of 1766–7 but he *was* accompanied by his wife, 'liv'd in the first company in Paris', and spent a lot on clothes and on china, furniture, tapestry and damasks for his London house. William Drake received £1,039 from his bankers between October 1768 and August 1769. The future seventh Earl of Salisbury was allowed £130 per month whilst abroad in 1770 and was given an additional sum of £400 because of the cost of staying in Paris. Five years later a tourist with more modest tastes wrote from Paris, 'I think one might live very comfortably from £300 a year or with a little management for £250'. In 1785 William Bennett did the accounts of the Rolles's trip to the Austrian Netherlands, Rhineland, Switzerland and France: 'what is called the little tour . . . He has performed it for about £550, which is less than £150 per month the sum generally allowed by persons who travel with an equipage.' James Burges's total costs for his trip to Paris and the Loire in 1771, in his second long vacation from Oxford, 'from leaving London to my return to it, amounted to no more than £89 1s 7d including every charge'.[50]

It is impossible to state the total cost to the nation of foreign travel. Lord North, later second Earl of Guildford, wrote from Rome in 1753 that in the recent Holy Year British tourists had drawn over £70,000 from one banker alone. Sixteen years later a London newspaper reported: 'A Gentleman who lately came from Calais assures us, that there are near 200 French remises to be sold there belonging to the English nobility and gentry, who leave them there at the end of their travels. This proves the vast sums of money left in France. Whether the English bring home anything deserving this expence, is a question that needs no answer.' In an undated fragment in his correspondence, presumably sent from France, William Blackett wrote, 'some time ago upon some occasion an inquiry was made how much money was spent in this country by strangers and it was computed at a million and a half sterling'. In 1785 William Blackett noted: 'If the calculation of the English who are settled or are travelling abroad as said to be delivered to Mr. Pitt, can be depended upon, they amount to 40,000 and if each man spends only £100 per ann: drain each year £4,000,000 hard money from the nation.'[51]

It was clear that a lot of money was spent abroad, but it is unclear whether the contemporary critics' accusations of extravagance were justified. Several travellers were convinced that their compatriots were extravagant. Bennett blamed the prevalence of beggars in Switzerland on tourism, 'This has arisen from the extravagance of the English, many of whom have thrown their money away in this country without either thought or use'. Captain John Barker complained from Brunswick in 1787: 'By the impositions through this part of Germany one perceives it to be the track of the English . . . I did not take that to be the character of the Germans; but it is our own countrymen have taught them.'[52]

On the other hand a mass of correspondence testifies to the efforts made to limit expenditure by parents, tutors and tourists. Those who were extravagant, such as Lord Dysart in 1728, were reprimanded severely. Others — Compton, Drake and Pelham among them — were constantly aware of parental supervision, and driven to defend their expenditure. Compton's tutor wrote in 1708: 'there's no avoiding spending what honour and necessity will have, and some allowance must be given to conveniency.' Thomas Pelham defended spending more than had been agreed: 'I flatter myself I am free from extravagance and that my expences are either necessary or such as fashion has made indispensable: I consider economy as much as possible and believe that in travelling, the continual change of place renders a fixed income very impolitick.'[53]

Costs were put up by factors largely outside tourists' control. Though by modern standards it was modest, there was a certain amount of inflation in eighteenth-century Europe. Throughout the century there were complaints of increased costs in Paris. 'Everything is very dear to what it has been', complained Edward Southwell in 1723. Forty years later Smollett wrote, 'Living at Paris, to the best of my recollection, is very near twice as dear as it was fifteen years ago'. In 1777 Thicknesse complained that over a decade most Parisian prices had risen by a third and many by 200 per cent. Judging from itemised expenditure figures these claims were overstatements, but no doubt it was difficult for tourists whose fathers had travelled, such as William Drake, to persuade them that the prices they remembered were no longer appropriate.[54] There were other reasons for higher charges. It was claimed in 1786 that anti-British feeling in the United Provinces was leading to 'exorbitant charges'. Increased tourist demand, such as that which crowded Neapolitan hotels in the early 1790s, probably played a greater role than tourist extravagance in pushing prices up. Francis Head reported from Rome in 1725 that the prices of antique coins had risen as a result of foreign demand, and that in Rome, because it was Holy Week, 'everything is excessively dear . . . lodgings, coaches are raised to more than double . . . what vast numbers of all nations are at present here'.[55] It was not only the British who travelled for pleasure. Another reason advanced for high costs was the attempt to impose upon strangers — Lord Carpenter complained of it in the Austrian Netherlands in 1717, and Thomas Pelham in Spain in 1776.[56]

How far costs influenced the decisions of tourists to visit particular areas or only to spend a certain amount of time in them is unclear. Lady Craven found Russia very cheap, but there was no rush of tourists there. Arthur Young pointed out, in 1787, that 'the comparative dearness and cheapness of different countries is a subject of considerable importance, but difficult to analize . . . What we meet with in France, is a cheap *mode of living*'. It was not that living abroad was expensive — one guidebook claimed that the author had only spent £150 in 18 months abroad — but that the 'mode of living' preferred by tourists was expensive. When Boswell planned a European tour in 1764 he wrote 'I would by no means be extravagant; I would only travel genteelly'. This aspiration was shared by most tourists and it inevitably involved expense. This expense invited emulation, aroused criticism and defined for many the nature of tourism: 'it is a general conceived notion in England, that it is necessary to have a considerable fortune to make the tour of France', claimed the guidebook cited above.[57] Tourism was a luxury because most tourists spent in accord with their social status and their lifestyle at home. However, it was possible for men of medium incomes to travel, such as Walker and Wharton, and after the Peace of Paris (1763) such men travelled in increasing numbers. The nature of tourism was altering before the Revolutionary Wars.

Costs clearly led some tourists to change their plans. John Pelham wrote to a relative from Nancy, 'I have heard such an account of Paris that I am quite out of conceat of going there. Everything is insufferable dear . . . I had much rather fall down the Rhine into Holland'. In 1734, George Stanhope turned down the suggestion of a trip from Paris into southern France on the grounds that he 'thought it too expensive'. Gibbon's shortage of money spoiled his Italian tour and led him to abandon a projected trip through southern France.[58] Most tourists did not however alter their plans for financial reasons. Those who travelled were on the whole those who could afford to travel, and their 'mode of living' as tourists matched this situation.

Notes

1. Fish to Sarah Marlborough, 11 Nov. 1726, BL, Add. 61444.
2. Journal of Dr. Grey, BL, Add. 5957, fo. 58; J. E. Smith, *A Sketch of a Tour on the Continent, in the years 1786 and 1787* (3 vols., 1793), I, 44.
3. *Mist's Weekly Journal*, 8 July (os) 1727.
4. *The Gazetteer and New Daily Advertiser*, 20 Aug. 1770; *The Nonsense of Common-Sense*, 3 Jan. (os) 1738.
5. *Daily Universal Register*, 5 Oct. 1786.
6. Gardner to Keith, 14 Sep. 1787, BL, Add. 35539.
7. Gardenstone, I, 11; BL, Stowe 790, fo. 163; *Tour of Holland* (1772), p. 237.

8. Thicknesse, 1768, p. 182.

9. James Hay, Compton's tutor, to George Compton, 5 Feb. 1708, BL, Add. 38507; Fenwick to Lady Haggerston, 8 April (os) 1718; Perceval to Daniel Dering, 17 June (os) 1718, Perceval to Clark, 16 April (os) 1726, Carteret to Wetstein, 27 June (os) 1728, BL, Add. 47028, 47031, 32415; Mellish to father, 7 Dec. 1730, 25 April; 2 May 1731; Pococke to mother, 13 June 1734, BL, Add. 22 798; Hatfield, *Index of Cecil Papers*, XI, 57; Wharton to Lloyd, 20 May, 23 Oct. 1775; Pelham to Lord Pelham, 18 Dec. 1775, 25 July, 24 Aug., 22 Oct., 29 Nov. 1776, 2 Aug. 1777, Lord to Thomas Pelham, 18 Sep. 1776, BL, Add. 33126—7; Drake to father, 25 Nov. 1768, Townson to William Drake senior, 28 Jan. 1769, Aylesbury, D/DR/8/2/4, 3/4.

10. Anon., BL, Stowe 790, fo. 75—6; *The Gentleman's Guide in his Tour through France by an Officer* . . . (7th ed., 1783), p. 8.

11. Blackett to Sir Edward Blackett, 4 Jan. 1785, Northumberland, ZBL 188/289.

12. Drummonds to Keith, 19 May 1778, Sidney Clive senior to Keith, 18 Nov. 1785, BL, Add. Mss. 35514, 35535; Pelham to Lord Pelham, 28 June 1777, Francis, 20 Nov. 1772, BL, Add. 33127, 40759; Wharton to Thomas Lloyd, 18 April 1776.

13. Barbara Countess of Jersey to Countess of Grantham, 5 May 1716, Herts. D/E Na F8; Wharton to Thomas Lloyd, 18 June 1775, Wharton jnl., Feb. 1775, Durham, Wharton; Thicknesse, 1768, pp. 180—3, 1777, I, pp. 10—11, 117, 1786, pp. 8—9.

14. Dering to Perceval, 25 Aug. 1723, BL, Add. 47030; Clavering to Lady Cowper, 13 March 1717, Henry of Nassau to Count William Maurice of Nassau, 17 May; 23 June 1732, Herts. D/EP F196, D/E Na F57.

15. Hay to George Compton, 20 May 1708, BL, Add. 38507; Stevens, p. 373; Richard, p. 184; Walker, p. 371.

16. Burnet to Sir Hans Sloane, 22 March 1720, BL, Sloane 4045; anon., BL, Add. 60522; Perceval to Daniel Dering, 4 Dec. 1725, 12 Feb. 1726, BL, Add. 47031.

17. Cradock, p. 252; Martyn, vii—viii; Hoare, CUL, Add. Mss. 3545, fo. 1; Bennett, 11 July 1785.

18. Bennett, 21 Sep., 29 Oct. 1785.

19. *Walpole-Cole correspondence*, I, 98.

20. Drummonds to Keith, 17 July 1778, Captain Sebright to Keith, 1 June 1787, BL, Add. 35514, 35538.

21. Bennett, 31 Aug. 1785.

22. *The Gentleman's Guide . . . by an Officer* (7th edn., 1783), p. 10; Riddell(?) jnl., 20 Nov. 1770, Northumberland, ZRW 62; Drake to father, 10 April 1769, Aylesbury, D/DR/8/2.

23. Brand to Wharton, 23 Nov. 1793, Durham, Wharton.

24. Carteret to Wetstein, 27 June (os) 1728, Hay to Compton, 1 Sep. 1707, BL, Add. 32415, 38507.

25. Francis, BL, Add. 40759, fo. 18, cf. fo. 2.

26. Spark Molesworth to Hugh Gregor, 24 March 1739, BL, Add. 61830; Fife, 21 Dec. 1765; Sixth Earl of Salisbury to Lady Brown, 27 May 1770, Hatfield, *Index* XI, 80; Edward Finch to Earl of Nottingham, 19 Nov. 1725, Leics. Finch Mss. DG/7/4952.

27. Shaw, 1709, pp. 9, 27; Grey jnl., BL, Add. 5957, fo. 55; Bennett, 7 July 1785.

28. In 1720 Glenorchy complained about the costs of Hanover and Lord Molesworth about those of Augsburg.

29. Walker, p. 381.

30. Shaw, 1709. p. 27; anon., jnl., BL, Add. 12130, fo. 11—12; Crewe jnl., BL, Add. 37926, fo. 25, 54, 60, 81; Leven, p. 329; Mrs Montagu, I, 111; St Vincent, BL, Add. 31192, fo. 11; Wharton to Thomas Lloyd, 4 April 1775; Wharton to Mrs

Wharton, 26 Feb., 19 March, 9 April 1775, Brand to Wharton, 14 Aug. 1792, Durham, Wharton; *Tour of Holland*, p. 137; Andrews, 1784, pp. 11, 338, 393–4, 500; Carpenter, p. 48.

31. Anon., Bodl. Ms. Eng. Misc. e 250, fo. 14; Hatfield, *Index*, X, 180; Perceval to Daniel Dering, 31 Aug. 1725, BL, Add. 47030; Hatfield, Accounts, 132/23; anon., BL, Add. 60522; Pococke, BL, Add. 22978, fo. 77, 78, 82, 87; John Ratcliff, CUL Add. Mss. 4216, fo. 3; Martyn, XX; Francis, BL, Add. 40759, fo. 13; *Tour of Holland*, p. 71; Wharton to mother, 26 Feb. 1775, Wharton jnl., Durham, Wharton; Thicknesse, 1777, I, 58, 35–6; Blackett to father, 2 June 1784, Northumberland, ZBL 188/239; Bennett, 15 Sep., 28 Aug. 1785; Gardenstone, I, 12, 19; Francis, fo. 2; Walker, p. 324; Young, I, 24, 41, 58, 70, 78, 90, 98, 101–2, 150–2.

32. Perceval to Daniel Dering, 26 Aug., 20 Oct. 1725, BL, Add. 47030; Hatfield, Accounts, 89/1; Martyn, xx; Pococke, BL, Add. 22978, fo. 82, 87; Smith jnl., CUL Add. Mss. 7621; Fife, p. 16; Francis, BL, Add. 40759, fo. 13; *Tour of Holland*, pp. 131–2; W. Fraser, *The Melvilles . . .*, I, 354; Wharton to mother, 26 Feb., 21 March; Wharton to W. Baker, 29 April 1775, Durham, Wharton; Blackett to father, 2 June 1784, Northumberland, ZBL 188/239; Bennett, 8 July 1785; Dewes jnl., Bodl. Mss. Eng. Misc. d. 213, p. 150; Gardenstone, I, 18–19; Walker, p. 145; Young, I, 96, 104.

33. Anon., BL, Add. 60522; Aberdeen, MacLaurain, fo. 196–7; *Tour of Holland*, pp. 253, 251; anon., BL, Add. 60522, Stowe 790, fo. 130; Add. 12130, fo. 50; Bennett, 29 Aug. 1785; Radcliffe, p. 17.

34. *Tour of Holland*, p. 248.

35. Hatfield, Accounts, 168/1; anon., BL, Add. 60522; Thicknesse, 1777, I, 17; Aberdeen, MacLaurin, fo. 198; Drake to father, Aylesbury, D/DR/8/2/2; *Tour of Holland*, p. 209; W. Fraser, *The Melvilles . . .*, I, 327; Smollett, p. 41; Accounts of Sir John Swinburne, 4th, Bt., Northumberland, ZSW 456, 13 Nov. 1749, 16 May 1750.

36. *Tour of Holland*, p. 246; Wharton to mother, 12 March 1775, Durham, Wharton; Stevens, p. 67; anon., BL, Add. 60522.

37. Walker, p. 391; Hoare, CUL Add. Mss. 3545, fo. 1.

38. Richard, p. 47.

39. Perceval to Daniel Dering, 31 Aug. 1725, BL, Add. 47030; Francis, BL, Add. 40759, fo. 13; *Tour of Holland*, p. 132; Smollett, p. 43; anon., BL, Add. 60522; Fish to Duchess of Marlborough, 12 Oct. 1727, BL, Add. 61444.

40. Pickersgill to sister, April [1761], Aylesbury, Saunders deposit.

41. Wharton to mother, 5 March 1775, Durham, Wharton; Spencer to Duchess, 27 Oct. (os) 1723, Molesworth bills, BL, Add. 61444, 61830; Swinburne, Northumberland, ZSW 456; Hatfield, Accounts, 89/1, 132/23; Fife, pp. 21, 39; Fish to Duchess of Marlborough, 11 Nov. 1726, BL, Add. 61444.

42. Mitchell, BL, Add. 58314, fo. 24–30; Wharton; Windham, p. 4.

43. Bennett, 30 June 1785.

44. Perceval to Daniel Dering, 20 Oct. 1725, BL, Add. 47031.

45. Fish to Sarah Marlborough, 30 Oct. 1727, BL, Add. 61444.

46. Southwell to Perceval, 9 April 1726, Perceval to Daniel Dering, 1 July (os) 1718, BL, Add. 47031, 47028; L. M. Wiggin, *The Faction of Cousins* (New Haven, 1958), p. 4; Nuneham to Lady Elizabeth Harcourt, undated, Aylesbury, D/LE E2/20.

47. Henry to Thomas Pelham, 21 Feb. 1775, Livingston to Keith, 14 Sep. 1785, BL, Add. 33126, 35535.

48. Brand to Wharton, 10 Sep. 1787.

49. Aylesbury, D/DR/8/3/3.

50. R. W. Ketton-Cremer, *Country Neighbourhood* (1951), p. 24; H. de la Harp,

Boston's tutor, to Earl of Grantham, 24 June 1716, Herts. D/E Na F8; John Thornton, Haggerston's tutor, to Francis Anderton, 18 Sep. 1718, Northumberland, ZH6 VII I: Spencer to Duchess of Marlborough, 29 April 1726, Sunderland to Spencer, 20 Sep. 1729, BL, Add. 61444, 61667; Hatfield, Accounts, 132/33; Lord Carteret to Wetstein, 7 April (os), 16 June (os), 22 Sep. (os) 1741, BL, Add. 32416; Fife, p. 39; Aylesbury, D/DR/8/4/2; Hatfield, *Index*, XI, 82, 88; Wharton to Brand, 17 March 1775; Bennett, 29 Oct. 1785; 'Memoirs of my own Life', Bodl., Bland Burges deposit, vol. 75, fo. 105.

51. North to Hallam, 21 Feb. 1753, BL, Add. 61980; *St. James' Chronicle*, 23 May 1769; Blackett, Northumberland, N BL, 188/239; Bennett, 27 Oct. 1785; M. Postlethwayt, *Great Britain's True System* (1757), p. 290; Stevens, p. 275; Delafaye to Waldegrave, 30 Nov. (os) 1732, Chewton.

52. Bennett, 6 Sep. 1785; Barker to Keith, 9 June 1787, BL, Add. 35538; *Tour of Holland*, p. 248; Andrews, 1784, p. 23; *Gentleman's Guide . . . by an Officer*, p. 3.

53. Hay to George Compton, 28 Nov. 1708, Thomas Pelham to Lord Pelham, 8 Feb., 2 Aug. (quote) 1777, BL, Add. 38507, 33127; William Drake to father, 25 Feb. 1778, Aylesbury, D/DR/8/2/7.

54. J. Gerard to Duke of Kent, 18 Jan. 1715, Lucas 30/8/28/1; Southwell to Perceval, 27 Sept. 1723, BL, Add. 47030; Smollett, p. 44; Thicknesse, 1777, II, 152.

55. *Daily Universal Register*, 22 July 1786; Head, 21 March 1725, Christ Church, Head-Wake correspondence.

56. Carpenter, pp. 32–3; Thomas to Lord Pelham, 16 Nov. 1776, BL, Add. 33127.

57. Young, I, 20; *Gentleman's Guide . . . by an Officer*, p. 2; Pottle (ed.), *Boswell in Holland*, p. 222.

58. Pelham to Thomas Pelham of Stanmer, BL, Add. 33085, fo. 41; Stanhope to Earl Stanhope, KAO Chevening Mss. U1590 C708/2.

8 SOCIAL AND POLITICAL REFLECTIONS

The road from Naples as far as Barletta is very good, for which the public is obliged to the King's liking the chase of Bovino; as it is obliged for the road from Naples to Rome, to His Majesty's being married; — Kings in these regions are not Kings of the people, but the People, People of the Kings.

Sir William Young, 1772.[1]

. . . there is a little policy working at such times at the Carnival, and it is actually a measure of Government, not merely to wink at excesses, but even to furnish the poorer sort with money to produce them; for the more debauched men are, the more abject and the more contented under their slavery they become, and, deluded by the false glare of riot and intemperance, the less likely are they to form reflections which in the end might be dangerous to their Tyrant! I know it is the fashion to say that the lower classes of people in France are happy and contented — I own I have my doubts about it. There is a sort of *rivalship* in gaicty, and probably the effect of habit; but they have many *actual* wants, and though they sing away their cares, it is like the moaning song, perhaps, of a poor weak child who puts himself to sleep that way.

Mrs Crewe, Paris, 1786.[2]

. . . the finest country in the world ruined by the badness of the government and people literally dying of hunger in the granary of Europe.

Sir James Hall, Sicily, 1785.[3]

In an important recent article Professor Müllenbrock has suggested that a shift in the nature of English travel literature took place during the eighteenth century. He claimed that in the opening decades of the century it was characterised by a political fervour directed against arbitrary power, and that in the second half of the century a shift occurred towards a more tolerant stance: 'English writers slowly groped their way towards a more conciliatory treatment of other countries.' Müllenbrock suggested that the 1760s 'saw the beginning of a tentative emancipation from the conventional Whig attitude towards the outside world'. English travel literature became more sympathetic to countries hitherto grossly stereotyped and 'former ideological prejudices were shed'.[4]

Müllenbrock's thesis is an important one, particularly as it draws attention to the need for an analysis of how the ideology of the Grand Tour altered with time. Britain's political situation vis-à-vis the continent changed dramatically in the eighteenth century. In the first years of the century, before Marlborough's victories, France under Louis XIV still represented a major threat to Britain and appeared capable of dominating Europe. However, Marlborough's victories, the peaceful accession of the Hanoverian dynasty (1714), the suppression of the 1715 Jacobite uprising, French weakness in the 1710s and early 1720s and the Anglo-French alliance of 1716–31 produced a period of relative self-confidence that reflected the diminution of the French threat.

In the 1730s and 1740s the situation changed. The collapse of the Anglo-French alliance in 1731, French successes in the war of the Polish Succession (1733–5) and the growth of French naval and colonial power in the 1730s reawakened British fears of France, which had never been entirely forgotten during the years of alliance. There was a marked increase in the expression of xenophobic sentiment in the press in the late 1730s. The War of the Austrian Succession (1740–8) was inconclusive politically, but it damaged British self-confidence. Britain failed to sweep Spain from the West Indies and British armies failed to repeat Marlborough's successes. It was not until the Seven Years War (1756–63) that Britain defeated France in the struggle for colonial hegemony. These victories led to a sense of national self-confidence that was tempered, but not obscured, by fears concerning domestic and European developments. Defeat and national isolation during the American Rebellion led to uncertainty and pessimism that did not lift until 1787, when growing signs of French internal difficulties and British success in the Dutch crisis, led to a revival in optimism.

Britain's international position experienced therefore considerable change and this was related closely to shifts in national self-confidence. The optimism of the early 1760s had been replaced by pessimism twenty years later. Any European commentator asked in 1780 to predict which European country would experience revolution before the end of the decade would have selected Britain, not France.

The degree to which these shifts were reflected in the attitudes of tourists is unclear. With printed works there is the difficulty often of establishing the date of authorship. Did printed journal entries relate to the period of the tour, which is not always easy to determine, or were they altered or written later? In some cases there was a substantial gap of time. Sacheverell Stevens began his tour in September 1738. His *Miscellaneous Remarks made on the Spot* . . . did not have a publication date, but the dedication was dated 3 July 1756. When such comments in the book as these were written is unclear,

> I beg leave to conclude with the following short reflection, which is, that if, from the foregoing faithful account of the wretched and miserable state of slavery and subjection, both ecclesiastical and civil, both in body and soul, other nations are reduced to by their arbitrary tyrannical governors, one single reader should be made sensible of the inestimable blessings he enjoys, be upon his guard against any attempts that may be made to deprive him of them, either by wicked ministers at home, or by enemies from abroad, and become a better subject, or a sincerer Christian and Protestant, it will afford me the highest satisfaction, and I shall flatter myself, that I have not altogether laboured or lived in vain.[5]

Such a statement makes blatant the ideological intentions of the author, as indeed did Stevens's dedication to the Princess Dowager of Wales,

> The following fathful Narrative will plainly shew under what a dreadful yoke the wretched people of other nations groan, their more than Egyptian task-masters having impiously robbed them of the use of that glorious faculty, their reason, deprived them of their properties, and all this under the sacred sanction of religion; . . . they thus miserably lie under the scourge of the tyrant's rod, and the merciless phangs of ecclesiastical power, . . .

However, despite these statements, Stevens's lengthy book is remarkably short of ideological comments and is largely devoted to the mechanics of tourism. It could be suggested that he added the conclusion, as he certainly added the dedication, at a later date, and that to concentrate upon them is to misunderstand the emphasis of the work. In some cases ideological comments could be treated as a convention that reflects what was expected in the genre rather than the opinions of the writers. There is often, with these comments, a sense of artificial interjection and conscious striving after effect. This is similar to some of the paeans to nature that occurred towards the end of the century, such as John Villiers's rhapsody on the sublime vastness of the Channel and the sense of grandeur that this awakened in his soul, when the reader would rather have expected vigorous puking.[6]

A consideration of unprinted tourist accounts reveals that political comment was not at the forefront of the tourists' attention. In so far as tourists made ideological remarks they tended to concentrate upon religious factors. These were both far more overt and more obviously differed from the situation in Britain. It was easier to note the plentiful presence of crucifixes and wayside shrines, the pomp, magnificence and alien quality of Catholic ceremonies and the large number of clerics than it was to perceive the role of the French Parlements, the nature of political power in German principalities or the fiscal system in their Italian counterparts. Furthermore once a tourist had noted the more obvious political differences, such as the greater number of soldiers in Berlin, there was little different about the political systems that he encountered in much of Europe that aroused notice and therefore comment. Prussia was Protestant, Austria and France Catholic. That was noticeable, but to the tourist there was scant difference between their political systems, in so far as he could judge them, and therefore nothing to comment upon. Comment centred upon states that were republics — the United Provinces, Switzerland, Genoa, Venice, Lucca, San Marino and Poland. Even in these cases most comments were brief and impressionistic. This was only to be expected, given the difficulty of assessing a foreign political system when most of the attempt to do so had to be conducted in a foreign language. A further problem was that tourists tended to visit only the major cities of states and so could often only grasp a metropolitan perspective on political developments.[7] The theme that Paris was not France was repeated by several writers because they feared that the attractions of life in Paris would blind susceptible tourists to the realities of life elsewhere in the country. How far tourists who visited Berlin and Vienna and stopped elsewhere in the Prussian and

Austrian dominions only to sleep (apart usually from a day in Prague) could hope to understand the political systems of these countries is unclear. The same was even more true for the small number of tourists who visited Denmark, Portugal, Russia and Sweden. Capitals displayed the power and prestige of monarchy and gave the impression of autocratic, often efficient, states. They were a poor guide to the compromise between monarchial centralisation and aristocratic particularism that underlay so much of the so-called absolutisms of the period. This was even more true of France, where the authority of the monarch was greatly limited. If they realised this, few tourists troubled to record it. They were however correct in stressing the manner in which Catholicism aided state authority. States such as France, Austria and Spain owed their political stability not so much to coercion, as to the ideological consensus of obedience and community that stemmed largely from Catholicism. By drawing attention to the interrelationships of Catholicism and political power, tourists perceived the strength and stability of many states. However, their conclusions concerning the impact of this relationship, particularly its supposed deleterious effects upon economy, society and morality, were often shallow and inaccurate, reflecting prejudice rather than perception.[8]

Tourists often had an opportunity to acquire a certain amount of political information. Well-connected tourists spent much of their time at courts or in court society. This was true of the German, Iberian and Scandinavian states, and of Russia, although it was not true of France, the Low Countries and Italy. The Brussels court of the Austrian Governor and the Hague Court of the Prince of Orange were visited, but were not centres of interest and activity for many tourists. British tourists in Italy were presented often to the Pope, the Kings of Naples and Sardinia, the Grand Duke of Tuscany, the Duke of Parma and Modena and the Governor of Milan, but their courts did not dominate the pastimes of British tourists to the peninsula, with the exception of the King of Sardinia's court at Turin. Versailles was visited by British tourists but few spent much time in court society. In Paris, however, there was no shortage of opportunities for acquiring information and opinion concerning political developments.

In court society aristocratic tourists could expect to be well treated. They would be received by the monarch, would dine often at court, would be permitted to attend court functions, particularly balls and royal hunting parties, would mix in a society of ministers and diplomats and have their activities supervised and entrées arranged by British envoys. These activities were regarded as an essential part of the social education of tourists and they could also be very enjoyable. Lord Pelham wrote to his son, Thomas, in 1777: 'I wish much to have you introduced to all Courts, for though they are not always equally agreeable yet the best company at every place must resort to Court.' The Earl of Essex found his visit to Munich in 1751 boring because of the absence of the court. Edward Southwell the younger encountered the same problem at Turin in 1725.[9]

Court society continued to be reasonably open to tourists even if diplomatic relations with Britain were tense. Despite a press report in 1725 that poor Anglo-Austrian relations had led to a bad reception for British tourists in Vienna, Edward Southwell the younger was well received the following year. The Duke of Richmond was extremely well received at Madrid in 1728, 'as no other stranger can boast of'. He was allowed to hunt with Philip V, a great honour.[10]

Southwell's good reception at Vienna reflected the strength and number of his letters of introduction. '. . . wherever he went, he found extraordinary reception being recommended with a portmantle full of letters to the greatest powers in every Court'. Indeed he took more than ten letters to Vienna. Letters of introduction were essential for a good reception in court society and they ensured the continued dominance by high-ranking tourists (with the addition of military men) of travel in Germany in the latter half of the century, at a time when increasing numbers of the 'middling orders' were visiting France, the Low Countries and Switzerland. A tourist recorded his arrival in Lunéville in August 1720: 'gave our letter to Baron Sauter who received us very civilly carried us to the play and got us presented to both their Royal Highnesses. The Duke spoke to us in German very civilly.' Two years later John Boteler wrote from Rheims that letters of introduction were essential for a traveller. In 1734, Richard Pococke had letters for the great Italian scholar, Muratori; Mitchell for the Sardinian foreign minister, Ormea. Thomas Pelham found his progress eased by numerous letters. He was taken to an assembly by the Governor of Corduba, given dinner by the Captain General of Spain, who arranged transport for him to Cadiz, and was given nine letters alone for Naples by a leading Spanish courtier. In Turin he found that 'Lord Grantham's letter to the Spanish Ambassador and Comte Massin's to a lady here has procured me the acquaintance of the first people in this Court . . .'. In Rome he benefited from a letter to the Spanish nuncio and in Genoa 'in respect to Society my letters from Spain procured me that of the first people here'. Unsurprisingly he stressed the importance of such introductions,

> . . . with regard to Paris . . . I find that it is necessary to be furnished with the most particular recommendations to gain admission into the society of the people of fashion, and that without a residence of some time your acquaintance with people of merit and distinction will be much confined; for the generality, not to say all the English, who have been at Paris lately have conducted themselves in such a manner as to be shunned universally and consequently obliged to live at publick places and in such *company* as may be found more or less in every town.

Despite Anglo-French hostilities, a letter introduced Philip Yorke to the hospitality of the French Cardinal Bernis the following year, whilst Charles Drake Garrard delayed his journey to Montpellier until he could receive the necessary letters. Brand, dissatisfied with the response to his letters in 1780, found them useful in Paris in 1781, Bologna in 1783 and The Hague in 1789–90, and suffered from the lack of them at Dijon in 1786 and Heidelberg in 1791. Aikin and Levett Hanson benefited from letters at Rotterdam and Milan respectively; Thicknesse and Townsend recommended them for Spain; and Andrews for France. Dalrymple sought a letter at Strasbourg in 1789 in order to refute a damaging 'report of my being a person of extreme low birth, who ought not to be taken notice of by anybody of rank and consequence in the town'.[11]

Letters of introduction could therefore serve to introduce tourists to the highest ranks of European society, and, as it was mainly from these ranks that ministers of princes were drawn, they provided ample opportunity to broaden political understanding.

Acquiring social skills, not political information, was the principal purpose of being at court, and the Earl of Huntingdon, who saw the Duchess of Parma perform in a palace production of an opera, or the numerous aristocrats who enjoyed primarily hunting with the court, were 'typical' tourists.[12] However, attendance at court did provide opportunities to meet the powerful. Lord Euston was received by Charles Emmanuel III of Sardinia in 1734 and the King discussed Anglo-Sardinian relations and the

international situation with the young man, leading a British diplomat to send a report on the conversation. Doubtless this reflected
the fact that Euston's father, the Duke of Grafton, George II's
Royal Chamberlain, was a royal favourite. Though in Thomas
Pelham's reception by the Austrian first minister, Count Kaunitz,
'all political questions are carefully avoided', when Pelham went to
see the Portuguese first minister, Pombal, at his country house he
was given an audience of four hours: Pombal 'talked a great deal of
the expulsion of the Jesuits out of Portugal and the attempt against
his own life in the execution of it with the firmness and composure
of an Old Roman'. When Lord Hervey discussed the abilities of
Charles Emmanuel III with George II and Queen Caroline in 1733,
he was able to speak with authority on the basis of 'the short
acquaintance he had with him five years ago at the Court of Turin'.
In a parliamentary debate on Anglo-Prussian relations eight years
later 'Ld. Baltimore said he knew the King of Prussia personally
and he was sure that a precipitate resolution of this House at the
end of the last session lost the King of Prussia to the Emperor'.[13]

Tourists who visited courts were not the only travellers who discussed politics. In 1714, James Hume had a long discussion with an
Irish merchant at St Malo concerning Anglo-French commercial
relations. In 1729 the British envoy in Brussels commented on
awareness of desire for the return of Gibraltar: 'Travellers observe
with amazement the general eagerness of the people, throughout
these countries, for the said restitution, and the invidious eye with
which they see Great Britain possessed of that place, as if their own
welfare was at stake by it.' The following year the Duke of
Norfolk, dining at the British envoy's in Paris remarked 'upon the
French hating of us'. In 1731, Thomas Robinson MP, who had
dined recently with Cardinal Fleury, the leading French minister,
commented on French hostility to Britain.

Swinton's journal contained many remarks on the political situation in Italy. In June 1731, travelling to Pisa, he was accompanied
by a Castilian aristocrat, who discussed recent Italian history with
him, and added: 'The English must never think of being friends
with the Spaniards till Gibraltar and Minorca were restored, but
withall added that the Spaniards could never take those places by
force of arms as long as the English continued masters of the sea.'
In 1740, Chesterfield referred in Parliament to the knowledge
acquired by travellers: 'Do not our common news-papers, does not
every traveller that comes from abroad, inform us, that our

conduct in the war is ridiculed and hooted at in every court, and in every city in Europe?' In Italy in 1769 William Drake was often asked why the British ministry was not supporting the Corsicans against France. In 1785 a newspaper cited as its source for a report that France was likely to support the Dutch against Austria, a letter that a London politician (possibly Shelburne) had received from his travelling son. The same year William Bennett dined at a table d'hôte in Lucerne and commented: 'there was a very large company, and a dispute about liberty begun by the French Marquiss who did not know what liberty was, and asserted his own nation was freer than ours. I was glad to see all the Swiss present inclined to the English side: . . .'[14]

As some tourists clearly *did* discuss politics, it is not surprising that criticism of travel was expressed on this account. On the grounds of politics, tourism could be attacked either because of specific views that a tourist might adopt, particularly Jacobite views, or because of the danger that he might sympathise with European political practices, particularly absolutism. One of the leading opposition London newspapers, the *Craftsman*, noted in 1728 of a tourist recently returned from Italy: 'I was extremely pleased to find, that notwithstanding his travels into countries of slavery and arbitrary power, he was still full of those noble and virtuous sentiments, which are so peculiar to us Englishmen and so much to our honour.' Nine years later a speaker in a fiscal debate in the Commons claimed,

. . . our travellers who make but very superficial enquiries into the manners or customs of any country they pass through, may perhaps imagine the people in France or Holland are more heavily, or more oppressively taxed, than the people of this Kingdom, because they hear the people complain there as well as they do here; but any gentleman who understands these things, and has made a proper enquiry, may soon be convinced of the contrary; . . .

Later in the century John Richard, writing at Bremen, suggested that northern Europe was of little interest to most tourists. His critique was an important one, as it was in Austria, Prussia and Russia that the most significant political developments were taking place in the second half of the century — until the French Revolution changed almost everything. Richard claimed: 'This part of the world would furnish no entertainment to a young traveller, who seeks no other end in his travels than amusement or gallantry, masquerades or operas; nor would he, in Westphalia or the neighbouring countries, be the admiration of the ladies, merely for being a coxcomb. Such persons do very wisely, in beginning their tour, by shutting their eyes till they arrive at Paris, and endeavouring to sleep between city and city till they arrive at Rome or Venice.'

It was certainly true that comparatively few tourists, other than military men, visited Berlin and St Petersburg. However it is by no means true that all those who visited France and Italy were motivated solely by hedonism, or that hedonistic interests were incompatible with perceptive observations.[15]

> It is the duty every man owes his country, to observe the methods of government used in other states, and adopt that which is founded on wisdom and true policy into their own . . . a strict regard is to be had to the particular turn of our own constitution; for what may be a necessary step in one state, may prove to be the destruction of another . . .
> Thomas Robinson, House of Commons, 1734.[16]

An assessment of the political reflections in accounts left by eighteenth-century British tourists suggests that Müllenbrock's concept of a stridently Whig travel literature becoming more conciliatory is not appropriate in the case of tourist accounts that were not designed for publication. Tourists were rarely as histrionic or rhetorical as travel literature in the early eighteenth century, but they manifested in general a tempered criticism of what they saw. This continued to be the case in the latter half of the century, although there are changes that can be discerned. Firstly, whereas in the first half of the century most political reflections related to the situation in France, Italy, Switzerland and the Low Countries, in the second half there was increased interest in the Empire, and in particular, in Austria and Prussia. The Emperor Joseph II's policies in the 1770s and 1780s attracted particular interest. His policies of secularism and 'Enlightened Despotism' came to the attention of many tourists in the Austrian Netherlands. Secondly, in the second half of the century, there was less stress on religious differences. The importance of confessional strife diminished markedly in Europe and the secular, often anti-clerical, policies of many Catholic rulers, symbolised by the expulsion of the Jesuits from the whole of Catholic Europe, rendered obsolete the picture of mutually reinforcing absolutism and Catholicism that was so strong an element in early eighteenth-century travel literature. In the case of this literature, it can be suggested that Müllenbrock over-emphasised the extent to which there was an ideological shift during the century. Although some works in the latter decades were relatively free from former ideological prejudices the majority were not, and the overwhelming assumption, stated frequently, was that Britain was the best country to live in.

In the first half of the century tourists agreed that much about the political system of most European states was inequitable. Royal authority was held to be too great and this was believed to be against the interests of the people, whose wretched condition was held up as evidence of the drawbacks of absolutism. In theory it could be accepted that all systems of government were relative. An anonymous description of Germany stated 'no Country or People can be said to be great or small, good or bad, unless when compared to others'. Joseph Shaw wrote: 'where the People are most wisely and best taken care of, according to their Climate, Situation, Religion, Laws and Customs, that seems the best Government, at least for that people: And hence it is that almighty God, who with watchful eyes governs the world, had ordained so many different forms of government in it.'[17] Such moderate statements did not prevent slashing attacks upon European autocracies from being printed. Shaw's vigorous denunciation of France and praise of Dutch social policy is understandable as Britain was then allied with the Dutch in a war against France. However, a similar stance, though less obsessively anti-French, was maintained during the years of the Anglo-French alliance. In 1722, the London Tory newspaper, *The Weekly Journal or Saturday's Post*, wrote,

A Traveller may, by the looks of the Inhabitants, know where Tyranny and where Freedom prevails; in the same air, the same soil, where only a little River divides the bounds of different dominions, may be seen the extreamest misery, and the greatest plenty . . . These things have made some men of sense of our own nation, who have travelled and observed the world, to become severe Republicans; they see Italy the richest soil in Europe, not half peopled; in Germany a man may travel many days and not find a bed to live upon; the poor people and their cattle have the same covering, and the same pillows. Another thing our travellers have observed, is, that all those Princes are not always men of the most elevated understandings;. . .

Five years later the ministerial *London Journal* printed a letter from Philopatris,

All our travellers observe, that though France and Italy are incomparable more rich and better furnished with all the pleasures and conveniences of life, than Switzerland is, yet Italy is almost quite dispeopled, and the people in it are reduced to a misery that scarce can be imagined by those that have not seen it; and France is, in a great measure dispeopled, and the inhabitants are reduced to a poverty that appears in all the marks in which it can shew itself, both in their houses, furniture, cloaths and looks . . .[18]

This uncompromising stance was not universal. Some printed accounts praised specific details of European political organisation, and others, such as the travels of Charles Thompson were relatively free of xenophobic rhetoric. Thompson noted that in Genoa wines were not adulterated because culprits were sent to the galleys. He did not comment on this either to condemn the severity of the action or to praise the effect of strong government. McKay wrote of the Flemings, 'They are an open, free-hearted people, like the English, and are great lovers of liberty; so that, though their religion is Roman-Catholick, they are not Priest-ridden' — a striking reversal of the usual association of absolutism and Catholism. Another writer who printed the stock contrast of happy Switzerland and unhappy Italy, nevertheless added: 'The Peasantry of France are not rich, but free; and they have the Laws of the kingdom to protect them.'[19]

The happiness of the French perplexed some tourists. Hume noted in 1714 that the French were happy, though oppressed. Twenty-five years later Stevens, travelling from Paris to Lyons, 'passed through several towns and villages, which had great appearance of poverty; but notwithstanding that the inhabitants were full of life and gaiety'. Such a contrast could be explained by reference to the strength and seductive appeal of Catholic indoctrination. Alternatively it could be suggested that absolutism was entirely appropriate for the French. Shaw wrote: 'the French Government, which is very severe, and as arbitrary as any under

Heaven, yet best for the French, whose natures are too wicked, and too insolent to be trusted with liberty; . . . hence it is that they are so much at Union, . . .' In 1729, George Lyttleton argued that: 'the French love that their monarch should be gallant, magnificent and ambitious, and do not care what price they pay for it, provided there be great news from Flanders and fine entertainments at Versailles.'[20]

Some tourists were interested in the political systems of the countries they visited. Several journals contain long, and somewhat boring, accounts of the constitutions and governmental systems encountered. There was particular interest in those Italian states whose constitution included a republican component and comments were made about their effectiveness. Mitchell described the governments of Bologna and Venice, Parker those of Bologna and Lucca. Edward Southwell the younger sent from Genoa some routine praise of republican liberty: 'Liberty makes even poverty tolerable, it makes a wilderness a standing water and water springs of a dry ground.' He was also capable, however, of sending from Turin brief comments on Victor Amadeus II, his policy, army, finances and government. Hervey, touring Italy with Stephen Fox, versified his comments in 1729,

> Throughout all Italy beside,
> What docs one find, but Want and Pride?
> Farces of Superstitious folly,
> Decay, Distress, and Melancholy:
> The Havock of Despotick Power,
> A Country rich, its owners poor;
> Unpeopled towns, and Lands untilled,
> Bodys uncloathed, and mouths unfilled.
> The nobles miserably great,
> In painted Domes, and empty state,
> Too proud to work, too poor to eat,
> No arts the meaner sort employ,
> They nought improve, nor ought enjoy.
> Each blown from misery grows a Saint,
> He prays from Idleness, and fasts from Want.

In contrast, the more sober, and certainly less poetic, Robert Trevor and William Mildmay commented on the political situation in Lorraine in 1728 and Italy in 1730, whilst another tourist attributed the Regent's unpopularity in 1720 to his moves against

French liberty. Hume claimed in 1714 that the French peasants were miserably oppressed by the Intendants and the tax-farmers, 'the meanest paying sometimes half their income to the Crown'. Perceval wrote from Amsterdam in 1718 'having cursorily run over Flanders and Holland, and seen the advantages which liberty and freedom in the exercise of religion bring to mankind'. In 1732 Waldegrave wrote from Paris: 'I was surprised the other day with a visit from mylord Onslow, and you will be more surprised when I tell you his Lordship is already half a Frenchman . . . he says he never saw such a country in his life and cannot praise this, without reflecting on his own . . . he praises everything excepting some inscriptions in the Place des Victoires, which he wants to have altered.' Unfortunately there is no indication as to what led to Onslow's change of mind. Mitchell's portrayal of France was far from simplistic. He noted limits on royal absolutism and commented on the dispute between the Parlement of Paris and the Crown: 'It is true the laws concerning private property, which regulate the succession, and contacts among men are still preserved entire, . . . The Parliament seems to be the only body in the kingdom that strikes for its libertys and privileges. The King treats them as a Court of Justice but does not care they meddle in state affairs.' Commenting on the royal seizure of papers belonging to a Benedictine monastery, a prelude to attempted despoliation, Mitchell wrote 'such proceedings occasioned very loud baulking even in France where property is not upon the surest footing'.

Some tourists did not therefore share the simplistic views of much travel literature. They appreciated the existence of political controversy within supposedly absolutist states, and realised that the impact of absolutism and Catholicism upon European societies was more complex than many claimed. A few praised aspects of state activity — Mildmay praised the French roads in 1748 — and some were driven by visiting Genoa and Venice to question the received wisdom of the superiority of republics.[21]

A variety of political reflections were expressed freely in the second half of the century. A good example of this was the continuing difference of opinion concerning the continental republics. Most could agree that Poland was not a praiseworthy state — Wraxall wrote of Cracow in 1778: 'It is half in ruins at this time; and the greatest happiness which can befall it would be that the

Emperor would take it into his own hands.' There were however mixed feelings concerning the United Provinces, Switzerland and the Italian republics. George Keate, who spent 1756 in Geneva, published five years later his *A Short Account of the Ancient History, Present Government, and Laws of the Republic of Geneva*, which presented the republic as the temple of virtues and liberty. In 1765 Thomas Pennant praised the Swiss custom of partible inheritance: 'which preserves an equality among these people. It reminds me of the comfortable feel of the Lacedemonian Legislator at seeing his levelling plan take place without a sign or any mark of discontent among those who so generously submitted to his regulations.'

Thicknesse claimed that the people of southern Europe were uglier than the British and the Swiss, and attributing this to either climate or liberty, he praised liberty enthusiastically. Bennett noted in Berne in 1785: 'There is a neatness and a care for the publick ease so conspicuous in all the works ordered by the Senate, the people seem so happy under their administration, that an aristocratic government begins to lose a great deal of the horror with which the dark and tyrannical councils of Venice and Genoa had inspired me.' There was, however, less enthusiasm for republics than there had been at the beginning of the century, and this change, though not noted by Müllenbrock, would help to substantiate his claim of a move away from Whig ideology. Possibly this partly reflected changes in the fortunes of various European states. The United Provinces, whether it was in 'decline' or not, became relatively poorer, its one time unique social and economic institutions were matched elsewhere, the state was affected by internal disorder, particularly in the 1750s and 1780s, and in 1780 joined the Americans and French in the anti-British camp. The splendours of Venice and Genoa became increasingly tarnished, and Genoa was badly damaged during the siege of 1747–8. Within Italy social, economic and political progress appeared to be most marked, not in the republics, but in the duchies of Milan and, in particular, Leopold's Tuscany. Tourists, such as Francis, making political points, contrasted Tuscany and the Papal States, rather than the republics and the non-republics. Increasing numbers of British tourists visited Switzerland but the civil disorders in Geneva in the 1760s and 1780s confused the political response to Switzerland. A hint of ambivalence is present in both Bennett's and Brand's account. Bennett noted that the clocks in Basle were an hour fast, 'preserved unaltered by that unwillingness to change which is a distinguishing feature in every democracy'. Brand claimed that the Swiss treated Lugano very badly. Oliver Goldsmith wrote of the republics of Genoa, Switzerland and the United Provinces: 'the people are slaves to laws of their own making, little less than in unmixed monarchies where they are slaves to the will of one subject to frailties like themselves.'

However, it is important not to overemphasise any shift in attitudes towards republics. The attitude of Whig tourists at the beginning of the century towards the Italian republics was one of ambivalence. Some noted signs of corruption and oppression, whilst the Catholicism, however anti-clerical, of Venice, Genoa and Lucca, differentiated them from the United Provinces and the bulk of the Swiss cantons. William Mildmay, in 1730, comdemned the distortion of the Genoese constitution by the nobles who sought to avoid burdens; He also thought that the frequent governmental changes in Lucca decreed by the constitution were bad for policy. Thus criticism of the Italian republics in the second half of the century was not new. It was rather the attitude to the Dutch that altered. One-time allies of Britain against Louis XIV, the Dutch were neutral in the Seven Years War and were replaced as Britain's Protestant ally by Prussia. This was paralleled by an alteration in tourist routes. At the beginning of the century the United Provinces and Geneva were commonly the only Protestant territories visited by British tourists and it was therefore understandable that the contrast between Protestantism and Catholicism should be confused with that between republicanism and absolutism. By the second half of the century, it became increasingly common to visit other Protestant states, mostly in Germany, and this altered the ideological experience of tourists. Prussia was an autocratic militaristic Protestant state, a new experience that clashed with the conventions of Whig ideology. Robert Molesworth had written about a similar state in the 1690s — Denmark — but Prussia was the first such state most British tourists had encountered.

As the conflation of republicanism and virtue was increasingly ignored, criticism of the Italian republics increased. In 1782, Andrew McDougall wrote from Venice: 'their government we could not possibly bear, sure there cannot be a greater shame for a free people (at least a people that call themselves so) than to suffer the first of their nation to be accused, without knowing by whom.' Walker launched a savage attack on the city five years later,

On the whole, though Venice is still a large and fine city, it is certainly not equal to what it had been; declination is visible in every feature of it; the people are too soft, luxurious, and indolent to cut any figure in trade; the pride of family is another bar against resurrection; and the great baits which make all gape, are the easy emoluments of office . . . Where the singularity of situation must necessarily beget an artificial and unnatural mode of life and living; it is no wonder that corruption and effeminacy originated here. To that place is Europe indebted for the refined system of rendering the multitude the slaves of the few, by the means of corruption, luxury, and effeminacy.

The more practical Pratt noted that living in the Prussian possession of Cleves was less expensive than in the United Provinces, and wrote 'in this instance, at least, whatever may be your political principles, you would prefer the despotic states to the Republics'.[22]

Many tourists condemned absolutism in the second half of the century. John Northall, who visited Naples in 1753, wrote: 'the prerogatives of the Crown are of such a nature, the authority of the nobility over their vassals so exorbitant, and, above all, the power and property of the clergy so excessive, that there are hardly any countries where the generality of the people are more dissolute in their morals, or more wretched in their circumstances: . . .' Nine years later Valltravers observed: 'We were greatly shocked at the scenes of Poverty Distress, and Despondence, which offered themselves to our view in the Austrian Netherlands, and in France.' Smollett was no apologist for the French system: 'The interruption which is given, in arbitrary governments, to the administration of justice, by the interposition of the great, has always a bad effect upon the morals of the common people. The peasants too are often rendered desperate and savage, by the misery they suffer from the oppression and tyranny of their landlords.'

The same year, 1763, Mrs Montagu wrote from Düsseldorf: 'It grieves one to see Princes so magnificent and luxurious while their subjects are so poor and so wretched.' Three years later the road from Calais to St Omer led to a fresh statement of the autocracy/Popery viewpoint: 'Great numbers of crosses and little images are stuck up everywhere along the side of the road, to which the people always pull off their hats, and in short you plainly discover everywhere under what an arbitrary Government they live, and how much they are bigotted to their religion.' In 1767 Charles James

Fox wrote from Florence, 'there had been a woman of fashion put in prison lately for f——g (I suppose rather too publickly) a piece of unexampled tyranny! and such as could happen in no place but this' an appropriate contrast to Robert Gray's subsequent praise of Leopold's legislation and legal reforms in Tuscany. Thicknesse wrote of France,

> Were the poor day-labourers and *vigenerons* capable, by their labour and industry, to keep themselves, their families, and their little habitations, in the same neat, simple manner that the industrious part of the poor in England do, France would be the most delightful country in the world, either, to pass through, or to reside in; but the extreme poverty of the poor, and the poor day-labourers in particular, renders their villages, nay even their great towns very filthy. The *fermiers generaux* oppress them beyond conception, and they toil from morning till night, exposed to the inclemency of all weathers, and yet live a much more wretched life than any of the African slaves, . . . But their lively disposition bears them through all with chearfulness, . . .

Sir William Young attacked the situation in Sicily in 1772 in conventional terms, 'feudal and ecclesiastic tyranny, . . . Industry sinking under united desolation, superstition and rapine'. Peckham, the author of the tour of Holland published that same year, attacked the French legal system, claiming that men of rank could 'almost depend on pardon', and drew attention to the social cost of good French roads: 'The roads are excellent, and untaxed with turnpikes; but these the poor peasants are obliged to make and to repair by the sweat of their brows, without even the prospect of advantage accruing to them from their labour.' Francis in 1772 questioned whether the Venetian system of anonymous denunciations was actually in use, observing: 'In most of our political systems, the theory of the constitution points one way, the practise another. If we rely upon the direction of the needle, without calculation of the variations, we shall always be mistaken.' In Ghent he wrote: 'We have passed through a rich, open corn country, in which the peasants, who cultivate the soil have not bread to eat. There is something uncommonly ingenious in a system of government, under which the people starve in the midst of plenty.' At the Comédie in Paris, Francis witnessed a small riot when the pit called for the author of the play, who was in prison. Troops restored 'what these people call peace and good order. Yet they made more resistance than I expected'. A week later he encountered difficulties in obtaining a passport to leave the country: 'Everything in this country is calculated for check and control.' St Vincent attacked 'the oppressive laws' under which the French peasant 'in general an inoffensive, peaceable, slave' lived.

A visit to Lisbon in 1775 led Thomas Pelham to praise Britain: 'with what joy and gratitude must every Englishman reflect on the happiness of his own nation in comparison of any other; when he sees in a country like this, the nobles from their greatness and tyranny exposed every hour to attacks from the people and the people from their poverty rendered the most abject slaves, . . . they are in general poor from the indolence that must necessarily follow so despotic a government . . .' The following year a tourist in France wrote,

> I am of opinion that the constitution of the government has more influence upon manners than is generally allowed to it, and that to this ought commonly to be referred what is attributed to climate and the natural character of nations. The distinction between noblesse and bourgeoisie in France, and the exclusion of the former from most means of acquiring wealth, have strong effects upon the national manner. They give the noblesse an exclusive right to pride with poverty: they give to the bourgeoisie an exclusive right to wealth with grossiéreté.

Noting the effect of the limited governmental authority in the Comtat, a Papal enclave in southern France, he observed: 'This freedom makes trade and agriculture flourish even under the government of the Pope, generally so notoriously blasting to both.' In 1779 John Moore delivered a harsh verdict on France: 'A candid Englishman, of whatever rank in life he may be, must see with indignation, that everything in this kingdom is arranged for the accommodation of the rich and powerful; and that little or no regard is paid to the comfort of citizens of an inferior station.' Five years later George Norman, returning via Courland from his trip to St Petersburg, commented on the oppression of the tenantry. The following year Petty noted the contrast between the wealth of Galicia and the poverty of the people. Visiting Liège in 1785, Bennett condemned the idea of an ecclesiastical principality: 'the ill effects of the Government are very apparent: an ecclesiastic elected by a Chapter of strangers, without hereditary right, and invested with absolute authority, can have little regard for the people whom chance has made his subjects: and if there should be a Prince Bishop who prefered their interests to his own, his plans would perhaps all be overthrown by the different views or caprice of his successor.'

The majority of political reflections in tourist accounts written in the years immediately preceeding the French Revolution, would not have been out of place at the beginning of the century. Space only permits a few examples. Lady Craven was very critical of Naples: 'At Naples, where the Government supplies nothing for the ease of its subjects, and where none are rich, because relative luxury conducts everyone to poverty; where public misery is concealed under national pomp; where indigence inhabits the palaces of the great as well as the cottages of the poor, — every one hurries after spectacles, diversion, and games; . . .' In 1786, St John contrasted British freedom and degenerate French luxury, and condemned the opulence of the Orangery at Versailles, a 'shameful' luxury when many of the poor had 'not a place to lay their heads in'. The following year Arthur Young attacked the tyranny of French *lettres de cachet* and Walker commented on 'the baleful hand of power and priestcraft' in Italy. The situation in Sicily was attacked by Watkins in 1788 and Brand in 1792, whilst Watkins also attributed the prevalence of crime in Italy to 'bad government and superstition'.[23]

Continuity in the critique of European society was the dominent theme, but alongside it there are also signs of a more tolerant attitude. Some travellers drew attention to the various possible responses. Gardenstone's views on France changed in response to the excellent burgundy he had with his dinner at Breteuil in September 1786. Entering Spain from France in 1791 Townshend noted: 'the face of the country immediately before me appeared desolate and barren, . . . I was at first inclined to attribute this dismal aspect of their want of industry, to some vice in their government, or to some error in their political oeconomy; but, upon examination, I soon discovered the real cause of this barrenness, in the hungry nature of the soil, and the want of those two inestimable feeders of vegetation, the limestone and the schist.'[24] Some tourists noted the happiness of those who were the victims of oppression. John Moore, Mrs Piozzi and Lord Gardenstone noted it in the case of the French; and Mrs Piozzi commented also on the happiness of the people of Milan.[25] A favourable response to specific aspects of absolutist rule was shown by several tourists. One wrote from Paris in 1764 to Sir John Cust, Speaker of the House of Commons: 'I find in general *here* that the free and independent persons in the kingdom begin to be weary of the extraordinary extension of the power *usurped* by *Parliaments*. The long and vexatious opposition they have given here to the Inoculation, and free exportation of grain has shown the majority to be no way qualified to conduct a great nation in its economical interests.' Five years later William Windham noted that in France, unlike Britain, the equivalent of the Vauxhall pleasure garden was taxed in order to support charitable purposes.

Wharton commented on the Parisian theatres in 1775: 'there is no mobbing they dare not be noisy for there are soldiers ready to arrest the troublesome person. This may appear a mark of despotism but it is yet comfortable to the peaceable spectators.' Three years later Philip Yorke wrote of Lucca: '. . . amongst these sumptuary regulations that of not wearing a sword is the most rational, and so convenient that I could wish it were adopted everywhere.' John Richard praised the simplicity of the Prussian law code and claimed that there were too many laws in Britain. Gardenstone praised French road laws: 'In this country all kinds of vehicles on the high-roads must give way to post-carriages, by the king's ordinance, which is constantly observed. — Our commonality are apt to spurn at such useful regulations — If they had a proper sense of liberty, they would at least be as well disposed to obey the acts of our legislature, as the French are to revere the royal edicts.' Brand clearly had a sympathy for continental orderly behaviour. He wrote of the Château d'If in Marseilles: 'a sort of Bastile, where a few state prisoners and young men whose excesses have procured them lodgement there at the recommendation of their father. This violation of liberty is very revolting to an Englishman but I am inclined to think that many of its victims rejoice in maturer age that their fathers had such a power.' One suspects that most tourists would have agreed with Fox's reflections on the Florentine Countess rather than Brand's comment; in that probably lay a lot of the tension between tourists and Bearleaders. At Prague Brand attended a fête given in honour of the Emperor: 'The wonderful order with which all this was conducted surprised and surprizes me still. I contrasted it with England and could not avoid some unpatriotic reflexions upon our want of police and our propensity to picking pockets and every species of theft.'[26]

There is no conclusion to the question of whether tourism served as a political education. Much depended on the inclinations of the tourist and the people whom he met, but the openness of European society to aristocratic travellers provided many opportunities for the acquisition of information and opinion. Lord Mandeville discussed Anglo-Austrian relations at Milan in 1758; the extensive European tour that he took during the recess of 1781 convinced Gilbert Elliot MP that European opinion favoured American independence; and Lord Wycombe wrote from Peterwardein in Austrian Serbia in 1786: 'It is . . . impossible for any man however incurious his disposition may be, to [gap in text] through this country the dissatisfaction which is everywhere produced by the new assessments that are about to be established. Whether this dissatisfaction results from real hardship or simply from the odium which constantly attends new calls for money' he did not know.[27] Whether the dispositions of others were similarly curious is unclear. Andrews thought it necessary to warn tourists against being dazzled by the glitter of Paris.[28] Wharton read Montesquieu's *L'Esprit des Lois* at Dijon because, 'I am going into different nations differently governed. That is the only book to enable me to judge of, and profit by seeing their governments'. There are few signs that others prepared themselves in the same fashion.[29] Peter Beckford stated that 'It is not in looking at pictures and statues only, that travelling is of use, but in examining the laws, customs, and manners of other countries, and comparing them with our own.'[30] The examination, however detailed, led most tourists to praise their own country. John Richard claimed that: '. . . from every nation, from even every circumstance, travellers will find many occasions to admire the constitution and comforts of their own country.' Pratt stated: '. . . in all which are justly called the comforts of life, Holland, Guelderland, Prussia, Germany, and other countries, are so many hundred years behind us, that we have just cause to be at once proud and grateful: proud of our happy island, and grateful for the benign government, under which it flourishes.'[31] Other factors, such as familiarity, friends and language, made tourists glad to return home, but the claims above were broadly true, though they must be set alongside the pleasures of European life that many tourists clearly enjoyed and the willingness of many tourists, particularly in the latter half of the century, to visit Europe more than once. There are innumerable instances of the latter. To give a few examples, one may name Sir Humphrey

Morice, Stephen Fox, James Caulfeild, fourth Viscount Charlemont, Joseph Leeson, first Earl of Milltown, Henry Ellison of Hebburn, Lord Pomfret, Mrs Crewe, Adam Walker, Lord Gardenstone, James, second Earl of Fife, David Garrick, Lord Perceval, Edward Southwell junior, Caroline, Lady Holland, James Bland Burges, Arthur Young, John Moore and William Mildmay.

Comments on the political situation in Europe were related closely often to reflections on social customs. As in the case of political reflections, there was a general sense that the British social order was better, accompanied by support for specific foreign social customs. Lord Charles Somerset (c. 1689–1710), grandson of the first Duke of Beaufort, visited Amsterdam in 1708 and praised the 'Rasphouse' where 'fellows that are above measure idle and debauched were forced to work'. He reflected: 'If we had this excellent way of managing idle vagabonds at their first beginning in wickedness, we should save ourselves frequently from losing our money and now and then our lives with it, and those miserable wretches from losing theirs on the Gallows, and with it a great venture of their afterbeing.' William Drake praised the Amsterdam prisons in 1769; Edmund Dewes a servant commended in 1776 the Berne system by which criminals were chained to wagons and made to clean the streets: 'I think such punishment in every country town, where prisoners are convicted, would have better effect than to send them all to the Thames in England.' Richard Garmston commented on the Berne system in 1787; and Thicknesse urged that Britain copy the prison system of the Austrian Netherlands.[32] Peckham praised the policing and firewatching of Amsterdam and Lady Craven the caution shown in dispensing drugs in Venice: 'You cannot buy a drug at the apothecaries here, without an order from a Physician. A very prudent caution against the madness of those who choose to finish their existence with a dose of laudanum, or their neighbours with one of arsenic.'[33]

Robert Wharton was amenable to many French customs. In Paris he parted from a Frenchman of his acquaintance: 'I had the honour to kiss him on each cheek, a ceremony which we should think rather ridiculous in England; but I have mentioned before, that it is quite the *Ton* here.' The previous day he had attended the Concert Spirituel and noted, as many tourists did in Paris, that 'the attention and silence of the audience was astonishing . . . I thought of the English audience and felt for my Countrymen.' From Dijon he reported: 'Gentlemen go out of a room full of company as quietly as possible without saying a word to anybody. This seems to be a good custom as it does not set all the company in a bustle as is the case often with us.' At Lyons he discovered, to his surprise, that women bathed in the Saône, and wrote home suggesting that British women adopt the habit of summer bathing and that the British adopt the French habit of a separate glass for each person at meals. Mrs Crewe noted in Paris 'much more attention and greater respect is paid to old age here than in London', and that old women were treated at suppers with good humour and cheerfulness by their juniors.[34]

Many continental customs were attacked. British tourists claimed frequently that not only were people less clean in their personal habits, but also that they were indelicate. The widespread habit, particularly in France, of urinating in public caused widespread comment and complaint. There was great surprise that the practice extended to women. Frankness also caused comment. Wharton wrote from Dijon: 'the people make not the least scruple of using the words, pisser, . . . I had a long dispute with an Abbé about delicacy in these affairs, which he said was highly ridiculous. "Every one, says he, knows that these things are natural and necessary, and it is therefore absurb to think of concealing them . . .".' Robert Gray noted of his visit to the Instituto in Bologna: 'We were disposed to make some comparison in favour of English ladies, when we observed with what sang-froid some Italian women, who accompanied us in the rooms of the Instituto, examined the monsters and nudities exposed to view. How offensive is it to see the female character devoid of delicacy, that timid and engaging charm which shrinks with sensibility from every object that might excite a blush, which is the peculiar grace of English women, and the great and fascinating ornament which secures those lasting attachments that we form in our country!'[35]

The swaddling of Italian infants, the nursing of their French counterparts, and the custom in both countries of dressing children like adults was attacked.[36] Gray claimed that Italian institutions for the relief of those incapable of working supported the indolent; Peter Wauchop in Lille in 1775 found 'their wooden shoes and dogs drawing carts are laughable enough'; and Lady Craven was scandalised by a 'very abominable' custom at St Pertsburg: 'noblemen, who are engaged to marry young ladies, . . . embrace them in the midst of a large company at a ball.' Sir William Young wrote: 'I am strange enough to imagine that the one and the other extreme, the

French Court and *Calabrian* Wood, may be regions equally barbarous; that happy medium alone, which teaches the genuine social duties of hospitality, unadulterated by new fangled ceremonies, and influences to mutual assistance and services, untainted by false and barbarous distinctions, and interests; that happy medium alone, is the true, best state or humanity civilized.' On a less elevated plane Mrs Crewe attacked the formality of Parisian etiquette in matters such as visiting and balls.[37]

Aside from specific issues, the general view was that British society was more free, less constrained by social distinctions and the privileges of rank. George Lyttelton wrote from Lyons of French social restrictions, the 'chimerical distinction between a gentleman and a marchand', whilst George Norman suggested that a major difference between Britain and the continent was the stress on rank in the latter.[38] There is little suggestion that these views changed during the century. Possibly the Anglomania that affected large areas of European aristocratic and intellectual society, particularly in France and Germany, in the latter half of the century, encouraged British tourists in a feeling of national self-confidence. There are no signs that tourists responded to seeing the Enlightened Despotisms by wishing to create one in Britain. Neither are there as many signs as might be expected that political reflections varied in response to Britain's international position. There were, it is true, some shifts in emphasis. It is difficult to imagine many tourists in the 1780s reiterating the second Lord Carpenter's statement of 1717 that he agreed with Addison that it was best to live under small commonwealths, although the virtues of enlightened government in states such as Baden and Tuscany were possibly not known to enough tourists to make them dissent from the second half of the maxim, that it was worse to live under small Princes.[39] It is also difficult to imagine many Bearleaders of the 1710s sharing Brand's reflection of 1790 on Lord Bruce's opinions during his Swiss tour, 'he is convinced that a peasant may be happy and will I hope benefit by the train of reflections which this expedition had at different times suggested'.[40]

Whatever the shifts most tourists remained convinced that Britain was the best country in Europe. Despite the hospitality they received and the access they were granted to European society at its highest reaches it would not be unfair to claim that most returned to Britain as better-informed xenophobes.

Notes

1. BL, Stowe 791, p. 15.
2. BL, Add. 37926, fo. 112.
3. Hall to Keith, 5 July 1785, BL, Add. 35534.
4. H. J. Müllenbrock, 'The political implications of the *Grand Tour*: Aspects of a specifically English contribution to the European travel literature of the age of Enlightenment', *Trema*, 9 (1984), pp. 7–21.
5. Stevens, p. 391.
6. [Villiers], *A Tour through part of France* (1789), p. 7.
7. John Mitford, travelling through France in 1776 wrote of 'the cursory view of a posting traveller'. Gloucester RO. D2002 F1.
8. [Lady Miller], *Letters from Italy in the Years 1770 and 1771* (3 vols., 1776), I, 14.
9. Pelham to Thomas, 5 Oct. 1777, BL, Add. 33127; Count Preysing, Bavarian foreign minister, to Count Haslang, Bavarian envoy in London, [5] July 1751, Munich, Bayr. Ges. London; Edward Southwell to Perceval, 2 Nov. 1725, BL, Add. 47031.
10. *Mist's Weekly Journal*, 25 Sep. (os) 1725; Southwell to Perceval, 27 July 1726, BL, Add. 47031; Keene to Delafaye, 13 Dec. 1728, PRO 94/99.
11. Perceval to brother, 21 Nov. (os) 1726, Southwell to Perceval, 27 July 1726, BL, Add. 47031; Anon., BL, Add. 60522; Boteler to Earl Cowper, 28 Sep. 1722, Herts. D/EP F53; Pelham to Lord Pelham, 3, 15 Oct. 1776, 8 Feb., 1 April, 26 July 1777, to Lady Pelham, 16 Sep. 1776, 15 March 1777, BL, Add. 33127; Yorke to Keith, 15 Dec. 1778, BL, Add. 35515; Garrard to Drake, 19 Oct. 1778, Aylesbury D/DR/8/10/6; Brand to Wharton [Nov.–Dec. 1780], 10 May 1781, 17 Nov. 1783, 14 March 1786, 15 Dec. 1789, 15 Feb. 1790, 26 Aug. 1791; Aikin, I, 84; Hanson to Keith, 10 Jan. 1788, BL, Add. 35540; Thicknesse, 1777, I, 136–42; J. Townsend, *A Journey through Spain* (3 vols., 1791), I, i; Andrews, 1785, p. 44; Dalrymple to Keith, 19 Oct. 1789, BL, Add. 35541.
12. Lady Mary Coke to Keith, 23 Nov. 1773, BL, Add. 35006; Southwell, BL, Add. 34753, fo. 6.
13. Villettes to Newcastle, 25 Dec. 1734, PRO 92/37; Pelham to Lord Pelham, 19 Dec. 1777, 30 Oct. 1775, BL, Add. 33127, 33126; R. R. Sedgewick (ed.), *Some Materials towards Memoirs of the Reign of King George II*, by John, Lord Hervey (3 vols., 1931), I, 220; Ryder diary, 18 Dec. 1741.
14. Hume, BL, Add. 29477, fo. 18; Daniel to Tilson, 20 April 1729, PRO 77/76; Waldegrave jnl., 1 Sep. 1730, Chewton; HMC, *Carlisle* pp. 89–90; Swinton, 7, 12, 15, 16, 29 Jan. (os), 21 Feb. (os), 21 March (os), 31 May (os), 7 June (os) 1731; Cobbett, 11, 822; *Daily Universal Register*, 5 Jan. 1785; Bennett, 31 Aug. 1785.
15. *Craftsman*, 6 July (os) 1728; Cobbett, 10, 173; Richard, *A Tour from London to Petersburg* (1780), pp. 198–9.
16. Cobbett, 9, 300.
17. *Present State of Germany*, I, xix; J. Shaw, p. xvi.
18. Shaw, xiii–xiv, 38; *Weekly Journal or Saturday's Post*, 15 Dec. (os) 1722; *London Journal*, 4 Nov. (os) 1727.
19. Carleton, pp. 249, 311; Thompson, I, 72; McKay, *A Journey Through the Austrian Netherlands* (1725), p. xxviii; *Present State of Germany*, II, 432.
20. Hume, BL, Add. 29477, fo. 23; Stevens, p. 67; Shaw, p. 150; M. Wyndham, I, 23; Mildmay jnl., Chelmsford, 15 M50/1302, p. 60.
21. BL, Add. 53816, fo. 61–4, 53815, fo. 25–41; BL, Stowe 750, fo. 356; Southwell to Perceval, 27, 2 Nov. 1725, Hervey to Lady Hervey, Trevor to Thomas Trevor, 27 Aug. 1728, BL, Add. 47031, 51345, fo. 18–19. 61684; Mildmay jnl.,

188   Social and Political Reflections

Chelmsford, 15M50/1303, pp. 15–18, 53–5; anon., BL, Stowe 790, fo. 9; Hume, Perceval to Chamberlayne, 9 July 1718, BL, Add. 29477, fo. 18, 47028; Waldegrave to Delafaye, 9 Aug., Waldegrave to Tilson, 15 Aug. (quote), Waldegrave to Essex, 12 Aug. 1732, PRO 78/200–1, BL, Add. 27732; Mitchell jnl., BL, Add. 58314, fo. 8, 24, 48.

22. Wraxall to Keith, 8 June 1778, BL, Add. 35514; G. R. de Beer (ed.), *Tour on the Continent 1765 by Thomas Pennant* (1948), p. 107; Thicknesse, 1777, I, 125–6; Bennett, 2 Sep., 12 Aug. 1785; Brand to Wharton, 21 July 1791; *Public Ledger*, 19 June 1760; Mildmay jnl., 15M50/1303, pp. 15, 32; McDougall to Keith, 27 Jan. 1782, BL, Add. 35515; Walker, pp. 173–4; Pratt, III, 80.

23. J. Northall, *Travels through Italy* (1766), p. 183; Smollett, p. 25; Montagu, I, 57; Tracy and Dettand, Bodl. Mss. Add. A366, fo. 4; Fox to Lord Fitzwilliam, 27 Oct. 1767, BL, Add. 47576; Gray, pp. 306–11; Thicknesse, 1768, pp. 43–4; Young, BL, Stowe, 791, pp. 116, 119; Tour, pp. 229–30; Francis, BL, Add. 40759, fo. 9, 2, 23–4; St Vincent, BL, Add. 31192, fo. 36; Pelham to Lord Pelham, 30 Oct. 3 Nov. 1775, BL, Add. 33126; Anon., BL, Add. 12130, fo. 49–50, 158; Moore, *A View of Society and Manners in France, Switzerland, and Germany* (2 vols., 1779), I, 32; Norman to his stepmother, 10 Sep. 1784, Kent, U310, C3; Bennett, 6 July 1785; Craven, I, 306–7; St John, pp. 127–8, 95, 36–7; Young, I, 55; Walker, pp. 330, 353; Watkins, I, 6, 358; Brand to Wharton, 3 April 1792.

24. Gardenstone, I, 13–15; Townshend, I, 89.

25. R. Anderson (ed.), *The Works of John Moore* (7 vols., Edinburgh, 1820), III, 1; Gardenstone, p. 13; Piozzi, *Observations and Reflections made in a Journey through France, Italy, and Germany*, pp. 9, 56.

26. W. R. to Cust, L. Cust, *Records of the Cust Family*, III (1927), p. 242; Windham, D/DZ EHC 20; Wharton to Miss Lloyd, 29 Feb. 1775; Yorke to Keith, 28 Sep. 1778, BL, Add. 35515; Richard, pp. 152–3; Gardenstone, I, 18; Brand to Wharton, late Aug. 1783; 14 Aug. 1792.

27. Otway, Mandeville's tutor, to the latter's father, the Duke of Manchester, 30 May 1758, Huntingdon, CRO dd M49 A and B, bundle 7; HP, II, 395; Wycombe to Keith, 12 April 1786, BL, Add. 35535.

28. Andrews, 1785, pp. 41–2.

29. Wharton to Thomas Wharton, 13 June 1775.

30. Beckford, *Familiar Letters from Italy, to a friend in England* (2 vols., Salisbury, 1805), I, 9.

31. Richard, p. 221; Pratt, II, 527.

32. Badminton, Somerset, 'An account of my Travels', pp. 14–15; Drake, Aylesbury, D/DR/8/20; Dewes, Bodl., Mss. Eng. Misc. d 213, pp. 84–5; Garmston, BL, Add. 30271, fo. 14; Thicknesse, 1786, p. 51.

33. *Tour of Holland*, pp. 73–4; Craven, 1789, I, 151–2.

34. Wharton to mother, 10, 9 April, 29 May, to Miss Raine, 31 Aug. 1775; Crewe, BL, Add. 37926, fo. 60.

35. Wharton to mother, 18 May 1775; Gray, p. 302.

36. Wharton to mother, 18 July 1775; Walker, p. 415; Thicknesse, 1768, p. 53; Brand to Wharton, 30 July 1779.

37. Gray, p. 255; Wauchop to Keith, 4 Nov. 1775, BL, Add. 35509; Craven, p. 183; Young, BL, Stowe, 791, pp. 40–1, Crewe, BL, Add. 37926, fo. 34–5, 44, 59, 67.

38. M. Wyndham, I, 25; Norman, 22 Sep. 1784, Kent CRO U310 C3.

39. Carpenter, Bodl. Mss. Douce 67, pp. 248–9.

40. Brand to Wharton, 25 Aug. 1790.

9 RELIGION

I have found . . . the Church of England very much esteemed by all the men of learning I met with abroad.
Dr James Walker, Lille, 1772.[1]

Last week I went to see the treasure of Saint Denis . . . whilst I was observing these curiosities with much attention; a Priest told me seriously that if I would but touch those Holy Relicks, it might convert me, upon which I replied, that if by touch I could but convert those precious stones into gold and silver for my own use, I should make a better use of them, upon which he laughed, and so ended our dispute upon Religion; upon which subject the women of this country as well as all other countries often dispute about, for they generally think that their own religion is the best and in France I have been often obliged to defend my religion against the Ladys, whose arguments and persons may be very powerful and persuasive in all cases except that of religion.
Edward Mellish, Paris, 1731.[2]

Anti-Catholicism was the prime ideological stance in eighteenth-century Britain. The methods, practices and aspirations of the Catholic church appear to have genuinely appalled many English-men of the period. Newspapers, sermons, processions, demonstrations and much correspondence reveal a response to Catholicism that was based not simply upon the repetition of trite anti-Catholic maxims but also upon a deep-felt repulsion. Catholicism was equated with autocracy; it drew on credulity and superstition and led to misery, poverty, clerical rule and oppression. The perceived danger from Catholicism was increased by historical factors, by the close association of Catholicism and Jacobitism and by the fact that Britain's principal enemies, France and Spain, were Catholic powers. That Britain also allied with Catholic powers — Austria (1702–11, 1731–3, 1741–56), France (1716–31), Portugal and Savoy-Piedmont — did not shake this perception. Catholicism therefore excited fear or unease. It also aroused interest and, at times, humour or ridicule. The last were most conspicuously

189

aroused by relics. Relics symbolised the inversion of reason that was held to characterise Catholicism. Credulity and superstition were seen both as the essential supports of a Catholic ascendancy and as the products of it. By means of a tight control over education and the propagation of religious practices that ensnared reason and deluded the senses, the Catholic church wove a poisonous web that entrapped the people of Catholic Europe. This was seen most clearly in the widespread respect for relics, which was regarded by most tourists as relic-worship.

Joseph Hume, an Anglican clergyman, was told at the Val-de-Grâce in Paris, in 1714, that the relics of James II of England that were kept there could cure, a neat portrayal of the threatening combination of Catholicism and Jacobitism. Colin MacLaurin was very sceptical about the relics he encountered at Auxerre and Dijon in 1722. Edward Mellish saw a relic in procession in Mons in 1731 and commented, 'we never pay so much honour to inaminate beings, neither would we be guilty of so much idolatry and superstition'. Two years earlier an Anglican cleric, Dr Joseph Atwell, Bearleader to the second Earl Cowper, scorned the relics of the eleven thousand virgins at Cologne and mocked those at Aachen. He wrote that the latter included: 'Some of the Virgin Mary's shifts (which by the way were not very clean) some of Jesus' swadling clothes . . . some of the Manna that fell in the wilderness and such trompery as would not be worth seeing, if it was not for the silver and jewels with which they are adorn'd.' Walker was similarly sceptical about the Aachen relics in 1787.

The zealous Tory and prominent Jacobite, Lord Quarendon, was sufficiently moved by the miracle of the blood of St Januarius at Naples, a relic that many British tourists mocked, to compose a blasphemous and witty poem. He recorded of his visit to Saumur in June 1739: 'Nothing worth observation except a Chapell to the Virgin which does great miracles, the walls are all surrounded with the Tabulae Votivae of persons sav'd from eminent dangers, . . . the whole quarter of the town consists of people whose only trade is to make chaplets, these when rubb'd over the Virgins lap are greatly efficacious, the Peres de l'Oratorie are the actors of this comedy which indeed they perform as if they themselves believe it.' Walter Stanhope mocked the French relics in 1769.[3]

Nunneries were another great source of interest. It was very common for tourists to visit them, particularly convents of British nuns, of which there were several in Northern France and the

Austrian Netherlands. Several tourists attended ceremonies in which women renounced the world to enter nunneries. James Hume visited the Dieppe convent of the Ursulines and talked with two English nuns in Dunkirk, in 1773, and stayed for two hours. Wharton and Lady Knight were both interested in nuns. Mrs Montagu, in the Earl of Bath's party to Spa in 1763, wrote: 'We visited the Nunnerys in every town; Mrs Carter constantly expressing the greatest abhorrence of their strict vows, and sequestered life . . .' The fascination that nunneries excited was speedily quenched. Those who visited nunneries discovered that most nuns were not beautiful, sensual women held against their will, and many were disappointed by their looks.[4]

In both guidebooks and private journals the general response to the Catholic Church was abhorrence coupled with respect for particular customs. James Hume was generally critical. He was unimpressed by the monastery he visited; by the lack of Sabbath observance; and by the appearance of Jesus on signs, pointing the way, for instance, to bars. He debated religion with a monk at Caen and witnessed the celebration of mass at Guingam: 'I stood behind a pillar and observed the old man's antick postures and grimaces, but could not hear what he mumbled, with his back turned to the people, who behaved themselves very devoutly though they understood not one word of what was said.' His reflections on French Catholicism were however mixed. After Ascension Day mass in Paris he wrote, 'he that sees and considers what the Roman Catholics call the service of God cannot choose but love the Church of England the better for it'. However he was also very impressed by the manner in which Catholics prayed at their bedside in inns and at home and thought this was 'extremely fit to be imitated by Protestants'. Thomas Pelham was as usual priggish; and Philip Francis facetious. The former wrote of 'the Roman Catholics, whose behaviour and manners may be made useful to a Protestant who compares them with his own', the latter, in Tuscany, 'after dinner discussed a few points of controversy, with a friar of the order of redemption. I thought he seemed edified with some inward workings of Grace which he discovered in my Signoria . . .'. Martin Ffolkes, who travelled to Venice via Germany and the Tyrol in 1733, wrote to the second Duke of Richmond, praising Bavarian architecture and painting, but attacking the superstition, ignorance and superficial devotion of Catholics. There was considerable ambiguity about religious art. Andrew Mitchell admired the paintings he saw in Italy, but nevertheless noted: 'One cannot help regretting (after seeing the vast profusion of paintings in these churches, by the ablest masters), the bestowing so much industry and art upon so silly subjects as the life and actions of one enthusiast and the fabulous martyrdom of a bigot. Corporal and ridiculous representation of the Deity serve to corrupt and debauch our ideas of him . . .'[5]

The sensual and physical appeal of Catholicism to tourists, who believed the religion to be irrational, evil and spiritually corrupt, posed a difficult problem of balance for them: many specific aspects of Catholic religion were commented upon unfavourably: pilgrimages, mariolatry[6] and scourging: 'One sees such processions, such penitents, and such nonsense, as is enough to give one ye gripes.'[7] Monasticism was also attacked. Monks were widely held to be idle in all but their greed.[8] Catholic religious observance was usually treated either as credulous superstition or as empty and formal. Tourists did not agree as to the extent of Catholic observance. Most thought the Catholics very religious, by their standards. Swinton wrote of 'the superstition and bigotry of the Ligornese'. Stanhope wrote from Paris, in 1769, that 'ye common people are ye most superstitious in ye world'.[9] And yet Garrick commented, in 1751, that the post boys near Paris did not take off their hats to the roadside crucifixes as those in Picardy had done; and Wharton on the same journey 24 years later noted that the peasants and a curé ignored these crucifixes. He presented the French as essentially hedonistic, eating meat in Lent: 'in short the study of this people seems to tend to this one point, the comfort and present happiness of themselves and all around them. As for care, of what kind ever, they seem utter enemies to it.'[10]

Some, but not all, tourists encountered hostility to Protestantism. Swinton was particularly conscious of religious struggle. In Genoa, where, according to him, the population was controlled by the Jesuits, he met Count Fiesco who 'complained much of the taxes and impositions yt were laid upon the Roman Catholics in England'. The following month he noted in Livorno: 'The natives of ys place are very insolent, and bear an implacable hatred to the English upon account of their religion, (not with standing they are the main support of ys place) in which, as in other Popish countries, they are spirited up by their ignorant and furiously zealous priests; which they frequently show by placing horns of a large size upon the most remarkable of the English monuments, and defiling them with odure and all manner of filth.' Swinton was in no doubt of the threat posed by Catholicism. In Genoa he noted in his journal,

What perfect pleasure it affords the Papists abroad to see the Protestant interest in England so weaken'd by our factions and intestine divisions at home — would all true Protestants consider ys, and could they but see the true proper genius of Popery, as 'tis exercised abroad, and observe how the Papists abroad are always on the watch to lay hold of and improve every opportunity yt offers itself of reestablishing their power and authority in England, I am persuaded, they would be more heartily disposed to a union amongst themselves.

In 1739, Sacheverell Stevens found himself one Sunday in an inn at Ponte Cento. He was told that he ought to go and hear mass, 'I heard them say that I was an Englishman, and consequently no Christian'. In 1740 two Englishmen in Calais 'were very much abused by the mob there, for not paying a proper respect to the host', which was being carried in the street to the house of a sick person.[11]

The conduct of some British travellers was such as not to help matters. In May 1726, the Presbyterian clergyman, Robert Wodrow, librarian of Glasgow University, noted

Provest Drummond tells me that he had the following account from one of the gentlemen, which hapened some years ago in Spain or Italy . . . Two Scots gentlemen were travelling in one of these places where Popery is in very great bigotry; and when they were coming to a famous church, the one of them would lay a wager with the other that he would ease nature on the steps of the alter, in a publick meeting, [when] some extraordinary relict or the hosty was exhibited. The other diswaded him but he insisted on it; and said he would venture, and the other should see his excrements should be honnoured as relicts, and the effect of a miracle. He prepared himself by taking somewhat laxative, and came in on a solemn day, thrumbled in to the very altar, and there voided himself. Very soon, we may be sure, a cry arose; and he only desired liberty to tell the occasion. He had his story ready for delivering, that for many days he had been under a violent consumption; that he believed nothing would relieve him but this; that as soon as he came to the relict or hostee, by faith in it, this cure was wrought. And, upon this, the priests presently took it as a miracle, and published it to the people, and he was the happiest that could get some of the excrements! This is another instance of the stupid bigotry and superstition of the Papists.

The accuracy of this account may be doubted but it is an interesting indication of what could be believed. Stevens, when he witnessed the miracle of St Januarius — the liquefaction of the Saint's blood — in Naples found several English captains of merchantmen swearing in English 'at the folly and superstition of the populace; they being my countrymen, in a very friendly manner I cautioned them against the risk they run, if they should happen to be understood . . . all the return I had for my friendly, salutary advice, was to be damned for a Papist'; Stevens himself was the innocent cause of disorder in a Paduan church for his dog leapt upon the back of a priest celebrating mass and attempted, unsuccessfully, to seize the host.[12]
Many tourists were clearly not too bothered by religious differences or treated them as curiosities, no more serious than the difference in food or language. Waldegrave's chaplain, Thompson, told Poole in Paris 'that the people who come here, generally leave their religion at London'. It is not clear how many tourists attended the Ambassadors' Chapels; very few left any account of doing so. Edward Mellish at Angers had to make do with his copy of the Common Prayer Book, but was not sure whether other Britons there had copies. The Duchess of Ancaster organised English prayers at Spa in 1785, and William Drake had a service in his Parisian hotel. Some tourists, such as James Essex, described Catholic ceremonies and processions without any criticism and others, such as Wharton, encountered hospitality and politeness from Catholic clerics.[13] The French Revolution led to an increased tolerance of Catholicism. Having visited Loretto with Lord Bruce in 1792 Brand wrote to Wharton from Pesaro,

Ld. B. has a sort of *awe* in seeing these kind of scenes which I never dare to touch upon but leave just as it is. I think it necessary only to drop a slight remark on the credulity of the Romish Church without exposing it much. Our friend *Jack* you know in tearing off the fringe in his rage made a terrible *Rent* in the paternal coat and in these times of turbulence and *Philosophy* everything that throws contempt even on the catholic church is as well avoided.

The following year, visiting Valombrosa, he joined with the monks in denouncing the Revolution. Pratt, who deplored the number of saints days, was moved by his abhorrence of the atheism of the Revolution and the havoc it had wreaked in the Rhineland, to praise some aspects of Catholicism. Attending a Catholic service near Cleves he was very impressed by Catholic piety. He claimed that 'the influence of the catholic faith on the subordinate ranks is, almost without an exception, a sober and sincere attention to the duties it enjoins'.[14]

Catholicism was not, of course, the only alien church that tourists encountered. However, compared to the wealth of comment on the Catholic church, the other Protestant churches attracted much less attention. James Porter visited Count Zinzendorff's Moravian settlement, and it was common for tourists in Amsterdam to sample the rich variety of church services on offer. Attending services in three different churches was one way to pass an Amsterdam Sunday. Few devoted as much attention to other Protestant churches as Anglican clerics did. Brand was particularly wide ranging: 'In 1779 he visited a Dutch Moravian settlement and 1787 delivered his opinion on the Lutheran clergy of Saxony: 'They are queer fellows are *Martin's* black servants. I think they have more pedantic stupidity in their looks than either Jack's or Peter's . . . I peeped into a church where one of them was catechizing some children and I never saw anything so outré as his manner and gesture.'[15]

Brand disliked the Netherlands — 'this vile country of canals and calvinism'.[16] Other Protestant travellers found more to praise in the Netherlands and in the Empire, particularly if they had just arrived from a Catholic country. It was common to contrast the Austrian Netherlands and the United Provinces (modern-day Netherlands). Perceval did so; whilst another tourist noted at Breda, 'were not a little rejoiced at our entering a Protestant country for several reasons'. Shaw claimed that an observant traveller could not help but notice the effect of Catholicism: 'as soon as he has left the *Dutch* Government, and comes into a Popish country by a looser freer air and weakness of manners, running through all sorts of people you meet, who are strangers to the wise and strict morality of the

Dutch, and which contributes so much to their power and riches.'
John Richard contrasted the United Provinces and the Bishopric of
Münster.[17]

Many were impressed by the Calvinism of Geneva, an important
factor in leading to so many being educated there. Caroline, Lady
Holland, wrote in 1767: 'At Geneva there appears to me to be
affluence without luxury, piety without superstition, great industry
and great cleanliness.'[18] Sacheverall Stevens was impressed by the
churches in Nürnberg, which were not excessively ornamented and
seemed 'more adapted to the plain, decent, and solemn worship of
the Protestants . . . than to the glaring ridiculous fopperies of
Popery'. John Richard was struck by the devotion of the carriers
on the road from Gdansk to Berlin and wrote: 'it is usual, in this
part of the world, to join in prayer and other devotion, in the
morning, on the road, and often at other times; religion does not
seem here the effect of hypocrisy or enthusiasm, but the natural
consequence of an early endeavour in parents to instil religious
motives in their children.'[19]

Some travellers, particularly clergymen, were concerned by the
plight of Protestant minorities in Europe. One tourist noted at
Nîmes, in 1776: 'Parties of soldiers are constantly sent to appre-
hend the priests and disperse the congregations; but always with
private orders not to find them.' Robert Wharton was interested in
the fate of the Protestants in southern France; and another tourist
visited a Protestant assembly in a valley near Nîmes, in 1785,
writing: 'This scene recalled the idea of those times when the primitive converts to our religion peformed the duties in defiance of
severe persecution.' Bennett discussed the situation with the
minister of the Bordeaux Protestant congregation.[20]

Most tourists did not however mention the fate of Protestant
minorities abroad, and in most cases an awareness of religious conflict stemmed either from personal experience or from the prevalent
ideology in Britain. Many tourists were of course treated well by
Catholics, and noted this in the case of Catholic clergy. In the
1770s, it became relatively common for Protestant tourists, who
were not Jacobites, to be received by the Pope. Philip Francis was
most impressed by his reception by Clement XIV in 1772. The Pope
told him that he would have supported Henry VIII, and Francis
noted that he: 'converses freely and amicably with heretics, and has
no idea of converting them . . . Though not a convert to the
doctrines of this Church, I am a Proselite to the Pope. Whoever has

the honour of conversing with him will see, that it is possible to be a Papist without being a Roman Catholic.' Philip Yorke was presented with six other British tourists in 1778: 'he was civil and polite and thanked Lord Lucan for the favours that had been lately shown to the Roman Catholics in Ireland. The only ceremony to which we were obliged to conform was that of taking off our swords and arms and hats and making genuflexion to his holiness on entering and going out of the room'.[21] Other Catholic clerics were also hospitable. Andrew McDougall was entertained in Bologna in 1782 by the Cardinal-Governor: 'he speaks very good English and seems to be much interested for the *Welldoing* of the nation.'[22]

Other tourists stressed confessional tension, often inadvertent, but sometimes dangerous. Parker, visiting the Vatican in July 1721, noted the wall painting of the murder of Admiral Coligny, the sixteenth-century Huguenot leader. If Sacheverell Stevens is to be believed, he was nearly mobbed in Montreuil, for a lack of respect displayed whilst visiting a church during mass, and in Rome for laughing at popular belief in a miracle. He was obliged also to conceal roast meat during Lent, and commented on the lack of respect shown to Protestant graves in Rome. Lord Nuneham witnessed a mass in Rheims, in 1754, and wrote to his sister: 'the ceremony is to me a most delightful amusement, I was again at sermon . . . in the evening . . . I just entered time enough to hear half the Discourse, which ended with an account of the heresies of Great Britain, in which we poor wretches were miserably clawed and abused. Was not I in luck? I assure you I thought myself so, for I love to hear arguments as well against as for.' Nuneham's mother Lady Harcourt was concerned about whether he would seek an audience with the Pope,

> I am glad to find you have no thoughts of kissing the holy toe. Those that have done it, I can't help saying, have acted with the greatest impropriety; for his power has never been acknowledged by the English Protestants since the reformation. Sir J. Dashwood acted in character when he did it, for a great Jacobite is not far from being a very good catholic, but as there is not many, I hope, of our nobility and gentry of that way of thinking, one can't help wondering they should take pains to make the world believe that they are so.

There were attempts to convert some visitors, such as Boswell, to Catholicism, and several tourists, particularly those who travelled by public transport, engaged in discussions on religious topics. One tourist recorded an interesting converation between his servant and a Rhône boatman. Samuel Smith visited the cathedral in Arras in 1752 and noted: 'I turned aside from the altar without bowing which greatly offended an old woman and made her complaints to the priest who was wiser than to take any notice.' John Villiers toured Cherbourg in 1788 with an Englishman whom he met there and wrote: 'a farce in the church; . . . Having never before been spectators at the ceremony of mass, I was at once entertained and astonished. We waited till the host was exposed, during the service; when being pointedly called upon, by two very zealous young priests, to kneel, my companion objected to it, and we retired.'[23]

Seeking to avoid difficulties, some writers urged tourists to adopt a tolerant stance towards Catholicism and an accommodating attitude towards its practices. Philip Thicknesse suggested that Protestants visiting Catholic churches should dip their fingers into the holy water and make the necessary sign of the cross. He also defended the principles of Catholicism: 'there is nothing so very alarming in the Roman Catholic religion to one who is a good Christian, when we hear their articles of faith expounded by men of sense and candour.' John Andrews condemned the habitual criticism of Catholic religious buildings: 'Many persons are apt to vent ill-natured reflections on their inspection of such places, and to assume a kind of traditional privilege to examine the severest strictures upon all that relates to them.' James Smith was particularly blunt on this point.

There is one subject which commonly makes a conspicuous figure in all travels to Italy, the absurdities and abuses of the Catholic religion. On this head many a Protestant writer seems to think himself privileged to let loose every species of sarcasm, censure and calumny, without any qualification or distinction. He censures a pretended infallible church as if himself and his own mode or fashion of belief alone were really infallible; he condemns a persecuting religion, while he himself persecutes it more uncharitably and unrelentingly with his pen or his tongue, than any churchman ever did a heretic with fire and faggot; and he execrates those who keep no faith with unbelievers, while he betrays the confidence of friendship and hospitality, and perverts the kindness of human nature (which gets the better even of religious antipathies) into a tool of ridicule against those who have exercised it in favour of himself. These errors, by far more disgraceful and blameable than errors of faith . . . He [Smith] directs his weapons, indeed, without reserve, against hypocrisy, tyranny, and imposition of all kinds, wherever they occur, and whatever church or sect they may happen to contaminate; but he endeavours to discriminate, between individuals and bodies of men, and while he laments or exposes the impositions and iniquities of any religion in dark and compt times, he by no means considers the present professors of that religion as answerable for them. Such a mode of judgment no one church or sect could be proof against. Still farther is he from laying the faults of any member of a church at the door of its other members. Those only who defend a bad system uncharitably, are answerable for all its defects; and those who make their own mode of faith a cloak for a conduct and spirit unworthy of any religion, deserve the blame which its mistaken and ill-informed zealots incur.

Persons who have never conversed with liberal Catholics at home or abroad, and take their ideas of them from partial accounts, written on days of animosity and party spirit, may do them great injustice. Those who have travelled in Catholic countries might easily show superstition and bigotry to be by no means universal among the thinking part of the community, if they thought themselves at liberty to disclose private conversations, or remarks made by themselves upon casual momentary actions or expressions, which more unequivocally display the true sentiments, than a deliberate discourse. But a man who should publish such anecdotes, would betray his own want of principle too much to deserve credit for anything he might relate, . . . those who make due concessions on doubtful points, are most likely to be honest and steady in essential ones. The most austere and fastidious zealots are often the most insincere.

These points were not accepted by all. Robert Gray wrote: 'The volcanic nature of the country about Rome tends to confirm the opinion of those who, from the language of St. John recollect that Rome, like Sodom, shall "be utterly burnt with fire," . . . Rome should be visited with the lantern of Christianity, that we may justly discriminate between the parade of religion and the real impiety of this dark, gloomy, and superstitious city.'[24]

There are some signs that religious antagonism became less of a theme in the accounts of many tourists in the second half of the century, but it is important not to exaggerate the scale of any change that took place. Jacobitism became a curiosity rather than an issue, and religious tension in Europe, which had been so important in the first half of the century, with prominent events, such as the 'Thorn massacre' of 1724 and the emigration from Salzburg of 1731–2, reported fully in the British press, became less significant after the Seven Year War. However, many travellers continued to stress the pernicious consequences of Catholicism. This was particularly marked in the case of southern Italy and Sicily, an area where British tourism spread in this period. Tourists, such as Watkins and Young, wrote of the dire consequence of feudal and ecclesiastical tyranny. Thomas Pelham, who praised the devotion of the Portuguese, nevertheless wrote to his father, 'with what joy and gratitude must every Englishman reflect on the happiness of his own nation in comparison of any other; when he sees in a country like this . . . Religion which should be the basis of all kingdoms made their ruin'. Bennett compared Zurich and Lucerne, writing of the latter: 'Within there is less industry and less riches. For Lucerne is Catholic, and I must say without partiality, that the different spirit of the two religions is very apparent in the two towns, as well as in almost all I have seen: Protestantism has every advantage by the comparison.'[25] Baltimore drew attention to a more mundane problem in 1764: 'Triers . . . It is a melancholy old city, crowded with churches and convents; so that as soon as I laid down to rest I was immediately waked by the tolling of a dozen belfries: a circumstance as contrary to sleep as would have been a battery of cannon: the same disturbance happened at Namur and in many other Roman Catholic cities.'[26]

Apart from the small number of tourists who visited the Turkish Empire, and came away in general with a somewhat unsympathetic view of Islam, the only non-Christian religion witnessed by tourists was Judaism. There were large Jewish communities in Dutch cities, such as Amsterdam, Italian cities, such as Venice and Rome, German cities, such as Frankfurt, and in Avignon. Given the presence of a sizeable Jewish community in London, Jewish practices should not have been strange to British tourists, but it is apparent from their accounts that, for many, the Jewish ceremonies they witnessed abroad were new. Pococke saw a circumcision at Rome, 'a most terrible execution'. Sacheverell Stevens wrote in Rome,

> I saw one day an odd kind of a ceremony performed with great
> pomp and solemnity; they carried about their Synagogue, a thing
> drest like a baby, with a rich embroidered cloak upon it, and a
> silver crown on the head, to which were affixed two scepters and
> silver bells hanging down them; the people, as it passed along,
> went up and kissed the cloak, and some rubbed their eyes with it;
> being carried to a kind of pulpit, they began to undress it, when it
> appeared to be only a large roll of parchment, filled with writing
> in a large Hebrew character; they all sat their hats on, and some
> with a piece of flannel over their shoulders, . . .[27]

A certain number of British tourists were Catholics. They followed the same routes as Protestant tourists, though fewer appear
to have visited the United Provinces. For many a visit to the
continent was linked to the education of children in schools and
convents, particularly in the Austrian Netherlands and northern
France. Nicholas Blundell visited his daughters in their French
school in 1723. On his return to Britain his 'luggage was searched
and some spiritual books and pictures taken from me to be
burned'. Henry, Lord Arundell, purchased a lot of religious paintings in Italy; the first Duke of Shrewsbury was married in Rome by
the Austrian nuncio; William Constable visited Italy, where he had
relations, on several occasions; Sir John Swinburne died at Paris;
his brother Henry published important accounts of his travels in
Spain and southern Italy; and Sir Carnaby Haggerston arranged at
Loretto the saying of masses that his mother desired.[28] Some
Catholic tourists displayed overt sympathy for the Jacobite cause,
but so did Protestant tourists, such as the Duke of Beaufort in
1726. The British envoy in Naples reported of the Earl of Stafford
in 1740 that he 'shews a disposition very different from most I have
met with of the same persuasion, and is not byassed in his principles, as to government, by the usual prejudices, which the religion
he professes, carrys with it'.[29] Often educated abroad, and many
with relatives abroad, Catholic tourists tended to be less critical of
continental society. Aside from their religious devotions and their
visits to foreign relatives — Sir John Swinburne's brother and
successor Edward was a Bordeaux merchant, his sister Anne a nun,
and he visited both of them — Catholic tourists did the same on the
whole as their Protestant compatriots.

Religion, as much as language, food and currency, helped to make the continent foreign. It was one of the major changes that tourists commented on as soon as they arrived in France. Religious symbols, such as crucifixes and shrines, were everywhere; as were religious personnel; processions were encountered frequently in the streets; religious buildings dominated towns. That tourists commented so often upon religious matters did not therefore reflect an obsession, but a response to the situation they encountered. Many were very hostile to Catholicism, many simply critical. Most discussed Catholicism without mentioning the situation in Britain, though Gardenstone commented in 1786: 'The Capuchins are respectful, generally modest in their applications, and very piously thankful, returning prayers as value for our charity; and what better pennyworths have we from our own established clergy?'[30] Possibly the lack of sympathy with and understanding for Catholicism led to an inadequate appreciation of many aspects of continental society and culture. This was not a feature of tourism that contemporary critics condemned; rather they drew attention to what they regarded as the ideological and religious dangers presented by travel to Catholic countries. Given the nature of British religious education and ideology, it is surprising that tourists were not more hostile to continental Catholicism.

Notes

1. Walker to Archbishop Wake, 2 July 1722, Christ Church, Wake Mss.
2. Mellish to mother, 12 May 1731.
3. Journal of Sir William Mildmay, Chelmsford RO 15M50/1303, p. 57; Drake, 10 April, 3 May 1769, Aylesbury, D/DR/8/2/11, 13; Thomas Pelham to mother, 19 Dec. 1776, BL, Add. 33127; James Fortrey to Perceval, 20 Nov. 1725, BL, Add. 47031; Black, 'The Catholic Threat and the British Press in the 1720s and 1730s', *Journal of Religious History*, 12 (1983); Hume, 28 April 1714, BL, Add. 29477; Maclaurin, fo. 191–2, 194; Edward to Joseph Mellish, 25 May 1731; Atwell to Lady Cowper, 28 Oct. 1729, Herts., D/EP 234; Walker, pp. 41, 410; Quarendon jnl., Oxford RO, Dillon papers, xx/a/7a; Walter Stanhope to mother, 11 July 1769, Bradford; Andrews, *Letters to a Young Gentleman*, pp. 282–3; Brand to Wharton, 11 Sep. 1790; Garmston, 23 Oct. 1787, BL, Add. 30271; Montagu, I, 55; Moore, II, 252; Thomas Wagstaffe to Lord Craven, 15 Oct. 1765, Aylesbury, D/6R/6.
4. Hume, 30 March 1714, BL, Add. 29477; Pococke, 13, 19 June 1734, BL, Add. 22978; Leven, I, 354; Wharton to Thomas Lloyd, 4 April 1775; Knight, pp. 17, 28–9; Montagu, I, 49; Carleton, *History*, pp. 245–8; *Gray Correspondence*, 30 March 1739; Swinton, 11 March (os) 1731.
5. Pelham to mother, 23 Nov. 1775, 19 Dec. 1776; Francis, 25 Oct. 1772, BL, Add. 33126–7, 40759; Swinton, 1 June (os) 1731; Mitchell, BL, Add. 58316, fo. 14,

40; Aikin, I, 89–90; Chelmsford, 15M50/1302, p. 7; Mildmay jnl.; Gray, p. 347; Wharton to Brand, 27; Perceval to Charles Dering, 25 June (os) 1718, BL, Add. 47028; Shaw, pp. 60, 74.

6. Garmston, 23 Oct. 1787, BL, Add. 30271; *Tour of Holland*, p. 230.

7. Earl of March, *A Duke and his friends: The life and letters of the second Duke of Richmond* (2 vols., 19–11), I, 175–6; Swinton, 12 March (os) 1731; Stevens, pp. 200–1, 209–10.

8. Wyndham, *Chronicles*, 125; *Tour of Holland*, pp. 106, 231; Northall, p. 118; Young, BL, Stowe, 791, p. 117; anon, 28 Dec. 1726, Bedford, L30/8/1; Mildmay jnl., 15M50/1302, p. 21, Young I, 36; Stevens, p. 52.

9. Swinton, 1 May (os) 1731; Stanhope, 21 June 1769, Bradford; Mitchell, BL, Add. 58314, fo. 47; Brand to Wharton, 14 March 1786; John Russell, *Letters from a Young Painter* (1748), p. 8; Stevens, p. 293; Smith jnl., CUL Add.7621, 9 July 1752.

10. Garrick, 1751, p. 5; Wharton to mother, 26 Feb., 5 March 1775; Andrews, *Letters to a Young Gentleman*, p. 84; Orrery, p. 113; St Vincent, BL, Add. 31192, fo. 38.

11. Swinton, 5 Feb. (os), 23 Jan. (os), 18 Jan. (os) 1731; Stevens, p. 157; *Newcastle Journal*, 28 June (os) 1740.

12. R. Wodrow, *Analecta, or Materials for a History of Remarkable Providences Mostly relating to Scotch Ministers and Christians*, III (Edinburgh, 1842), 305–6; Stevens, pp. 298, 340.

13. Poole, I, 50; Mellish to mother, 19 Feb. 1731; Essex, pp. 51–4; Wharton to mother, 1 May 1775; Bennett, 10 July 1785; Townson to Drake, 12 Oct. 1768, Aylesbury, D/DR/8/3/1.

14. Brand to Wharton, 21 May 1792, 3 Aug. 1793; Pratt, pp. 101–7, 231.

15. Brand to Wharton, 27 Aug. 1779, 10 Sep. 1787, 4 June 1780.

16. Brand to Wharton, 15 Dec. 1789.

17. Anon., BL, Stowe, 790, fo. 158; Shaw, p. 72; Perceval to Chamberlayne, 9 July 1718, Perceval to Daniel Dering, 5 June (os) 1726, BL, Add. 47028, 47031; Richard, p. 202.

18. Holland, BL, Add. 51445 B, fo. 10.

19. Stevens, p. 375; Richard, p. 143.

20. Anon., BL, Add. 12130, fo. 81; Wharton to Brand, 5 May, Brand to Wharton, 27 May, 16 July 1783; anon., 20 March 1785, Bodl. Mss. Eng. Misc. F55; Bennett, 3 Oct. 1785; J. E. Smith, I, 140.

21. Francis, BL, Add. 40759, fo. 16–17, 25–7; Yorke to Keith, 15 Dec. 1778, BL, Add. 35515; *Daily Universal Register*, 17 Jan. 1785.

22. McDougall to Keith, 27 Jan. 1782, BL, Add. 35515; Shaw, p. 92; Stevens, p. 52.

23. Stevens, pp. 6, 221–2, 163, 187; Nuneham to sister, D/LE E2 No. 5; *Harcourt*, III, 82–3; anon., BL, Add. 12130, fo. 66; Smith, 22 July 1752, CUL Add. Mss. 7621; Villiers, p. 31–2; Thicknesse, 1768, p. 73.

24. Thicknesse, 1786, p. 182; Andrews, 1784, p. 243; Smith, I, xxv–xxviii; Gray, pp. 380, 425, 385, 402–3.

25. Pelham, BL, Add. 33126, fo. 178–9; Bennett, 29, 30 Aug. 1785.

26. *A Tour to the East* (1767), p. 165.

27. Pococke, BL, Add. 22978, fo. 75; Stevens, pp. 192–3; Mitchell, BL, Add. 58319, fo. 60; Aikin, I, 80, 82.

28. T. E. Gibson (ed.), *Blundell's Diary* (Liverpool, 1895), p. 196.

29. Allen to Newcastle, 22 March; 22 May 1740, PRO 93/10.

30. Gardenstone, I, 15.

10 THE ARTS

. . . notwithstanding all I had seen in Italy and came almost surfeited with Paintings, the Pictures at the Palais Royal, the Luxembourg Galleries, and in many private collections could not but charm me; yet I do not profess myself a General Admirer either of French Painting or Statues.

Henry Ellison, 1781.[1]

There was a dead Christ over a door most horridly natural the gaping wounds, the blood settling in the extremities, all quite shocking. Painters had not yet learnt to improve and soften nature.

Bennett, Basle public library, 11 August 1785.

Music

. . . à quoy aboutit pour les Anglois tous ces voyages en Italie, qu'à y prendre le gout de la peinture, des statues, et de la musique, toutes choses qui n'engagent qu'à des depenses.

St Saphorin, envoy in Vienna, 1722.[2]

The most fashionable music in eighteenth-century Britain was foreign, principally Italian opera and German orchestral music. British tourists expected to attend musical performances whilst abroad, and to enjoy the music that they heard. Music played a large part for many tourists and it is clear that many were observant and sensitive critics of what they heard.

Opera

The opera with the old style of French music than which, nothing in nature can be more disagreeable; For my part I could not help asking the Gentleman who sat next me whether they were singing an air or a Recitative it mattered not which for both are equally detestable . . . the eye is the only organ to be pleased at the French opera . . .

Wharton (Paris) to Miss Lloyd, 29 February 1775.

Alongside Italian painting the opera dominated the cultural consciousness of British tourists. There are far more references to it than to other forms of music, and, in so far as comparisons are possible, it attracted more interest, for most tourists, than architecture. Opera was a sensitive political and cultural issue in Britain. The preference of aristocratic society for this expensive Catholic foreign art form led to widespread condemnation, particularly in the second quarter of the century. Opera was held to be an unnatural art, an attitude expressed most strongly in press criticism of the popularity of Italian castrati. Aristocratic preference for opera led to attacks on the supposed abandonment of British culture in favour of a pernicious, effeminate import. Little of this criticism was voiced by aristocratic British tourists, though the second Earl Cowper's response to the opera in Rome in 1730 was that it was very disagreeable to see men 'drest in women's cloaths'. The majority of the attacks made by tourists on opera, as opposed to criticism of specific performances, came from tourists who were not members of the British elite. The Anglican clergyman Robert Gray visiting Rome criticised the idea of men dancing dressed as women. Walker, visiting Italy in 1787, launched savage attacks on opera,

> . . . of all the seminaries appropriated to the wise purpose of propagating folly, none ever equalled the Italian Opera: Here, indeed, the god Fashion displays his mental triumph! Reason is led into captivity by the ears! Virtue and public spirit take opiates from the hands of Circe! — and effeminacy, lewdness, and perverted ideas gambol in the train! Let the monarch who wishes to render himself despotic over tame and unreflecting slaves, give countenance to this school of softness and debility: . . . though the sneers of wit stigmatize the absurdity of whimpering in Recitativo — the accompanying groan uttered as echo from the mechanic Orchestra — Caesar degraded by tall plumes, an hoop-petticoat, or by uttering artificial love like a snivelling schoolboy — more ridiculous and absurd the better — it will dispose the mind to that finical trifling, that simpering vacuity of conversation — that yielding softness, and tender compliance to every proposition not understood — that makes men — like the Venetians.[3]

Such sentiments were voiced by few. Most tourists sought to

attend the opera in all the towns that they visited, and many altered their route in order to attend specific performances and hear famous singers perform. It was the singers that commanded attention rather than performances of specific operas. Opera played a large role in tourism in Italy — it was one of the principal attractions of the peninsula, the prime glory of modern, as opposed to ancient, Italy. Particular towns that attracted tourists as a result of their operas were Bologna, Reggio, Milan and Naples. Allen noted in 1729 'a good many English Gentlemen at Milan in order to take the diversion of the opera'. The Earl of Essex went to Bologna in 1733 to hear 'the finest opera that ever was heard, and a vast deal of company, there was 32 English'. Earlier that year Earl Stanhope wrote from Milan 'The opera is the chief entertainment of all the strangers here'. The following year Stanhope's brother George referred to British tourists travelling in order to hear the celebrated castrati Farinelli.[4]

In Paris, at the beginning of the century, Joseph Shaw attended 'several Operas, whose musick pleased not my ears, and is much inferior to the *English* and *Italian*, but their Dancing superior'. In 1709, Lord Charles Somerset visited the opera in Bologna: 'which appeared to me extraordinary delicate and fine; but was esteemed by them but as one of the middle rank, so much does the excellent musick of this country excell any that we can pretend to, that I am sure 'twould be the highest vanity for us in England to compare the best of any of our new Operas to that which was counted but indifferent among the Italians.' Anthony Grey attended a very expensive opera in Vienna in 1716; and the following year Lord Carpenter found in Bologna 'a very fine opera. I went to it every night: the singing and musick was incomparable'. Viscount Parker visited Reggio in July 1720 in order to attend the opera; and another tourist was very impressed that year by the chief dancer at the opera in Valenciennes. Edward Southwell attended the Paris opera in 1723; and Lord Boyle visiting it two years later complained about the noisy audience. In 1726, Lord Perceval was upset that the Lille opera was not performing: 'These amusements which perhaps I should not mind if I were settled at home, have their value with strangers being a refreshment from their fatigue of travelling.' Swinton was delighted by the opera at Genoa which he attended on several occasions. Earl Stanhope found the audience very noisy, the orchestra very good and the dancers poor at Milan, where he also attended rehearsals.

Harcourt claimed, in 1734, that opera was 'very fine in most parts of Italy'. That year Richard Pococke attended the opera at Rome (where the Pretender was a member of the audience), was disappointed by the opera at Venice, and travelled to Vicenza (as did Sir Harry Lyddal and Sir Hugh Smithson) 'to hear the opera of the famous Faranelli'. Mitchell attended the opera at Paris: 'the most frequented of all the spectacles, the connoisseurs in music cannot bear it, the lovers of dancing admire it . . . The scenes and decorations are very beautiful and the dresses of the actors very rich. — The house is large and very well contrived . . . The French are very bigotted to their own music, I have seen the musicians hissed for playing one Italian air.' Sacheverell Stevens was pleased by the Siena opera, 'the singing is extremely fine, the performance noble, and the scenery magnificent'. David Garrick thought the singing in Paris very bad in 1751.

The following year Samuel Smith visited the Paris opera, sharing a box with four British friends. They thought the performance and opera house worse than those in London. Nevertheless they made themselves 'very merry . . . a Courtisan came into our box with whom I had some conversation and invited her to our hotel'. Two years later he heard an 'Italian opera tolerably well performed' at Frankfurt. Orrery preferred British to Italian opera, and complained, in 1754, that the audience at the Florence opera was too noisy for him to hear the production. Joshua Pickersgill complained, in 1761, that the tragic opera was only changed once during the Turin carnival and he ascribed audience noise to their consequent boredom with the repetition; he was however pleased by the low price of admission. Henry Ellison and William Drake attended the opera at Rotterdam and Padua, in 1768 and 1769, respectively. William Windham was pleased by the decoration of the opera house and the quality of the dancing in Paris in the latter year. Francis attended several opera houses in Italy: at Naples he 'saw an opera at the King's theatre did not hear a sound, from the vast size of the house'; at Livorno he 'saw a miserable thing they called an opera buffa'; he was pleased by the opera house at Lucca; but at Turin 'killed the evening at a comic opera' (though he enjoyed the same production when he saw it the following evening).

Wharton was not very impressed by the Parisian opera in 1775: 'The music at the Opera when it is true French music is detestable. The Dances are very "superbes et magnifiques".' Thomas Pelham attended the opera at Florence in 1777: 'it is tolerable and by far the best I have heard in Italy for that at Naples the great school for music was abominable; the management of the theatre being in the hands of people whose only interest is to get money; and who consequently are satisfied provided that their house be full.' At Bologna he visited the elderly Farinelli. The following year Philip Yorke 'heard the Gabrielli sing in the opera of Armida' at Lucca and found that the opera at Venice was 'the only place where one sees the society of the place'. Charles Drake Garrard compared the London and Paris opera in 1779, to the advantage of the former — whilst Henry Ellison suggested that the sets of the Paris opera were better than the music. Brand was critical of the quality of the Parisian singing he heard in 1781 and 1783, though reasonably pleased with the operas he attended at Turin and Alessandria in the latter year. In 1784 he was shocked by the representation of God on stage at Bologna and went en route from Venice to Geneva with Sir James Graham and Sir James Hall 'by Mantua on purpose to hear Marchesi in the opera of the Fair . . . all fell asleep during the performance! The heat was intense and we were fatigued beyond all conception'. In 1787, Brand attended a performance of an Italian opera at Brunswick; and, in 1790, 'had an excellent opera' at Florence and went to Bologna partly to hear the famous Italian tenor David perform. The following year he heard a good German opera in Frankfurt and attacked the excessive flourishes of Italian opera singing: 'This is the degenerate taste of Italy, where methinks everything else is equally degenerate.' However, the following year he praised an oratorio he heard in Palermo and a burletta in Milan. In May 1793, Brand heard David sing at Florence and wrote: 'I think him too French in his manner of passing from the extreme of sweetness to that coarse bellowing which he calls expression and force.' Later in the year, at Milan, he 'feasted on a charming Burletta of more sense as well as humour than the general run of those great products of whim and caprice'.

Bennett and the Rolles, visiting Paris in 1785, went

. . . to the Opera of the Danaides. The music loud and noisy in the French taste, and the singers screamed past all power of simile to represent. The scenery was very good, no people understanding the jeu de theatre or tricks of the stage, so well as the French. We had in the dark scenes not above one light, and in the bright ones above twenty large chandeliers, so as to make a wonderful contrast, nor was there the least error or blunder in changing the scenes, except once when a candle pulled up too hastily, was very near to setting fire to a whole grove of trees. The stage being deeper than ours, was filled sometimes with fifty persons, a great advantage to the Chorus's and bustling parts; but not equal to the theatre at Turin, where they can (by throwing back partitions) open a large field behind the playhouse, and introduce upon occasion a body of Cavalry. Our Opera ended with a representation of Hell, in which the fifty Danaides were hauled and pulled about as if the Devils had been going to ravish them. Several of them in the violence of the French action being literally thrown flat upon their backs; and they were all at last buried in such a shower of fire, that I wonder the Playhouse was not burned to the ground. We paid somewhat more than 6 shillings each for our places, and were on the whole well entertained.

That spring James Dawkins wrote from Dresden, 'after having left Vienna, it is not an easy matter to be pleased with an opera'.

The appeal of the opera was widespread though for a variety of reasons. Lord Dalrymple was not the only tourist who chased the 'filles de l'opera'. Bennett wrote in Paris, in October 1785, of: 'Madame de Gazon, a lively little opera singer well known to many young Englishmen who have shared her favours, and as *Gazon* signifies turf, are said by the wits of Paris to have been on the *turf*. Mr L: lately a fellow commoner of Trinity, an heir to one of the first fortunes in Durham is the reigning favourite at present.' Arthur Young attended the opera; St John claimed that it did not gratify the mind; Peter Beckford praised Italian opera; Robert Gray heard the great singer Crescentini, at Bologna, and had his pocket picked; Edward Chapman visited the opera a lot in Italy in 1792; Robert Arbuthnot complained about 'the vile screaming of the French singers' at Brussels; James Robson praised the performance of a comic opera he saw in Geneva; and Richard Garmston deplored the dancers showing their legs in France and Turin, and the 'very tiresome' five-hour-long performance of a serious opera in Naples, where the female dancers displayed their behinds. He did however praise the scenery and the dancing at the Rome opera. Mrs Crewe left a fascinating account of the Parisian opera in the mid-1780s.

Gluck and Piccini are now the favourite Composers here. Their taste in Music is, I think, much improved within these ten or twelve years, and their Theatres on that account much worth going to. — I still think, however, one may trace a great deal of the abominable French stile of composition: but this is more, perhaps, in the manner of expression: than in the composition itself. The Dancing is very fine, . . .

. . . been at the great Opera last night — a more striking entertainment, take it for all in all, I never saw. It is certain our stage almost every year affords one or two singers, which connoiseurs may think compensate for all droning recitative, and insipid Dancers, Gestures and Scenery, but indeed, since Sachini and Gluck are the composers of their Opera here, and since the performers have left off the strange and disgusting French manner of singing, it is impossible not to be often delighted with the great Opera at Paris. That which I saw last night is called Dordanus; a piece tho not remarkably well written, yet full of Interest — and here I must venture to observe that, in my opinion, the Greek Model, which has had so much said for and against it, seems to be quite calculated for an opera — The Strophes and Antistrophes last night had a remarkable effect upon all the Audience — and as no opera can ever produce that sort of sympathy which regulated Tragedies, and other dramatic Representations, being more like reality, are formed to excite, what can be wished for, than to be quite overwhelmed with sounds of harmony and influenced by a system, as it were formed *'to elevate and surprise'* They have a very full Orchestra here, and a new Instrument in it which, I think, is called un Trombeau — It has a mixed sound of Drum and Trumpet and produced great effect. The scenery of this Theatre is remarkably magnificent and the Machinery is managed with infinite Dexterity. As to Dancing, that has always been in the greatest Perfection here, and one is not shocked, as with us, at an immense distance between the leaders and Figurantes. I cannot quit this subject without expressing a wish that something of this kind of opera was attempted in *our* language.

. . . Surely people would be more affected by Distress conveyed in a language they understand than by mere sounds which are all our fine operas have to bestow upon the generality of Auditors . . . Here indeed the audience, even to the lowest of them, by the shouts which they frequently send forth, and the many inconveniences which they contentedly suffer on crowded

nights, sufficiently prove how capable they are of tasting this
species of entertainment —[5]

It is clear that tourists expected a high standard of performance,
and were a critical and appreciative audience. In no sense can they
be described as provincial or as praising whatever they saw. This
stemmed from the high level of musical culture in London and the
well-developed awareness of operatic technique. In opera, as in
much else, British tourists were part of an international society in
which cultural forms were common even if cultural suppositions,
particularly in the case of religion, were very different.

Other Musical Forms

Much to my surprise, I hear little or no music; there is ten times
more in London all the year round, than in any city in Italy,
except perhaps during the Carnival. Neither do the Italians
appear to me half so fond of music as the English though I
believe they understand it better. They have no such thing as
Ballad-singing; except upon a few particular days; nor an opera
but at particular seasons, and then they never listen to it. I fancy
we import all the music from Italy, as we do all the claret from
France. These commodities are not to be found upon the spot
where they grow, but among the people who can purchase them.
I say this upon my own experience only, which I admit is not very
great.

Francis, Italy, 'Hints to Travellers', 1772.[6]

The musical experiences of British tourists were dominated by
opera, but many enjoyed other aspects of the continent's varied
musical life. Some of this can best be described as exotic. Thomas
Pelham, on his way from Madrid to Cadiz saw the gypsies who
visited the inns of southern Spain 'and entertain Travellers with
Fandangos, Sequidillas etc.'.[7] Lady Craven heard the Prince of
Wallachia's orchestra in 1786; and was much struck at St
Petersburg by the extraordinary sounds produced by horns. Most
tourists, however, heard music similar to that which they could
hear in Britain — for, as a character in a London play of 1737 complained: 'The reigning Taste's all *Italian*. Music has engrossed the
attention of the whole people: The Duchess and her woman, the
Duke and his postilion, are equally infected — The contagion first
took root in the shallow noddles of such of our itinerant coxcombs

as were incapable of more virtuous impressions.'[8] It was certainly true that some tourists were effective in spreading interest in foreign music. John, Earl of Orrery, wrote from Cork in 1737,

> . . . we have a Bishop, who, as he has travelled beyond the Alps, has brought home with him, to the amazement of our mercantile fraternity, the arts and sciences that are the ornament of Italy and the admiration of the European world. He eats, drinks and sleeps in taste. He has pictures by Monte Carlo, Morat, music by Corelli, castles in the air by Vitruvius; and on high-days and holidays we have the honour of catching cold at a Venetian door . . . Under the reign of Dr. Clayton we sing catches, read *Pastor Fido*, and talk of love.[9]

As a Tory, Orrery was sceptical about the value of such foreign cultural importations. Such scepticism was shared by others. Sarah Marlborough was opposed to her younger grandsons being taught architecture and music 'which are all things proper for people that have time upon their hands and like passing it in idleness rather than in what will be profitable'.[10] Despite these criticisms tourists attended concerts abroad and took music lessons. Walker, whose critical comments upon opera have already been quoted, heard a concert in the Louvre in November 1787, and his response was very positive: 'Am just returned in great rapture I fear the French outdo us in music!' Paris was a major centre of music and many tourists attended concerts there. Perceval and his wife were frequent attenders in 1725–6, and enjoyed the concerts. They also hired a music master, presumably for their sons. Mitchell was very impressed by the Concert Spirituel, though Mrs Crewe was less impressed by the sacred music she heard,

> I went to the Kings Chapel to hear a high mass yesterday morning — The music was fine, but the drums and fiddles in my opinion spoiled the effect which good choirs ought to have — It was indeed far from 'Dissolving the Soul in Ecstacies' or bringing 'all Heaven before our Eyes'. However it was harmony for all that, and good in its Gothic way.[11]

Italy, 'this country of Musick' as Francis Head described it in 1724, offered many opportunities for the music lover. Swinton, who attended a concert in Pisa, was delighted by the musical lovers he heard in Livorno. In 1775 Wharton heard in Rome some apprentice barbers give a very good vocal serenade for a few women. He also attended some small private concerts where Boccherini quintets were played. Nine years later Brand complained from the same city 'there is nothing to be heard but now and then an Oratorio with a wretched band and worse voices', but he added three weeks later: 'The holy week is at last over that season of wonder and enjoyment for all that are not blind or deaf. The first verse of the Miserere frightened me it so far exceeded all ideas I had formed of it.' Seven years later he rushed to Venice, travelling, against his custom, by night, to hear an oratorio by Anfossi at Venice. He was delighted with the performance: 'I never expect so long as I live to hear such music and such execution. The accompanied recitatives especially were beyond all conception expressive. I assure you such a Jonas as *Bianca Sacchetti* might turn more to repentance than the preaching of ten metropolitans . . .' Four years earlier James Robson had been pleased by the oratorio he heard in Venice.[12]

Music was not of course confined to Paris and Italy. Harry Digby attended a concert at Vienna in 1751 'of which I shall say nothing as in musick I have no opinion'. Brand attended concerts and purchased music in the same city in 1787.[13] He attended concerts at Geneva in 1780 and was amazed by a solo on the doublebass which he heard at an excellent concert at The Hague in 1790. In his letters Brand also described the musical life of the Germans and a concert he heard in Salzburg.

Not all music was orchestral. Richard Garmston's supper at Mâcon was accompanied by a band, and many tourists left accounts of the rich and varied musical life of the continent. Most enjoyed the music that they heard, though, like so many of the tourist pastimes, it was confined largely to the major cities.[14]

Painting

I am in high spirits at the thoughts of seeing Italy in so short a time, ever since I can remember I have been wishing to go into a country, where my fondness for painting and antiquities will be so indulged, I expect every day a letter from Mr. Knapton with a catalogue of all the finest galleries and his remarks on them, for I intend not only to improve my taste, but my judgement, by the fine originals I expect to see there, I have attempted all sorts of painting since I left England.

Lord Nuneham to his sister, 1755.[15]

I went last week with my Spanish master to see the pictures in the palace which are exceedingly fine and very valuable from having the works of some masters who are almost unknown in any other collection; I intend visiting them often not only with a view of learning their different perfections or faults, but of a talking Spanish on subjects different from what I should meet with at home.

Thomas Pelham, Madrid, 1776.[16]

Italian paintings were valued greatly in Britain, where they were regarded as the best example of their art. For many tourists seeing these paintings was a major motive for their trip to Italy. Whereas French cooking and Italian opera could be sampled in London, it was necessary to visit Italy in order to appreciate, to any degree, Italian art and architecture. This was despite the increasing number of Italian paintings that were imported into Britain in the eighteenth century. Many tourists purchased paintings and they were willing to buy paintings on most topics, including religious ones. Furthermore tourists were willing to commission paintings by Italian artists, such as Batoni, and by British artists resident abroad. Many British artists travelled in Europe. Most, such as William Kent, Alexander Cozens, Gavin Hamilton, Jonathan Skelton, Allan Ramsay, Joshua Reynolds, Richard Wilson, Wright of Derby, Francis Towne, Thomas Jones and Joseph Wilton visited Italy but some travelled further afield. Willey Beverley accompanied Sir Richard Worsley to Constantinople in 1785. Lady Craven noted that Worsley 'had a person with him to take views'.[17] British tourists employed painters for a variety of reasons. Many wanted their portraits painted, often in elevating poses in classical surroundings. These portraits were usually painted in Italy, often in Rome, by artists such as Batoni, David, Nazzari, Rosalba, Dupra, Masucci, Mengs and Trevinsani.[18] The British were in no way unique in this: at Vienna there is a splendid portrait of the future Joseph II and his brother Leopold, painted whilst on their Grand Tour. Many of the portraits were extremely good, and William Bentinck wrote to his mother, 'I have also sent you my picture done by Rosalba and which will always be worth something for the painting'.[19] Others commissioned paintings of places that they had seen. The painter George Robertson accompanied the Duke of Dorset and William Beckford and painted various scenes. Some commissioned reproductions of paintings that they liked. Sir Richard Hoare had copies made of many of the Raphael frescoes in the Vatican in 1793, and Brand commissioned a copy of a painting in Florence.[20]

The purchase of paintings was concentrated in Italy. Some, such as Lord Camelford in 1788, admired but did not buy,[21] but others such as the Second Marquis of Rockingham, Henry Arundell and Henry Blundell bought many. Charles Townley purchased copies of three paintings, including a Titian, at Florence in August 1786; James Robson bought some old drawings and some Piranesi prints in Rome in 1787; and the third Duke of Beaufort, visiting Italy in the late 1720s, purchased paintings by Raphael, Leonardo, Veronese, Palma Vecchio, Caravaggio, Domenichino, Rosa and Reni, many of whose works were also acquired by British tourists. Parker in Padua in September 1720 'bought some pictures amongst which there is a very fine deluge of Guilo Romano which everybody here thinks cheap at the price I gave for it viz: a hundred pistoles'.[22] Agents, often ciceroni (guides), such as Parker and Byres in Rome and McSwinny in Venice, assisted in arranging purchases. Lady Pomfret wrote in Rome, 1741: 'Mr. Parker is a Gentleman who goes about with the English to show them what is most remarkable assisting them also in buying what picture paintings and other curiosities that they fancy most.'[23]

Some of the paintings purchased, as with some of the medals and some of the supposedly antique statues, were fakes. They were manufactured in considerable quantities in Italy and purchased often by gullible tourists misled by dishonest guides. Northall wrote, in 1753, of young British aristocrats deceived in Rome by antiquarian guides into purchasing copies, rather than originals, of works by Raphael, Titian and Michelangelo. In his 'Hints to a Traveller', Francis warned: 'We English, before we see Italy, are apt to think that we can purchase the best works of the great masters, and that many of them have actually been brought away within these few years. There cannot be a grosser mistake. The Italians are too cunning to suffer the market to be removed out of Italy. As for parting with a valuable antique statue, they would much sooner give up their seven sacraments. Pope could make his people Protestants much more easily, than persuade them to let the

Apollo go out of Rome . . . The best pieces we have in England are I believe only good copies.'[24] Francis's suggestion was linked to a feeling that many tourists did not truly appreciate art, and that their pretensions to culture were superficial and dangerous, dangerous in that it left them open to the possibility of being tricked into purchasing fakes and that it led them to neglect British in favour of foreign culture. Thus, the terms cognoscenti and connoisseur became terms of abuse. Francis wrote: 'To a man really curious in the polite arts, Rome alone must be an inexhaustible fund of entertainment; but what can be more disgustful, than to see our young people give themselves the airs of cognoscenti.' Cultural pretentiousness was mocked in the *Connoisseur*, a London weekly of 1754–6, and by Hogarth.[25] This criticism must be set alongside the often exaggerated praise of the cultural sensitivity of British tourists.

Art interest and purchases were not confined to Italy. Robert Trevor, who purchased prints and books in Paris in 1728, had more ambitious plans on a trip to Lorraine that August,

> In passing through Nancy . . . I took some pains to hunt after Callot's engravings, thinking it probable I might find some very fair originals of that master in a city, where he generally lived . . . but I found but few and they happening to be in the hands of persons, that knew the value of their countrymens pieces, were very dear. Among others there were his three great sieges complete, but as they were pasted upon cloth, and framed, they were too great an embarras for a traveller to carry about with him in posting; but it was a great mortification to me to leave them.

Bennett and the Rolles, visiting Berne in 1785, 'called on Aberli the Painter of the coloured views of Swisserland, . . . and all of us laid out some money with him'.[26] Outside Italy, British tourists were most interested in the art of the Austrian Netherlands, where the themes of the paintings, principally religious, were similar. The paintings of Rubens, in particular those in Antwerp Cathedral, were praised greatly. Peckham wrote of Rubens' descent from the cross, 'the varied expressions of the same passions in the different countenances of the weeping matrons surpass our imagination'. John Aikin wrote of the Rubens in the Cathedral, 'It is impossible to conceive painting to go beyond this; but the solemnity of the effect is somewhat diminished by being shown the portraits of Ruben's three wives among the figures . . . The Madonna of Rubens must excite emotions in the most insensible'. Brand was similarly struck in 1779: 'The instant I got into the Cathedral of Antwerp I lost my breath and stood still with wonder. The superb altars, the colossal statues the pictures, the solemnity of the people and all together deprived me of all my faculties; I gaped and stared . . . The descent of the Cross in the Cathedral by Rubens and the Christ in the Church of the Beguinage by Vandyke and either of them worth a journey from England.'

Tourists also praised paintings in other towns, such as Bruges, Brussels and Ghent. Walker liked the paintings in the Cathedral at Ghent, including Rubens' St Sebastian: 'the anxiety of an old woman looking on, exhibit an expression such as I never saw before on canvas!'[27] Walker however also drew attention to a major problem in appreciating the art of this region: the prominence of Catholic themes. He wrote of the church of St Pierre in Ghent: 'The tapistry and Paintings in the Church, denoting the triumph of Popery over Luther and Calvin makes one forget the absurdity of the subject in the excellence of the pieces.' Perceval enjoyed visiting the churches of the Austrian Netherlands: 'where the paintings sculpture, and other ornaments surpass imagination; but the bigotry of the people is so great that what we admire we cannot like.' Brand, as an Anglican clergyman, was forced to defend his views on Antwerp paintings,

. . . the letter in which you abuse my affection for the Antwerp churches: but you cannot think me so absurd as to have the least affection for the Roman Catholic religion. There is surely a wide difference between the admiration of fine painting, scuplture and music and the adoration of a full dressed Virgin, be she wax, Ivory or even Ebony (for such I have seen) or the silver lillies of St. John or golden rule and compasses of St. Joseph. Though we pitied the people who could submit to the absurdities we saw every day and had a hearty contempt for the fat, bloated, heavy-eyed monks and shuddered at passing a confessing chair yet we had the greatest pleasure imaginable in viewing the ecstasies of St. Augustine, St. Francis and St. Theresa. And I assure you that I lament very much the necessity under which the reformers were under of banishing pictures from their churches.[28]

Few French paintings outside Paris were mentioned, though Pourbus' Death of St George in Dunkirk was praised in 1720, and James Hume in 1714 attacked the representation of God in a painting at Nantes.[29] In Paris there were many paintings to be seen: a large number were in churches, but it was possible for well-dressed tourists, often without any letter of introduction, to gain access to private houses where paintings could be viewed. The Luxembourg palace was open to visitors twice weekly. Andrews wrote in the early 1780s: 'no people display more willingness to exhibit their stores of this kind than the French, especially to foreigners. They consider themselves as bound in a particular manner to satisfy the curiosity of such as visit France — looking upon these exhibitions of their artists, as proofs of the superior ingenuity of the natives, they are desirous you should carry away with you an ocular conviction how much they excel all other people.'[30] In 1726 Perceval was very impressed by Le Brun's Mary Magdalen in the Carmelite church. Two years later Robert Trevor was impressed by the Duke of Orleans' collection at the Palais Royal, 'a cabinet of the finest pictures I ever yet saw'. Garrick showed less enthusiasm in 1751: 'No Hotel has so good a collection of pictures as there is at Chiswick. In general rubbish to 'em.' William Drake was impressed by Guido's Salutation and Le Brun's Magdalen in 1768, and also praised Charles Vanloo's St Borromeo taking the sacrament to the plague sufferers, which he saw at Notre Dame: 'the zeal and sympathy of the good man, the extreme sickliness of the patient, who is brought out in her bed to receive the sacrament, the languishing of several other persons visited by this terrible calamity, are most naturally and inimitably expressed.' Wharton was told, in 1775, to look out for 'the Vision of Ezechiel in the Palais Royal Collection, (which is said to be the second in Europe,)' and he commented on the prevalence of religious themes. Six years later Brand attacked 'the studied attitudes' of French paintings.[31]

The two principal German galleries that attracted tourists were both at Catholic courts: Düsseldorf and Dresden. In the first half of the century Düsseldorf was the most visited, as a trip to Düsseldorf, Cologne and Aachen was a convenient appendage to a tour in the Low Countries. Later in the century Dresden became more important. The Wittelsbachs largely abandoned their palace at Düsseldorf, whilst Augustus III of Saxony (1733–63) created a superb collection at Dresden, largely by purchasing paintings from

Italians such as the Duke of Modena. Lord Charles Somerset found in Düsseldorf, in 1708, 'three or four large chambers filled with the most curious collection of original pictures by the hands of the best and most famous masters in all parts of Europe'.[32] Sir James Hall visited Dresden in 1783,

> I stopt above a week at Dresden to see the pictures and went no less than eight times to the cabinet where I found full employment for my time — there is a very fine collection of the best masters of both schools — I made it my business to study the Italians — I believe I have picked up some knowledge — but what I value more I have learnt a good deal of diffidence in judging of pictures as I saw many that were certainly very fine that I should have thought nothing of if I had seen them in another place.

Brand wrote four years later,

> The Gallery of Pictures you know is one of the first in Europe. The great Raphael of the Virgin, St. Sixtus and St. Barbe, the famous *Notte* of Corregio and other spoils of the Modena collection are very fine. I spent four mornings there deliciously. Of the Flemish school too there are some very fine things. You have no doubt heard of the famous Rembrant of the Rape of Ganymede. The poor boys fright is wonderfully expressed in his *face* but that was not enough for a Dutch painter! But let us not be too partial. There is a young Bacchus by Guido as indelicate as this Ganymede.[33]

Few tourists visited Spain but Thomas Pelham benefited in his artistic appreciation from his meeting with Mengs, with whom he went to see the paintings in the royal palace at Madrid.[34] Just as most tourists ignored German Renaissance paintings so the Dutch school found far less favour than Italianate paintings. Visiting The Hague in 1779, Brand regretted the small number of Italian masters, and his response to 'the burlesque Flemish-painting' he described there was ambiguous.[35]

Those who travelled to the United Provinces tended to visit the major accessible collections, such as that of the Prince of Orange at The Hague. Henry Ellison found that gaining access to private collections in Rotterdam was not free from difficulty. He wrote of one owner: 'the Gentleman being strongly prejudiced in favour of a bad Painter, to recommend ourselves to him we were obliged to commend at the expense of truth by which means we ingratiated ourselves with him so much, that he gave us an invitation to make a second visit to his Pictures etc., a favour he does not often grant.' Hugh Dunthorne has drawn attention to greater interest in Dutch art than in the seventeenth century, but a comparison of tourist comments with those made in Italy and the Austrian Netherlands suggests that the appeal of Dutch art was not as great for most tourists.

Italy was therefore the centre of interest for those interested in paintings. As in the Austrian Netherlands difficulties were created for some by the prevalence of religious themes, though many of those who complained were Anglican clergymen. Catholic art was believed by many to represent a threat. Even Samuel Davies, an American non-conformist clergyman touring Britain on a fund-raising mission, was affected. At the University of Glasgow he saw: 'a collection of pictures lately imported from France. One was the picture of the dead body of Christ taken off the Cross and carrying [sic] to the Sepulchre. The prints of the nails in his hands and feet, the stab of the spear in his side, the effusion of the blood, etc. were so lively that they unavoidably excited a sort of popish devotion in me.'[36]

Swinton attacked the obscene pictures and statues that he found in Italian churches. Sacheverell Stevens's response to the statue of God at the altar of Florence cathedral was a mixed one: 'prodigiously fine; the statue of the first, on reflection somewhat shocks a Protestant, to see the infinite, visible, and ineffable Deity, represented in stone! Whether this be consistent with Christianity, of which the members of the Romish Church pretend to be the only true professors, might safely enough be left to the determination even of the most bigotted papist, if he would only give himself time to reflect a little seriously, what an offence and stumbling-block these kind of representations are, and eternally will be, to Jews and Mahometans.' Gray attacked the Catholic priesthood for teaching 'their wealthy followers to display their idle vanity in costly presepios or representations of the circumstances of Christ's nativity'. Most tourists did not share these views; few were Anglican divines whilst those who had converted to Islam or Judahism were eccentrics.[37]

Italian art was accessible. Much of it was in religious establishments which were, bar a few nunneries, open, whilst access was freely given to ducal collections, such as the Uffizi, or private collections such as those in the palaces of Genoa and Venice. Walker noted in 1787: 'we found the palaces of the noble Venetians very open to our curiosity, and their pride no way hurt by the presents their domestics exacted from us.'[38]

Judging from their correspondence and journals, many tourists were discerning critics. Parker's comments on Raphael and his criticism of Michelangelo's Last Judgement were relatively intelligent. Mitchell, revisiting Bologna in 1734, criticised the lighting and hanging of the paintings (as Thomas Pelham was to do in Madrid), and noted that he was no longer so impressed by paintings that he had once admired. Mitchell was unable to decide whether he had been 'satiated by the vast variety of paintings in these churches and palaces of Rome, or the taste refined by frequent looking upon the works of the best masters'. Lord Nuneham, who had executed a landscape in crayon in the Rhineland, went repeatedly to the Uffizi in 1756. Caroline, Lady Holland, praised Corregio's Marriage of St Catherine at Parma, whilst William Drake wrote from Bologna in 1769: 'We have found here good amusement in the picture-way, having seen the principal works of the great masters of the Lombard school.' Francis observed in Rome three years later: 'As for Pictures and Statues, I have really seen so many that I remember nothing. In a very large mixed company, one seldom contracts a lasting acquaintance.' Curzon noted of Loretto: 'the *profane parts* in the Apothecary's shop are most admirably, and most lewdly painted by Raphael.' Thomas Pelham was impressed by the paintings in Genoa and Parma and benefited from Mengs's advice in touring Rome. Philip Yorke spent over a week examining the paintings at Bologna; and Andrew McDougall over ten days in Florence in 1783: 'I by no means pretend to be a *connoisseur*, either in painting or sculpture, but at the same time, they give me great pleasure; I believe some of my countrymen pretend to receive a great deal more pleasure, than what is real, and wish to have the name of *connoisseurs*, by praising the noted pictures, but before they begin, they have the good sense, (in general) to enquire the name of the painter.' Five years later James Robson was impressed by the paintings in Mantua, but condemned the hanging of Romano's Battle of the Giants in the ducal palace: 'which though esteemed an inestimable composition amongst the connoisseurs, I think looses all its grandeur and majesty in so small a room, by bringing such monstrous figures of human form, down to a level with the eye, nay even to the floor you walk upon. For want of height and distance they loose much of their dignity of character, and so does the scenery that accompanys them.' Lady Craven regretted that she could not spend three months in Genoa examining the paintings in the palaces at her leisure and copying a few of them.

Neglecting the appeals of antiquity and pleasure, James Smith, President of the Linnaean Society, wrote: 'The fine arts must always make a principal feature in an Italian tour; indeed that country itself would hardly be amusing, nor would an account of it be interesting, to those who are quite devoid of taste and curiosity on this subject.'

Many tourists, including Robert Gray and Philip Francis, compared the Medici Venus and Titian's Venus in the Uffizi. Walker left an interesting account of his response to Raphael's St Cecilia, which hung in Bologna:

> The curtain drawing, I must confess I expected to have fell on my knees with admiration! — but I find it is an education of some time and application to learn to see — I stood a quarter of an hour between doubt of my own, or other peoples tastes. My own is certainly, defective; for I must honestly confess, at the end of the said quarter of an hour, I found my refractory opinion as obstinate as at first. Can that have no excellence which all the world admires, and has admired for this 250 years?
>
> For the future I shall be doubtful what I say of pictures when in *this* I can find nothing but a vulgar Wench looking as if she was selling the organ she holds in her hand, to three insipid bystanders, and was abusing them for not bidding her enough for it. St. Peter looks as if he was considering whether the instrument was worth the money.
>
> St. John, like an ignorant boy, who liked a tune, but knew nothing about the value of an organ. St. Mary and her companion seeming to wait for another tune before they quitted the sale, etc.

Brand's responses varied. In 1790 he wrote from Pisa,

> From Milan we went by Placentia Parma Modena and Bologna to Florence. I suppose that in those days of rapture when I first

set foot on Italian ground I rav'd much about Corregio and
Carucci and Guide and Guerino. If I am more moderate now it is
not that I have felt less pleasure in seeing these wonderful works
a second time but from the conviction that words can very ill
express the impressions which they make and that there are few
things more ridiculous than an affected description of a picture.

[The following year he added,]

The Italian painters the Italian sculptures the Italian poets are
all too many idolaters of affectation. With such divine models
before their eyes they only worship extravagance and the
Raphaels and Michaelangelos serve only to lead them still further
from nature.[39]

Clearly responses to painting, as to other arts, varied. If only for
this reason the excessively stereotyped nature of the debate on the
virtues of travel and on the nature of Britain's cultural relationship
with the continent must be questioned. Whatever the supposed
cultural threat, money and patronage were clearly critical issues.
'There is no being a virtuoso, or gratifying that itch in building,
medals, statuary, or painting, upon the foot of a moderate estate',
warned the Bishop of Chichester in 1739.[40] Aside from the cost to
the individual patron there was also the cost to the community.
This was particularly an issue in the cases of paintings and of
opera, for most famous opera singers were foreigners and they
were held to take their large payments abroad. Architecture was a
less contentious issue, largely because the money was spent on
buildings in Britain, and because the leading architects of the
century patronised by the British elite were British.

Architecture and Other Arts

All the fine houses are shacked in the English manner, and not
that odious one of Paris, where using no putty, they fit their
panes with paper and paste, which with the soil of flies and dust
of the streets takes off the beauty of their built palaces, and has
indeed a beggarly look.

Perceval, Ghent, 1726.[41]

Many of our modern houses have been built from Italian models,
without the least reference or conformity to the change of

country. On account of heat in Italy, it is necessary to have but few windows. This must ever make a building not only appear heavy, but of course produce a contrary effect to that which ought to be sought for in a northern clime; besides, windows in England are of themselves a great ornament, where they are always glazed, and not unfrequently with the finest plate glass.

Joseph Cradock.[42]

Architectural ability was one of the attributes of gentility in eighteenth-century Britain, and many members of the elite were knowledgeable enough to play a role in the construction or alteration of stately houses. Much of British architecture, in the design both of houses and of their interiors, was heavily influenced by continental models, particularly those of Palladio. Tourists paid great attention to Palladian buildings and, particularly in the first half of the century, a visit to Vicenza was considered an essential part of the Italian section of the Grand Tour. This was not only true for the British. The Swedish tourist Tessin was advised to go to Vicenza in 1716 because of the Palladian buildings.[43] Some tourists discussed architecture with foreign architects. Sir Carnaby Haggerston planned, in 1718, to discuss his seat and gardens at Haggerston and possible changes to them with Italian architects. In 1734, Andrew Mitchell described a lazaretto being built in Ancona, noting, 'the architect Antonio Vanitelli is a Civil sensible man, he shewed me the plan and elevation of it'. The Earl-Bishop of Derry planned the rebuilding of Ickworth whilst in Italy.[44] Many clearly appreciated the buildings that they saw on the continent. Brand was very impressed by the new church of St Geneviève in Paris: 'It is very fine — the Corinthian order shines in all its purity and just proportions — There are no buildings near it. It is seen to great advantage and does infinite honour to the taste of the architect.'[45] *Mist's Weekly Journal* condemned the uncritical nature of British tourists in Paris: 'they commonly take a turn to Versailles, Marli etc. and gaze at the fine Buildings and Statues of these places, with the same wonder that a country fellow does at some strange sight, without considering, or acquiring the least knowledge into, the design of the architect, or skill of the statuary.'[46] Far from being uncritical many tourists comdemned the buildings that they saw. William Young wrote of Gallipoli in southern Italy: 'The churches in the town are of a bad taste of architecture, as are all public buildings in this part of Italy, heavy charged with profusion of minute work; in short the very reverse of that simplicity which characterized the Greek orders in their ancient pure taste.' Peter Wauchop, visiting Lille, claimed that 'the nasty small windows disfigure all the houses'. Bennett thought that French architecture was too heavy, that their cathedrals and monastries were worse than their British counterparts. He wrote, '. . . the cathedrals of Viviers, Valence, Avignon, Limoges, Cahors, Vienne, Toulouse, and even Lyons itself, would hardly be esteemed an ornament in any of our principal market towns.' He objected to the addition of classical parts to Gothic cathedrals, as in Orléans, and to 'those clumsy awkward domes, with which so many of the French buildings . . . are spoiled'. Many other tourists objected to the characteristic French roofs; one wrote of 'that most deforming protuberance of summit with which the northern parts of France abound'.[47]

Italian buildings were also criticised. Walker thought Milan 'not a beautiful city; it is built of brick, and plastered smooth over like most towns in Italy'. Robson thought Verona cathedral 'a heavy lumpish building' and wrote of its Paduan counterpart, 'the cathedral is but a heavy dull building much in want of cleanliness and repair'. Brand wrote of Turin: 'if the houses in general are well built, in the churches and palaces there is a wonderful deficiency of good taste. The materials the marbles especially are costly and rich but everything is cut into angles and broken curves sometimes concave sometimes convex but always deviating from elegance and simplicity.'[48]

Tastes varied, but, in general, there was a preference for the classical over the Gothic that led most tourists to ignore or dislike the architecture of Germany, most of provincial France, and some of northern Italy. Old towns were disliked; the preference was for wide, straight streets, as in Turin or the newer sections of Marseilles. Narrow, twisting streets were associated with dirt, disease and poverty. Wharton disliked Mâcon, and Maclaurin disliked Sens for that reason. Charles Drake Garrard wrote of Toulouse and Montauban, in 1779, 'they are both of ancient structure and consequently have nothing strikingly beautiful'. Arthur Young shared these prejudices, which were understandable given eighteenth-century problems with cleanliness and fire. Of Abbeville he wrote: 'it is old and disagreeably built; many of the houses of wood, with a greater air of antiquity than I remember to have seen, their brethren in England have been long ago demolished.' In the

Dordogne, he noted: 'The view of Brive, from the hill, is so fine, that it gives the expectation of a beautiful little town, and the gaiety of the environs encourages the idea; but, on entering, such a contrast is found as disgusts completely. Close, ill built, crooked, dirty, stinking streets exclude the sun, and almost the air, from every habitation, except a few tolerable ones on the promenade.' Cahors was 'bad; the streets neither wide nor straight . . . Lodeve, a dirty, ugly, ill built town, with crooked close streets'.[49] Pamiers and Poitiers were also condemned.

Many of the buildings that tourists admired were relatively modern — St Paul's in London, the Invalides in Paris, palaces such as Versailles and the Belvederes. The response to older buildings was unfavourable generally, unless they dated from classical times. The strong influence of a classical education and of a public ideology that drew strongly on classical images and themes can be seen in the accounts of many tourists. It played an important role in every Italian trip and represented a significant aspect of the appeal of Italy, counteracting the pernicious consequences of Italy being the seat of catholicism.

Outside Italy there were few classical remains that were visited regularly other than those in the south of France: Nîmes and the Pont du Gard. St John visited a Roman camp in eastern France, whilst the sixth Earl of Salisbury visited Roman sites near Besançon and in Savoy. At Aix-les-Bains he found the remains of a Roman temple dedicated to Diana, and at Avanche 'a very high marble pillar, which seems to me to have belonged to a gate of some fine temple'. James Hume was very impressed by the statues on classical themes in the garden at Versailles, 'to carry a young scholar thither would be an excellent introduction to Ovid's Metamorphoses'. Thomas Pelham was keen to see the Roman remains of Andalusia. Having discussed with Lord Grantham the route he should take in Spain, he wrote: 'we have agreed that I shall see the south of Spain, which is not only a very interesting tour from it's having been the scene of so many transactions in the Roman History and consequently retaining many curious antiquities but likewise as being the most fruitful and commercial part of modern Spain.'[50]

The Italian classical remains and sites that most tourists saw were Roman. The large number of sites near Naples was the furthest south that most went. It was only a small number of tourists, and those mostly later in the century, that visited the Greek sites in Sicily, and only a small number (one of whom was Sir William

Young) visited those in Apulia and Calabria. Giving his reasons why he liked travelling in Italy, Lord Carpenter wrote,

> above all the ancient inscriptions: ruins: and antiquities: which are very curious and instructive to one that takes delight in such things: Most of the places have been famous for some notable action: they are easily found out by one that travels for his instruction: and will take a little pains and be curious: . . . I took a great deal of pleasure in comparing the descriptions that are given us by the ancient authors of particular places as rivers mountains etc. with what they are at present. I found that time had made such vast alterations in landscapes that it was not easy to know them by the descriptions.

Francis Head noted of Italy, 'one meets almost everywhere with some marks of the old Roman greatness'. Edward Southwell junior visited Rome in 1726:

> I have spent 3 months with great pleasure and some profit among the ancient and modern curiosities of this famous city, which have cost me daily reading and application and filled 140 pages in my journal, and I must own these heaps of magnificent ruins, and the view of so many places not only renowned for the actions and fate of so many heroes, but by the pens of so famous writers do fill the mind with great ideas of the Roman grandure as also with various reflections upon the vicissitudes of all human things.
>
> By the remains of above 40 temples one sees how devout and magnificent the Romans were in their religion, but their palaces, circus's amphitheaters and baths, testify that they were no less luxurious in their diversions. Their aquaducts which convey water 10, 17, 22, 35, and 45 miles, and their paved causeways which reached 30, 40 and even 180 miles to Capua, and some of which were the expence of one private man, are noble monuments of a publick spirit and disinterested regard to the good of ones country, and the triumphal-arches pillars and statues which were erected to the Patriots at home and the avengers abroad, are instances of the gratitude and honour the Romans paid those benefactors by whose means they reaped the advantages of war and the blessings of peace. There is a sensible pleasure in viewing the place where Marius Curtius leaped into

the Gulph, and devoted himself to the safety of his country.

He was also moved by visiting other similar sites, such as that of
Pompey's statue. Andrew Mitchell verified Virgil's description of
the falls of Terni in 1734, but found it 'difficult to trace the situation of Marseille as described by Caesar'. Sacheverell Stevens
described Virgil's tomb near Naples and the Sybil's grotto.
Frederick Calvert, the sixth Lord Baltimore, matched his predeces-
sor's Baltic cruise by a tour to Greece, Constantinople and the
Balkans and wrote, 'what I saw in my travels recalled strongly to
my rememberance the classical erudition I was so happy as to
receive at *Eton College*'. William Drake and James Robson had
very differing responses to Mantua, Virgil's birthplace. The first
noted in 1769 that it 'afforded us no small pleasure, as one
naturally interests oneself in the most minute things that regard
famous persons'. The second was less encouraged by his visit to
classic ground in 1787: 'but now alas! not a stone nor monument to
stamp it sterling; a mere hovel adjoining to a cottage. How
frequently the traveller and antiquarian are disappointed in their
pursuits and expectations. We expected to feel as it were an
electrical shock on approaching the sacred turf once pressed by the
favourite poet of antiquity'. Francis wrote a Latin epigram on an
antique stone lion he saw in Florence. Wraxall found that the
Neapolitan sites still resembled closely the descriptions in Pliny,
Strabo and Virgil and wrote of 'the celebrity of the surrounding
country in Roman fable and history. All these circumstances con-
spire to charm the mind and warm the imagination'. Sir James Hall
was delighted by Agrigentum, Richard Garmston and Lord
Belgrave viewed Virgilian sights; and Thomas Watkins referred
continually to the classics in his description of Sicilian towns such
as Syracuse. His party 'arrived at the banks of the Rubicon, with
Lucan in our hands'. Sir Richard Hoare repeated Horace's journey
from Rome to Taranto; and Brand was very impressed by the
classical sites in Sicily.[51]

Given this strong interest in the classics, the appeal of Italy and
of the remains of ancient buildings is not surprising. Classical
sculptures were also of great interest — famous examples were
described frequently, and many sculptures, including not a few
fakes, were purchased. William Weddell, a leading member of the
Society of Dilettanti, 'a club for which the nominal qualification is
having been in Italy, and the real one, being drunk',[52] sent 19 cases

of classical statuary back to Britain. There was also an interest in ancient coins many of which were purchased in Italy.

Acquiring knowledge of the arts was a reason advanced to justify tourism.[53] Judging from surviving letters and journals many tourists were not uncritical purchasers and praisers of continental art. The length of foreign tours, the guidance available, both from experienced Bearleaders, such as Coxe, Brand, Lyte, Townson, Brydone, Livingstone and Clephane, and from local guides, such as Byres and Parker in Rome, and the interest of most tourists helped to ensure that many acquired considerable experience in assessing operas, paintings and buildings. Some were more critical than others, but standards were high in general and tourism served to enrich the British elite culturally. Whether that was in the interest of British culture is a different question and one that aroused heated debate at the time.

Notes

1. Ellison to brother George, 13 June 1781, Gateshead, Ellison, A11 No. 2.

2. St Saphorin to Townshend, 28 Nov. 1722, PRO 80/47.

3. Cowper to sister, 10 March 1730, Herts., D/EP 234; Gray, P 424; Walker, pp. 178–9, 378.

4. Allen to Newcastle, 3 Sep. 1729, PRO 92/33; Essex to his agent Thomas Bowen, 30 June 1733, Stanhope to Essex, 6 Jan. 1733, BL, Add. 60387, 27732; Stanhope to Earl Stanhope, 25 Oct. 1734, Kent, U1590 C708/2.

5. Shaw, *Letters to a Nobleman*, p. 105; Somerset to Lady Coventry, 21 July 1709, Badminton; Carpenter, Bodl. Mss. Douce 67, p. 145; anon, BL, Add. 60522; Southwell, BL, Add. 34753, fo. 14; Cork and Orrery I, 43; Perceval to Daniel Dering, 22 May (os) 1726, BL, Add. 47031; Swinton, 24, 26, 27 May (os) 1731; Harcourt, III, 26; Mitchell, BL, Add. 58314, fo. 29–30; Stevens, p. 99; Garrick, p. 8; Smith, CUL Add. Mss. 7621, 14 July 1752, 23 Sep. 1754; Orrery, 11, 57, 140; Pickersgill to sister, April 1761, Oct. 1768, Aylesbury, Saunders; Gateshead, Ellison, A15 No. 22; Francis, BL, Add. 40759, fo. 15, 19, 21; Wharton to Brand, 17 March; Wharton to Thomas Lloyd (Quote), 24 March 1775; Pelham to mother, 8 Sep., 2 Oct. 1777, BL, Add. 33127; Yorke to Keith, 28 Sep.; 27 May 1778, BL, Add. 35514–5; Drake, Ayesbury, D/DR/8/10/11-12; Gateshead, Ellison, A 11, No. 2; Brand to Wharton, 10 May 1781; Wharton to Brand, 4 June 1781; Brand to Wharton, 2 Feb., 24 Oct., 17 Nov. 1783, 16 May, June 1784, 18 Oct. 1787, 6 Dec. 1790, 26 Aug. 1791, 3 April, 5 Oct. 1792, 25 May, 24 Sep. 1793, Bennett, 14 Oct. 1785; Dawkins to Keith, 5 April 1785, BL, Add. 35534; Bennett, 15 Oct. 1785; Young, I, 10, 76; Beckford, II, 381; Gray, pp. 298–9; Arbuthnot to Keith, 6 May 1787, Robson, 30 July 1787, Garmston, 6 Oct., 4 Nov. 1787, 28 Jan. 1788, Crewe, BL, Add. 35538, 38837, 30271, 37926, fo. 43, 51–3.

6. BL, Add. 40759, fo. 31.

7. Pelham to mother, 28 Sep. 1776, BL, Add. 33127.

8. Lynch, *The Independent Patriot*, p. 2.

9. Cork and Orrery, I, 206–7.

10. Marlborough to Fish, 12 Oct. (os) 1727, BL, Add. 61444.

11. Walker, p. 432; Perceval to Edward Southwell, 30 Oct. 1725, Perceval to Daniel Dering, 16, 23 April, 4 May 1726, BL, Add. 47031; Mitchell, BL, Add. 58314, fo. 29; Crewe, BL, Add. 37926, fo. 84.

12. Swinton, 10 March (os), 9 May (os) 1731; Wharton to Brand, 15 Nov. 1775; Brand to Wharton, 26 March, 17 April 1784; 14 Oct. 1791; Robson, 24 Aug. 1787, BL, Add. 38837; Knight, p. 176.

13. Digby to Hanbury-Williams, 25 Dec. 1751, BL, Add. 51393; Brand to Wharton, 27 June, 4 Aug. 1787.

14. Brand to Wharton, 10, 20 Jan. 1780; 9 April 1790; 26 Aug., 22 Sep. 1791; Garmston, 4 July 1787, BL, Add. 30271.

15. Aylesbury, D/LE E2/16.

16. Pelham to his mother, 26 Feb. 1776, BL, Add. 33126.

17. Craven, I, 170; Ainslie to Keith, 3 Dec. 1785, BL, Add. 35535.

18. *Pompeo Batoni and his British Patrons* (1982), Catalogue of Kenwood exhibition; *Souvenirs of the Grand Tour* (1982), Wildenstein catalogue.

19. Bentinck to mother, 28 April 1727, BL, Eg. 1711.

20. Brand to Wharton, 23 Nov. 1793.

21. Camelford to William Pitt, 10 Feb. 1788, CUL Add. 6958.

22. Bodl. Mss. Add. D71, fo. 45; Robson, 7 Sep. 1787, BL, Add. 38837; O. Sitwell, *Sing High! Sing Low!* (1944).

23. Pomfret, Leics., DG7, Finch D5; McSwing correspondence with second Duke of Richmond, Chichester, Goodwood Mss. 105, vol. I; Pears, 'Patronage and learning in the Virtuoso Republic; John Talman in Italy, 1709–1712', *Oxford Art Journal*, 5 (1982), pp. 27–9.

24. Northall, p. 127; Francis, BL, Add. 40759, fo. 30.

25. Francis, BL, Add. 40759, fo. 30; L. Bertelsen, 'Have at you all: or, Bonnell Thornton's journalism', *Huntington Library Quarterly*, 44 (1981), pp. 269–72; R. Paulson, *Hogarth: His Life, Art, and Times* (2 vols., New Haven, 1971), II, 153–87.

26. Trevor to half-brother Thomas, 27 Aug., 3 July 1728, BL, Add. 61684; Bennett, 3 Sep. 1785.

27. *Tour of Holland*, pp. 98–9; Aikin, I, 89–90; Brand to Wharton, 12 Sep. 1779; anon., BL, Add. 60522; Bennett, 24 June 1785; Walker, p. 17.

28. Walker, p. 19; Perceval to Charles Dering, 25 June (os) 1718, BL, Add. 47028; Brand to Wharton, 16 Oct. 1779.

29. Anon., BL, Add. 60522; Hume, BL, Add. fo. 14.

30. *Tour of Holland*, p. 143; Andrews, 1784, p. 204–5.

31. Perceval to Daniel Dering, 9 April 1726, Trevor to Thomas Trevor, 3 July 1728, BL, Add. 47031, 61684; Garrick, p. 33; Drake/D/DR/8/2; Wharton to Thomas Wharton, 19 April 1775; Brand to Wharton, 10 May 1781.

32. Somerset to Lady Coventry, 24 Nov. 1708, Badminton; Daniel Dering to Perceval, 20 Aug. 1723, BL, Add. 47030; anon., BL, Stowe, 790, fo. 111.

33. Hall to Wharton, 6 Oct. 1783; Brand to Wharton, 10 Sep. 1787, 11 Sep. 1792.

34. Pelham to mother, 26 Feb., 28 July, to father, 29 Feb., 1776, BL, Add. 33126–7.

35. Brand to Wharton, 30 July 1779; H. Dunthorne, 'British travellers in eighteenth-century Holland: tourism and the appreciation of Dutch Culture', *British Journal for Eighteenth-century studies*, 5 (1982), pp. 80–1; Henry Ellison junior to Henry Ellison senior, Gateshead, Ellison, A15, No. 22.

36. G. W. Pilcher (ed.), *The Reverend Samuel Davies Abroad. The Diary of a Journey to England and Scotland, 1735–55* (Urbana, 1967), p. 102.

37. Swinton, 1 June (os) 1731; Stevens, pp. 111–2; Gray, p. 402.

38. Walker, p. 169; Orrery, p. 90.

39. Parker, BL, Stowe, 750, fo. 378; Swinton, 3 March (os) 1731; Mitchell, BL, Add. 58319, fo. 33; Nuneham, Aylesbury, D/LE E2/16, 20; Holland, BL, Add. 51445 B, fo. 8; Drake, Aylesbury, D/DR/8/2/16; Francis to Dr Campbell, 17 Oct., 1772, Curzon to Keith, 17 Oct. 1777; Pelham to mother, 15 March, to father, 1 April 1777, Yorke to Keith, 12 May 1779, McDougall to Keith, 27 Jan. 1782, Robson, 19 Aug. 1787, BL, Add. 40759, 35512, 33127, 35516, 35525, 38837; Craven, p. 88; J. E. Smith, *A Sketch of a Tour on the Continent in the years 1786 and 1787* (3 vols., 1793), I, xix; Gray, p. 312; Walker, pp. 188–9; Brand to Wharton, 6 Dec. 1790, undated (1791); Camelford to Pitt, 10 Feb. 1788, CUL Add. Mss. 6958.

40. HMC *Hare*, p. 249.

41. Perceval to Daniel Dering, 22 May (os) 1726, BL, Add. 47031.

42. Cradock, *Literary and Miscellaneous Memoirs* (1826), p. 57–8.

43. Stevens, pp. 360–1; Francis, 8, 9 Aug. 1772, Robson, 31 Aug. 1787, BL, Add. 38837; Walker, pp. 134–6.

44. Haggerston, 26 Nov. 1718; Mitchell, BL, Add. 58319, fo. 23.

45. Brand to Wharton, 10 May 1781.

46. *Mists*, 18 Sep. (os) 1725.

47. BL, Stowe, 791, pp. 27–8; Wauchop to Keith, 4 Nov. 1775, BL, Add. 35509; Bennett, 16 Sep., 8, 11, 17 Oct. 1785; anon., BL, Add. 12130, fo. 183.

48. Walker, p. 379; Robson, 19, 22 Aug. 1787, BL, Add. 38837; Brand to Wharton, 31 March 1787.

49. Wharton to Thomas Lloyd, 14 Aug. 1775; Brand to Wharton, 31 March 1787; Thompson, I, 45–6, 55, 90; MacLaurin, fo. 189; Drake, Alyesbury, D/DR/8/10/10; Young, I, 5, 17, 19, 51, 53, 63.

50. Salisbury, Hatfield, Cecil Papers, Mss. 340; Hume, BL, Add. 29477, fo. 27; Pelham to father, 11 March 1776, BL, Add. 33126.

51. Carpenter, Bodl. Mss. Douce, 67, p. 153; Christ Church, Head to Wake, 9 March 1725; Southwell to Perceval, 9 April 1726, BL, Add. 47031; Mitchell, BL, Add. 58319, fo. 7. 78; Stevens, pp. 313, 319–20; Baltimore, *A Tour to the East, in the years 1763 and 1764, with Remarks on the City of Constantinople and the Turks* (1767), ii–iii; Drake, Aylesbury, D/DR/8/2/17; Robson, 19 Aug. 1787, BL, Add. 38837; Francis, BL, Add. 40759, fo. 28; Wraxall to Keith, 22 June 1779, BL, Add. 35516; Hall to Wharton, 2 Aug. 1785; Brand to Wharton, undated; Garmston, 16 Nov., 1787, Belgrave to Keith, 19 May 1787, BL, Add. 30271, 35538; Watkins, *Travels through Swisserland*, II (1792), 97; Hoare, CUL Add. Mss. 3549; Brand to Wharton, 3, 22 April 1792.

52. Horace Walpole to Mann, *Walpole-Mann*, II, 211.

53. [Hurd], *Dialogues on the uses of Foreign Travel; Considered as a part of An English Gentleman's Education* . . . (1764), p. 57.

11 THE DEBATE OVER THE GRAND TOUR: CONCLUSIONS

There are indeed some that go abroad meerly to eat and sleep: and think if they have been at the places it is enough for them: of this number are generally those that travel young with governors: who sometimes come home as knowing as they went out.

Lord Carpenter, 1717.[1]

The misfortune is, that young men who want experience; and have not the happiness to be under the influence of somebody, who should have an authority over them, they are guided by their own humours and make themselves appear in the world to great disadvantage, and commit many follies, which they may possibly live long enough to repent of, but can never retrieve.

Edward Carteret on Lord Dysart, 1728.[2]

. . . those are the best of our countrymen that are not *much* altered by their continental peregrinations.

John Boyd on Wraxall, 1787.[3]

Tourism was attacked on many grounds, ranging from cost to culture, the dangers from Catholicism to the dangers from venereal disease. Much criticism was expressed in public: in print, the theatre and even in Parliament. Others expressed their criticisms privately: guardians, parents, diplomats and tourists themselves. In turn tourism was defended, both in print and privately, though this defence was never as vigorous nor as bitter as much of the printed assault. Most of the criticism related to a more general attack on Hanoverian society and culture and, in particular, on foreign influences, such as French food and Italian opera, and their supposed pernicious effects. Very little criticism referred solely to tourism. It is difficult to assess changes in the content or quality of the criticism. Most of the themes remained remarkedly constant. This was due partly to constant features of tourism, such as its cost and the loss of wealth to the country, and partly to the quality of xenophobia, a fusion of conservatism and vigour. Strong criticism continued to be expressed in the second half of the century, but it appears to have been less constant a theme than in the 1720s and 1730s. In that period London opposition newspapers, such as the *Craftsman* and *Mist's Weekly Journal*, attacked tourism on many occasions.

The Benefits of Tourism

Our joyous situation . . . you see two of the happiest fellows in life having left every care behind them in their native land, in high spirits, breathing the most delicious air in the world, in a fine summer-morning, rolling along on a broad smooth causeway considerably elevated above the plain, as it were on purpose to show us the adjacent country to the greatest advantage.

Nixon, near Paris, 1750.[4]

From both trouble and pleasure I assuredly derived instruction; and on many occasions I have essentially profited from this my first entrance into the world. To many perhaps the experiment might have been dangerous: to me fortunately it proved of the most real and lasting advantage.

As I now attained the age of 21, my good father, who was earnest to qualify me in every respect for my approaching entrance into the active world, proposed to me a second tour, . . . The variety of scenes through which I had lately passed, the society into which I had been introduced, and the manners and information which I had acquired, made me on my return extremely acceptable to all my old friends, and procured me the acquaintance of many, to whom I otherwise had small pretensions to be known . . .

James Bland Burges, 'Memoirs'.[5]

Those who defended tourism stressed rarely the pleasures of foreign travel. Such a stress would have appeared trivial, and to defend the heavy cost of tourism it was necessary to advance reasons more consequential than those of enjoyment. It was not a motive that could be proposed usually to parents or guardians, nor one that could be advanced by moralists. A certain amount of (self-)deception without doubt played a role in the discussion of motives for travel. As with travel to Bath, many tourists who sought cures for their health were also influenced by the desire to travel, and, particularly in the case of Aachen and Spa, to socialise. The relationship between the debate over travel and the actual views of tourists is a complex one, and the latter are difficult often to elucidate. Many journals that were not published in the eighteenth century were nevertheless written for others to read. St Vincent's is a good example. MacLaurin hoped that his account would be of interest to friends and relations. Perceval congratulated Edward Southwell junior on his description of Geneva and wrote of the 'pattern it gives my son how to write when it becomes his turn to voyage as you do'.[6] Unpublished defences of tourism tend to advance reasons similar to those in contemporary printed material.

The principal motives advanced for foreign travel were that it equipped the traveller socially and provided him with useful knowledge and attainments. It was partly for this reason that many had part of their formal education, at school, academy or university, abroad, though other factors played an important role, such as the traditional preference of the Scots for Dutch universities[7] and the wish of Catholics to educate their children abroad. Foreign education was not free from hazard. There was a risk of conversion to Catholicism, as happened to the third Earl of Cardigan in 1703–4. Stevens was particularly worried about the dangers posed by foreign education.

> I cannot help thinking it worthy the consideration of the legislature, to prevent, as much as possible, the sending our young people, of both sexes, into foreign parts to receive their education: they imbibe such principles, both religious and political, that, on their return, make them enemies to the mild religion and government of their native country.[10]

Despite these dangers many were educated abroad. One tourist found six British students at the Academy in Lunéville in 1720.[11] Academies at Angers, Besançon, Blois, Colmar, Caen, Turin, Vandeuil, Paris, Tours, Hamburg and Brunswick received British students; so also did universities such as Leipzig, Göttingen, Leyden, Wittenberg and Utrecht. The quality of the education varied. Brand criticised the Academy at Brunswick, but Philip Yorke praised the lectures he attended at Leyden, and the second Earl of Dartmouth was impressed by those he heard at Leipzig. Many hired language teachers. Haggerston did so at Rome. Lord

Harrold and John Clavering studied French in 1715 in Geneva and Hanover respectively.[12] Sir John Blair was boarded in a French house in Paris in 1787 in order to hear 'no other language spoken at Table'. His guardians wished him to be educated 'in such a manner as to fit him for availing himself' of prospects of employment but 'at the same time that due attention is to be had to procure him every accomplishment otherwise suitable to his fortune and expectations'. Arbuthnot, Blair's tutor, did not think it sufficient for him to be trained as a man of business, 'to those qualities should I think be added an acquaintance with human affairs in general, and with the polite arts, which may place him above professional peculiarities of manner, or professional littleness of character'.[13] Such an ambiguity existed generally. Tourists were expected to improve themselves and to behave like gentlemen. The two were believed to be compatible and mutually supporting, but there was often a tension between them, particularly in the matter of expenditure. Sarah Marlborough was sceptical of the value of tourism. She wrote to her grandsons' Bearleader, Fish: 'I never thought travelling was of much use but to teach them perfectly the language and to keep them out of harms way, while they are so young that they cannot keep the best company in England, and to make them see that nothing is so agreeable as England take it alltogether, but what I value more than anything you will see abroad is the constant application to what Mr Chais will read and teach them.' Charles, second Viscount Fane, urged the Spencers, then at The Hague, to accompany him to Paris. Fish reported that Fane,

> . . . reckoned up several advantages we should find there, such as . . . better opportunities of growing perfect in the French, better masters for mathematics (which he has a mind to apply himself to for some time) and for any exercise of accomplishment that any of us might have a mind to advance or perfect ourselves in such as dancing, fencing, drawing, architecture, fortification, music, the knowledge of medals, painting, sculpture, antiquity, or whatever we would . . . Mr Charles [Spencer] gave his voice strongly for Paris as well as for the reasons Mr Fane gave as because he thought there would be a great many agreeable entertainments . . . which would keep us in better humour and better spirits for the mornings' application.

Sarah Marlborough was not so sure,

Useful learning is what I have always earnestly recommended, and next to that . . . good company is the most desirable thing. But I should naturally have thought, that the worse the company is at any place, and the duller, the more likely it would be for young men to apply themselves . . . The mathematics I have always thought was the most desirable knowledge . . . To speak the French language perfectly well is certainly very agreeable and upon many occasions will be more useful even than Latin . . . Dancing gives men a good air; and fencing should be learnt, because it is possible that it may be of use . . . I give you full power to go where you will, since I believe, that wherever the children are they will be very idle, and notwithstanding all the pains that I have taken, they will never know anything that is of any more consequence than a Toupee, a laced coat, or a puppet-show.[14]

Sarah Marlborough's harsh words may have been justified for her grandsons, all of whom proved disappointments, and two of whom gambled heavily whilst abroad.

Other tourists achieved a better balance. Mellish engaged dancing and fencing masters in Paris, but he also worked hard to improve his knowledge of French. Robert Wharton, who translated Montesquieu 'backwards and forwards', informed his uncle that he did not 'think a lesson in the art of walking, bowing, giving, receiving, standing etc. avec bonne grace, too ridiculous to receive'. He took, lessons in riding 'a la Françoise' in response to his uncle's wishes. The scholarly Thomas Pelham had lessons in dancing and perspective in Turin.[15] He was convinced of the value of travel. From Spain he informed his father,

I think it very necessary and right that every young man should know that there are other countries than those he lives in; that there are rational creatures out of his island and though men are very different in themselves they live all under the same heavens and are governed by the same all seeing Providence; — the seing those countries which are famous as scenes of so many actions in History are highly conducive to the enlarging and opening of the understanding — the total change in the face of those countries is the most convincing proofs of the uncertainty of things in this world; the flourishing state of some and the miseries and wretchedness of others is the best cure for a mind prejudiced with an idea that no country is equal to his own, and shew in the strongest light that happiness is not confined to one quarter of the globe, and that a Spaniard may be as easy in servitude as an Englishman in liberty. In short visiting other countrys is the best indeed the only way of learning how to weigh the perfections and imperfections of our own. — In respect to societies, few I fear are open to a young traveller that he can gain any improvement from; In Italy I believe none; and should only be *visited* as a country of fame without any regard to its inhabitants; and I much doubt whether in any nation a young man who comes there only for a few weeks or months will gain much from the company he will live with . . .[16]

Others disagreed and felt that young tourists could benefit greatly from the social life that they might enjoy. Edward Carteret hoped in the case of Lord Dysart 'that affability, and good breeding will introduce him into the best of company which is the greatest advantage that can be acquired by travelling into foreign countrys'. Sholto Douglas wrote from Turin, 'the principal advantage I shall reap here is I fancy an *easier air* in company, as I am to be introduced to the king and the principal nobility at the return of the court'. In 1778, Lord Pembroke thanked Keith for looking after his son in Vienna: 'The good company, to which you have introduced him, must be of the greatest consequence to him at his period of life'.[17] Aside from mixing in society tourism could also be of use in acquiring information. Martin Sherlock, in his *New Letters from an English Traveller* claimed,

Nothing is so useful as travelling to those who know how to profit by it. Nature is seen in all her shades, and in all her extremes. If the mind of the traveller be virtuous, it will be confirmed in the love of virtue, and in the abhorrence of vice; because he will everywhere see that virtue is esteemed by the persons who practise it the least. If the traveller has the seeds of one or of several talents, he will find men of the first merit in every line, who will think it a pleasure to encourage and unfold those seeds, and to communicate knowledge . . . The traveller has, besides, the advantage of making continual comparisons, which strengthen his judgment extremely; . . . it is more than probable that every man who goes to exhibit his insignificancy in foreign countries, without parts, and without an object, will collect there only vices, follies, and absurdities.

Commentators differed on what was held to be useful information. Joseph Marshall, possibly a pseudonym, was a proponent of
the school that argued that only tips on turnip cultivation were
useful. Peter Beckford stated,

> It is not in looking at pictures and statues only, that travelling is
> of use, but in examining the laws, customs, and manners of other
> countries, and comparing them with our own. Agriculture,
> Natural History, Trade, Commerce, Arts, and Sciences, all
> present themselves under various forms to improve and enlarge
> the understanding; while a continual habit of receiving favours
> will put us in good humour with the rest of the world, remove
> our prejudices, increase our sensibility, and inspire in us that
> general benevolence which renders mankind so serviceable to one
> another.

Lord Carpenter and Thomas Pelham both stressed the classical
heritage of Italy. The former wrote in 1717,

> There is certainly more pleasure and advantages in travelling in
> Italy than in any other country whatsoever: you see greater
> varietys in nature than anywhere else: besides the prodigious
> diversity of Governments: the fine paintings and sculptures: but
> above all the ancient inscriptions: ruins: and antiquitys: which
> are very curious and instructive to one that takes delight in such
> things: . . .

Sixty years later, Pelham wrote to his mother from Rome: 'the
great use I found is the obtaining clearer ideas of the Roman
magnificence than history conveys, and the reflections that must
necessarily arise on the comparing our situation with theirs, with
the melancholy thoughts of the imperfection and instability of
every work of man.'[18]
Beneficial comparisons were held to be an important aspect of
foreign travel. Robert Poole discovered in 1741 that the Sabbath
was profaned a lot in Paris. He had hitherto thought the situation
in London bad, but he found that it was worse in Paris:

> Hence travelling is of use to enable a person to form juster

notions of things, and to see in what respect his own country exceeds, or is exceeded by others, whereby the better to value what is valuable, and disregard what is not so. And hence I am enabled to have juster notions from experience, by comparison, concerning religion, in regard to the exterior part of it, now, than before I could . . .

Thomas Pelham also found travel useful in comparing Protestantism and Catholicism — a comparison many critics of tourism feared. He wrote to his mother '. . . I think that the comparing them together and weighing the perfections and imperfections of Romish and Protestant tenets may enable a private man to arrive at a nearer pitch of Christianity — let a Protestant engraft the zeal of a Roman on the sincerity of his own faith and in my opinion he can not be a very bad Christian.' John Richard claimed that,

> The pleasures of travelling are certainly beyond common conception; from every nation, from even every circumstance, travellers will find many occasions to admire the constitution and comforts of their own country. To a traveller of observation many things appear of consequence which others esteem as trifles. Happy will he be on his return, if he can retain and follow good examples he has met with, and forget the bad ones.

Arthur Young's first foreign trip confirmed him in 'the idea, that to know our own country well, we must see something of others. Nations figure by comparison'. The ever-hyperbolic John Villiers noted in Cherbourg in 1778: 'We know not the value of our privileges, . . . till we have felt the loss of them; and every young man ought to go abroad, to make him the more attached to his own country. I find everything here so extremely inferior, that I glow with pride and rapture, when I think I am an Englishman.'[19]

There were social benefits in Britain for those who returned having been polished by continental society. Lady Mary Wortley Montagu wrote of how lords newly arrived from abroad won the admiration of women at court. Many agreed with Mr Classic, a character in Samuel Foote's *The Englishman at Paris*, in praising the advantages of a visit to Paris: 'I think a short residence here a very necessary part in every man of fashion's education.' Mrs Crewe drew attention to the powerful appeal of snobbery, the manner in which the returned tourist appeared part of a charmed exotic world. Bored at a Versailles ceremony she wrote,

> It will, at all events, serve to vapour about when I get to England
> — Oh! how shall I show off amongst you all with 'my Alps, my
> Appenines, and River Po'! or, at least, My Spa, my Brussells,
> and the River Seine! Not one of which, however, between you
> and me, is worth an evenings walk over poor Philip's Hill, when
> one makes some new remark upon Beeston Castle, and find out
> that the Welsh Hills are pretty objects from that spot.

The countryside near Crewe Hall clearly appealed to her, but
when she contemplated her return to it she wrote: 'I shall show off
with my Paris fashions, and make you believe anything I please!'[20]

The benefits of travel and the processes by which these benefits
were to be acquired were not often explained. Edward Southwell
junior returned from his travels 'very much improved'; John
Rogerson hoped that by travelling his nephew's 'mind may be
opened and his acquaintance with the world enlarged'; John Moore
argued that 'one end of travelling is to free the mind from vulgar
prejudices'.[21] There was little agreement as to how best to achieve
these noble aims. It was agreed in general that it was best to avoid
the company of other tourists, but comments varied on the dangers
of mixing in local society. There were also differences of opinion
concerning how long tourists should spend in particular towns.
Perceval, an experienced tourist, argued that 'to travel to purpose
men should fix at Courts, and not loose their time in lesser towns
where nothing but the outside of houses and inside of churches is to
be seen'.[22] Most could agree that tourists should seek to acquire
political information, but the means by which they were to do this
were unclear. *Mist's Weekly Journal* claimed that tourists simply
wenched and drank: 'If you ask them questions concerning the laws
or governments of the countries they have visited, you will find
they know no more of those matters than they do of Terra Australis
incognita; . . .'[23] This was true of many tourists, but others
acquired a lot of information, often through the hospitality of
British envoys. The Earl of Morton wrote from Warsaw, in 1782: 'I
shall certainly use my utmost endeavours to form a proper notion
of the state and constitution of this country.' Bennett determined
to read a history of European treaties as soon as he returned home,

It is astonishing how interested one becomes in the fate of a country, when one has travelled through it. All the books in the world will never inspire the warmth, or give the information and I have learned more in a three month tour, than I could by silent meditation for half a century.[24]

Difficult as it was to explain the exact benefits of travel, many were agreed, nevertheless, that not to travel was bad, and that it led to boorishness and narrow-mindedness. Baltimore wrote of the Turks: 'They are enthusiasts in their religion, they look on those who differ from them as despicable as dogs, hogs, and devils. This is from want of travelling; for they are in the most deplorable ignorance of other nations . . .' Thomson observed of the Danes: 'They are much addicted to intemperance in drinking, and convivial entertainments; but their nobility, who now begin to visit the other courts of Europe, are gradually refining from the vulgar habits of their ancestors.'[25]

The defence of tourism was conducted therefore on a variety of fronts. Its principal characteristic was an idealistic one. Few advanced pragmatic defences, such as that tourism enabled young men to sow their wild oats abroad or kept heirs from seeking to influence the management of parental estates. Instead the defence of tourism, unlike much of the attack upon it, was conducted on an elevated and often abstract plane. Lynch's *Independent Patriot* which satirised the cultural gullibility of many tourists, was dedicated nevertheless to Burlington, for whom travel served only 'to improve his mind for the embellishment of his country'. The variety of benefits that were assumed to derive from tourism stemmed largely from the differing assumptions and interests of tourists. It was hoped that Henry Nassau, Viscount Boston, would acquire social knowledge and manners that would be useful to him for the rest of his life. Perceval was pleased that his eldest son gained in Paris an interest in seals and 'virtuosoship'. Robson noted: 'I hope this tour into foreign parts will have its uses upon conduct in life in future, and teach me humiliation and submission to the will of heaven'. The Reverend William Cole acquired from his visit to Paris the habit of burning the incense used in French churches in his house after dinner to remove the smell of cooking.[26] Whatever the benefits were believed to be they were rarely stated as vigorously as the criticisms.

Criticism

> Travelling has for some time I think been much in fashion with
> our Gentry; I doubt whether they improve much by it, but this I
> am sure of, that it must carry a good deal of money abroad.
>
> Charles Delafaye, 1732.[27]

> I suppose a little tour to Italy, will be the next excursion; it
> furnishes rather an additional fund for elegant amusement in
> private life than anything useful.
>
> Lord Findlater to James Oswald
re latter's son, 1768.[28]

Much of the printed criticism of tourism was xenophobic in content
and intention. It was witty and interesting often, but related only
tangentially to tourism. Tourism was treated as but one example of
a generalised failure to defend the integrity of British life and
society in the face of all things foreign.[29] Tourism was a good
instance of this, in the eyes of critics, but it was less striking and
possibly less immediately apparent to a metropolitan audience,
than opera. Specific discussion of the merits of particular routes or
particular activities whilst abroad was less common. Tourists were
aware of the generalised debate within Britain though it is difficult
to ascertain how far this influenced them. Wharton wrote from
Dijon that he did not wish to act in a manner similar to that which
was attacked in print.[30] However, in general, tourists were
influenced not so much by a printed criticism, as by the advice or
entreaties of parents, guardians and Bearleaders. Many of these
were disenchanted with tourism, not so much for xenophobic
reasons, as for others linked to cost. Edward Mellish's father and
uncle were clearly sceptical about the value of travel,

> I do not apprehend real advantages from seeing fine paintings
> and buildings, can yet be of any real advantage to you in the life
> you are like to lead hereafter and may . . . give you a taste of
> living beyond your circumstances . . . a habit of negligence in
> your own affairs, which is but too often seen amongst very agree-
> able Gentlemen which have spent a great deal of time in travel-
> ling, and have by it improved themselves in every valuable quali-
> fication, but that one the most essential, which is, solid good
> Judgement.[31]

Possibly there is a social bias in the evidence. Most of the criticism of tourists comes from those who could not be described as being at the highest reaches of society, diplomats such as Robert Murray Keith, and travellers such as Robert Wharton, Philip Francis, Arthur Young, John Macky, Thomas Watkins and Thomas Pennant. Andrews attacked 'the frivolous pursuits of the plurality of our travellers'; and Pennant attacked those educated at the Academy of Geneva,

> . . . it is folly to send here the grown up youth of our country as many parents have done. They come here corrupted by the dissipation of our island, spurn at all discipline, and either give themselves up to the rural sports of the country or abandon their studies for the enervating pleasures of the South of France, unknown to their friends who are regretting the unaccountable expenses of an education they were taught to believe was as reasonable as it was good.[32]

Whether these views were shared by those at the top of the social pyramid, the parents of Keith's 'brawny beef-eating barons' without any 'notion of taste or elegance', or of Wharton's 'Jolly-boys', is unclear. Judging from the attitudes of parents such as Sarah Marlborough, the first Earl of Grantham, the first Earl of Macclesfield, the fourth Earl of Northampton and Lord Thomas Pelham, many were prudent and not prepared to see their heirs waste their estate in folly and dissipation. There were other tourists whose parents or guardians could not control them or did not seek to do so. Possibly the extent of tourist 'vice' was exaggerated, and many tourists should have been castigated rather for sloth and a failure to consider seriously what they saw, than for wenching, drinking and gambling. The Earl of Essex was criticised in 1752 for being very given to 'loitring away his time'. Garrick recorded of one of his days in Paris, 'did very little this day but idle and eat and drink'.[33] These appear to have been more common than the 'vices' castigated by many, but because they were less provocative they received less attention. Many critics could not accept that tourism, despite the ideology of education and improvement, was primarily a holiday. Francis noted at Florence in 1772: 'Travelling perhaps may polish the manners of our youth: but quaere whether the Italian polish be worth the price we pay for it.' Brand complained in 1790,

Shall we be driving post from place to place, living in noisy dirty Inns, grumbling (perchance swearing) at postboys and visiting vast snowy mountains . . . And all this to acquire what? At best a little knowledge of Geography — Alas Alas! How strange a system of Education have I engaged in — surely there is no situation worse.

Lady Knight wrote from Rome three years later: 'I am very apt to think that the present mode of travelling is turned rather to amusement than to improvement.'[34]

Because tourism was debated largely as a means of education and not as a holiday, the debate on its merit appears often to be remote from the activities of many tourists and to be somewhat artificial. Furthermore the debate became increasingly irrelevant as the nature of tourism altered during the century. In the first half of the century tourism was dominated by the classical Grand Tour — young men travelling with tutors for several years in order to finish their education. In the second half of the century, many still travelled in this manner, but there were also larger numbers of other tourists: travellers not on their first trip, women, older tourists, families, those of the 'middling sort' who tended to make short visits. These groups, usually unaccompanied by any guide, except in major cities where they might hire a laquais de place, did not stress education as a prime motive for travel. Instead enjoyment and amusement came increasingly to the fore. Possibly this was linked to a discernible shift in guidebooks towards a less didactic and more practical pattern that devoted more stress to information such as prices, transport and conversion rates. Arthur Young was naive in attacking 'those whose political reveries are . . . caught flying as they are whirled through Europe in post-chaises'. According to him they failed to tackle questions concerning the bases of French power.[35]

Young and many other critics failed to appreciate the shift in social values that appear to have underlain changes in attitudes towards travel. There was a growing acceptance by tourists that the purposes of travel were not primarily educational. It was quite acceptable for William Drake to inform his father, a former tourist, in 1769 that he stayed in Florence longer than anticipated 'in order to see a little the humours of a masque Ball'.[36] Such actions had always been common; but in the second half of the century tourists appear to have regarded them as appropriate activities that did not need defending.

Conclusions

Travellers always buy experience which no books can give.

Bennett, 9 August 1785.

Foreign travel is knowledge to a wise man, and foppery to a fool.

Cradock, *Memoirs*, p. 67.

For a historian trained in diplomatic archives, tourism is a strange topic largely because the accounts left by tourists are so disparate. Despite contemporary criticisms that they stayed together too much and were insufficiently perceptive, there is an astonishing variety in the written remains that they left behind. It is difficult after reading the accounts of tourists such as Mitchell, Parker, Perceval, Southwell, Holroyd and Lichfield, to accept John Stoye's characterisation of British travellers (albeit of the previous century) as 'receiving the same memories or images, learning to share the same stock of historical commonplaces'.[37] Many tourists were intelligent and perceptive and left informed accounts of what interested them: agricultural methods, a popular topic,[38] or opera, court society or religious ceremonies. These accounts were often prefaced or concluded by statements that the situation in Britain was better, but such remarks do not vitiate the interesting accounts that accompany them. Given the extraordinary variety of tourists and their writings it is difficult to summarise the evidence on such questions as how far they were affected by the experience of travel. It is reasonable to suggest that the consequences of having a large number of the men of the upper orders abroad during their formative years must have been considerable. Clearly exposure to foreign influences was lessened by the employment of Bearleaders, the majority of whom were British, the preference for the company of other British tourists, the tendency to visit towns where there were reasonable numbers of such tourists, the habit of attending educational establishments patronised by compatriots, and the important entertainment role of British diplomats in courts such as Vienna. Nevertheless, a large number of tourists met and conversed with foreigners as social equals and attended ceremonies or visited institutions which it was more difficult to attend and visit in Britain — such as Italian operas and Catholic ceremonies. The cultural influence of this appears to have been considerable. Predisposed by an education in the classics to take an interest in the past achievements of Italian society, the upper orders, through tourism, became aware of the current achievements of European society and culture. Some of this awareness was faddish: the large numbers of tourists who visited Voltaire at Ferney, and who made a pilgrimage to Rousseau's tomb at Ermenonville, the somewhat uncritical praise that some lavished on the domestic and religious policies of Joseph II. However British tourists had sufficient self-confidence and national pride not to praise things simply because they were foreign; *pace* contemporary critics, there was relatively little unthinking assumption of foreign customs, manners and mores. Rather the upper orders were open to continental influences and willing to consider foreign habits. It is important not to exaggerate the openness of British society at the highest ranks and to contrast it too sharply with a supposedly more xenophobic and less open climate of opinion among the lower orders. The position varied by individual and there are signs of shifts in attitude; though, for as long as the history of eighteenth-century xenophobia remains unwritten, it is difficult to assess the attitudes of particular groups in society. Nevertheless, the upper orders do appear to have been relatively open to foreign influences and it could be suggested that tourism played a significant part in this process.

'As to travelling, it is only eligible from the difficulty of finding employing for a young man not yet of age', Lady Polwarth argued in 1778.[39] The importance of this aspect of the Grand Tour has often been overlooked. Tourism clearly served an important social purpose for the sons of the landed property owners, a group not always appreciated by the urban 'middling orders', who left many of the surviving accounts of tourism. However it would be a mistake to present the Grand Tour as a simple response to this important social problem. Evidence of a major demographic crisis in the upper orders in the early eighteenth-century, of many landed families finding it difficult to ensure direct male descent,[40] would suggest that there were significant social reasons why sons should not be sent abroad on a lengthy and often hazardous Grand Tour, which sometimes, as with the Duchy of Somerset, led to deaths that produced a breach in the direct line of succession. There is insufficient evidence surviving to permit any conclusive statement of why sons were nevertheless sent abroad, but it could be suggested that social emulation and a viewpoint of foreign travel as a means of education and, particularly of social finishing, were the key factors. This conflation of social and educational aspects was possibly crucial in the development of the concept of the Grand Tour in its classic mould — education for aristocratic youth — but during the course of the eighteenth century the stress on educational aspects declined. Historians such as Plumb and Malcolmson have pointed to the greater importance of leisure activities in eighteenth-century British society. Leisure clearly became more of an accepted aspect of foreign travel. This was not acceptable to many contemporary critics, but their views had little apparent effect on the activities of tourists. It was clear by the second half of the century that tourists travelled not only 'to see and hear everything that is to be seen and heard',[47] but also to enjoy themselves.

Notes

1. Bodl. Mss. Douce 67, pp. 153−4.
2. Carteret to Wetstein, 8 Aug. (os) 1728, BL, Add. 32415.
3. Boyd to Keith, 17 July 1787, BL, Add. 35538.
4. Nixon, BL, Add. 39225, fo. 87.
5. Burges, Bodl. Dep. Bland Burges, vol. 75, fo. 105, 107, 165.
6. MacLaurin, fo. 187; Perceval to Southwell, 1 Dec. (os) 1725, BL, Add. 47031.
7. Mitchell, Balgonie.
8. Haggerston; Bennett, 7 July 1785.
9. *North Country Journal*, 10 Sep. (os) 1737; Smollett, p. 16; Mrs Montagu, II, 127.
10. Stevens, p. 6; St Saphorin to Townshend, 28 Nov. 1722, PRO 80/47; B. Skerrett to Mrs James Wallace, 17 Oct. 1776, Northumberland, ZHW/2/3.
11. Anon, BL, Add. 60522; Southwell, BL, Add. 34753, fo. 7; Fish to Marlborough, 11 Nov. 1726,BL, Add. 61444.
12. Haggerston, Northumberland, 24 May 1718; Clavering to Lady Cowper, Herts., Panshanger, D/EP F196.
13. Robert Arbuthnot to Keith, 10 Nov. 1787, BL, Add. 35539.
14. Marlborough to Fish, 26 June (os), Fish to Marlborough, 12 Oct., Marlborough to Fish, 12 Oct. (os) 1727, BL, Add. 61444.
15. Mellish to father, 25 April 1731; Wharton to Thomas Wharton, 19 May; Wharton to mother, 29 May 1775; Pelham to father, 15 Feb. 1777, BL, Add. 33127.
16. Pelham to father, 2 June 1776, to mother, 27 May 1777, BL, Add. 33126.
17. Carteret to Wetstein, 27 June (os) 1728, Douglas to Keith, 23 Sep. 1775, Pembroke to Keith, 1778, BL, Add. 32415, 35509, 35515.
18. Sherlock, *New Letters* (1781), pp. 147−9, 152; Beckford, I, 9; Carpenter, Bodl. Mss. Douce 67, pp. 152−3; Pelham, 23 April 1777, BL, Add. 33127; Sherlock, *Letters from an English Traveller* (1780), p. 173.
19. Poole, I, 50; Pelham, 4 Dec. 1775, BL, Add. 33126; Richard, p. 221; Young, I, 99; Villiers, p. 33; Wharton to Miss Raine, 7 Oct. 1775.
20. R. Halsband (ed.), *Montagu correspondence* (3 vols., Oxford, 1966), II, 100; Foote, I, i; Crewe, BL, Add. 37926, fo. 71, 104; Lynch, *Independent Patriot* (1737), pp. 44, 50.

21. Perceval to brother, 21 Nov. (os) 1726, Rogerson to Keith, 27 May 1788, BL, Add. 47031, 35540; Moore, *Collected Works*, I, 358.

22. Perceval to Southwell, senior, 22 Jan. 1726, BL, Add. 47031.

23. *Mist's*, 18 Sep. (os) 1725.

24. Morton to Keith, 28 Aug. 1782, Hanbury-Williams to Lord Holland, 23 March 1752, BL, Add. 35526, 51393; Bennett, 4 Aug. 1785.

25. Baltimore, *Tour to the East*, p. 76; Thomson, p. 27; Hurd, pp. 41–2.

26. De la Harp, Boston's tutor, to Earl of Grantham, 24 June, 3 Nov. 1716, Herts., D/E Na F8; Perceval to Edward Southwell, senior, 7 May (os) 1726, Robson, 1 Sep. 1787, BL, Add. 47031, 38837; F. G. Stokes, *The Bletcheley Diary of the Rev. William Cole* (1931), p. 23; Hurd, pp. 51–5; Andrews, 1784, pp. 4–5, 16–17.

27. Delafaye to Waldegrave, 30 Nov. (os) 1732, Chewton.

28. *Memorials of . . . James Oswald*, (Edinburgh, 1825), p. 206.

29. *Mist's Weekly Journal*, 14 Aug. (os), 18 Sep. (os) 1725, 8 July (os) 1727; *Craftsman*, 6 July (os) 1728, 7 July (os) 1739, 12 July (os) 1740; *London Journal*, 7 Aug. (os) 1731; Rolt, *John Lindesay, Earl of Crawford*, p. 96; Lynch, *Independent Patriot*, p. 27; J. M. Smythe, *The Rival Modes* (1727).

30. Wharton to Dr Baker, 20 May 1775.

31. J. to E. Mellish, 15 April; John Gore to E. Mellish, 10 Dec. 1730.

32. Keith to Bradshaw, 13 Oct. 1773; G. Smyth (ed.), *Memoirs*, I, 446; E. Carteret to Wetstein, 27 Sep. (os) 1728, BL, Add. 32415; Knight, p. 179; Watkins, 22 April 1788; J. Macky, *A Journey through England* (5th edn., 1732), iv; Andrews, 1784, pp. 16, 5; Pennant, pp. 69, 84; Wharton to Dr Baker, 12 March, Wharton to Thomas Wharton, 13 June, Wharton to Thomas Lloyd, 30 June 1775; Dundas to his son, G. Omond, *Arniston Memoirs*, (Edinburgh, 1887), p. 80.

33. Hanbury-Williams to Lord Holland, 11 June 1752, BL, Add. 51393; Garrick, 1751, p. 34.

34. Francis, 2 Nov. 1772, BL, Add. 40759; Brand to Wharton, 9 April 1790; Knight, p. 179.

35. Young, I, iii.

36. Aylesbury, D/DR/8/2/6.

37. Stoye, *English Travellers Abroad, 1604–1667* (1952), p. 18.

38. Robert to Thomas Trevor, 28 Sep. 1728; Pococke, Mitchell, St Vincent, Robson, BL, Add. 61684, 22978, fo. 76, 58319, fo. 12, 31192, fo. 3, 22, 38837, fo. 49; Bennett, 27 Oct. 1785.

39. Polwarth, 27 March 1778, Cambridge RO 408.

40. T. H. Hollingsworth, *The Demography of the British Peerage*, supplement to *Population Studies*, 18 (1964); Hollingsworth, 'Mortality among Peerage Families since 1600', *Population Studies*, 32 (1977); L. and J. C. Stone, *An Open Elite? England 1540–1880* (1984), pp. 96–104.

41. Lady Margaret Fordyce to Keith, 27 July 1783, BL, Add. 35529.

SELECTIVE BIBLIOGRAPHY

For reasons of space only some of the primary and secondary material used has been mentioned. It is hoped to produce a detailed bibliography on the subject.

There are no references to newspaper, pamphlet, parliamentary and theatrical material, nor to material in the Public Record Office and in foreign archives. Unless otherwise stated the place of publication is London.

Manuscript Sources

Aberdeen, University Library, Diary of Colin Maclaurin, Journal of George Ogilvie
Aylesbury, Buckinghamshire County Record Office, Craven, Drake, Lee, Saunders papers
Badminton, Badminton House, Beaufort papers
Bangor, University Library, Penrhos letters
Bedford, Bedfordshire County Record Office, Lucas papers
Birmingham, Central Library, Malies diary
Bradford, Public Library, Spencer Stanhope, Tong papers
Bristol, Avon County Record Office, Harford journal
Bury-St-Edmunds, West Suffolk County Record Office, Grafton, Hervey papers, Mason journal
Cambridge, Cambridgeshire County Record Office, Chapman diary, Green diary, Townley journal, Polwarth letters; Fitzwilliam Museum, William Fitzwilliam journal; University Library, Hoare, Ratcliff, Smith papers
Carlisle, Cumbria Record Office, Nelson letters
Chelmsford, Essex County Record Office, Barrett, Braybrooke, DuCane, Mildmay papers
Chewton Mendip, Chewton House, Waldegrave papers
Chichester, West Sussex County Record Office, Goodwood papers; anon. (additional manuscripts 7236—7)
Durham, University Library, Wharton papers
Edinburgh, Scottish Record Office, anon. (GD 26/6/233; 38/1/1253/14; 267/7/20), Barclay (GD 18), Clark, Clerk (GD 18), Coke, Dalhousie, Dalrymple, Deskford, Grant (GD 248), Morton, Oliphant, Stair papers
Gateshead, Public Library, Ellison papers
Gloucester, Gloucestershire County Record Office, anon. (D1799/A325, C7), Blathwayt, Freeman, Mitford, Wetenhall papers
Hatfield, Hatfield House, Cecil papers
Hertford, Hertfordshire County Record Office, Leake, Panshanger papers
Huntingdon, Huntingdonshire County Record Office, Manchester papers
Ipswich, East Suffolk County Record Office, Leathes papers
Kidderminster, Public Library, Knight notebooks
Leeds, Vyner papers

Leicester, Leicestershire County Record Office, anon. diary (DG7/4/12), Finch
papers
Lincoln, Lincolnshire County Record Office, Massingberd papers
London, British Library, additional manuscripts: anon. (12130, 60522), Althorp,
Blenheim, Burnet, Caryll, Compton, Crewe, Dysart, Egmont, Essex, Finch-
Hatton, Flaxman, Fox, Francis, Garmston, Grantham, Grey, Hardwicke,
Holland House, Hume, Keith, Macclesfield, Mitchell, Newcastle, Nixon, Pelham,
Spark Molesworth, Pococke, Rainsford, Robson, St Vincent, Southwell, Suffolk,
Ward, Wetstein, Whitworth papers; Egerton manuscripts: Bentinck, Southwell
papers; Sloane manuscripts: letters of Sir Hans Sloane, vol. 4045; Stowe
manuscripts: anon., journal, vol. 790;
University Library, anon., journal, ms. 491
Maidstone, Kent County Record Office, Norman, Polhill, Stanhope, Twisden
papers
Manchester, John Rylands Library, Stanley journal
Matlock, Derbyshire County Record Office, anon., journal, D2375 M/76/186
Newcastle, Northumberland County Record Office, Blackett, St Paul, Haggerston
papers.
Norwich, Norfolk County Record Office. Gurney, Ketton-Cremer papers
Nottingham, Nottinghamshire County Record Office, Rolleston papers;
University Library, anon., journal (Me/2L/2a), Mellish letters
Oxford, Bodleian Library, anon. (Ms. Eng. Misc. d. 213), Bennett, Bland, Burges,
Butler, Carpenter, Folkes, Milles, Rawlinson, Tracy papers;
Christ Church Library, Wake papers;
County Record Office, Quarendon papers;
Wadham College Library, Swinton papers
Preston, Lancashire Record Office, Farington papers
Reading, Berkshire County Record Office, anon., notebook D/EBT F26, anon.,
poem D/EBT Z6
Stafford, Staffordshire County Record Office, anon., journal (DD/SH 67/19
C/2480), Kemys-Tynte, Wadham, Wyndham papers
Wigan, Town Hall, Leigh, anon. (D/DZ), Windham papers
Winchester, Hampshire County Record Office, Mildmay papers

Private Collections

1. Glenbervie papers
2. Journal of Major Richard Creed

Guidebooks and Published Travel Accounts and Correspondence

Aikin in L. Aikin (ed.), *Memoir of John Aikin M.D.* (2 vols. 1823), I, 69–95.
J. Andrews, *Letters to a Young Gentleman on his setting out for France* (1784).
J. Andrews, *A Comparative View of the French and English Nations* (1785).
Anon., 'Sketch of a Fortnight's Excursion to Paris in 1788', *Gentleman's Magazine*,
67 (1797), pp. 723–35, 908–9.
A.R., *The Curiosities of Paris* (1758, 1760).
J. Armstrong (alias Lancelot Temple), *A Short Ramble through some parts of
France and Italy* (1771).

Lord Baltimore, *A Tour to the East* (1767).

P. Beckford, *Letters and Observations written in a short Tour through France and Italy* (1786).

P. Beckford, *Familiar Letters from Italy to a friend in England* (2 vols., Salisbury, 1805).

W. Beckford, *Italy, with sketches of Spain and Portugal* (Paris, 1834).

W. Beckford in G. Chapman (ed.), *The Travel Diaries of William Beckford* (2 vols., 1928).

Berry in T. Lewis (ed.), *Extracts from the Journals and Correspondence of Miss Berry* (3 vols., 1865).

Boswell in F. A. Pottle (ed.), *Boswell on the Grand Tour* (1953, 1955).

Boswell in F. A. Pottle (ed.), *Boswell in Holland 1763–1764)* (1952).

J. Breval, *Remarks on several parts of Europe* (1726).

P. Brydone, *A Tour through Sicily and Malta* (2 vols., 1775).

Burney in C. H. Glover (ed.), *Dr. Charles Burney's Continental Travels 1770–1772* (1927).

Calderwood in A. Fergusson (ed.), *Letters and Journals of Mrs. Calderwood* (Edinburgh, 1884).

Coke, *The Letters and Journals of Lady Mary Coke* (4 vols., Edinburgh, 1889–96).

W. Cole in F. G. Stokes (ed.), *A Journal of My Journey to Paris in the Year 1765* (1931).

W. Coxe, *Travels in Switzerland* (3 vols., 1789).

W. Coxe, *Travels into Poland, Russia, Sweden, and Denmark* (3 vols., 1784, 90).

Joseph Cradock, *Literary and Miscellaneous Memoirs* (1826).

Mrs Cradock, journal, translated and edited by O. Balleygiuer as *La Vie Française à la veille de la révolution* (Paris, 1911).

E. Craven, *A Journey through the Crimea to Constantinople* (Dublin, 1789).

E. Craven, *Memoirs of the Margravine of Anspach* (2 vols., 1826).

Crawford in R. Rolt, *Memoirs of the Life of the Right Honourable John Lindesay, Earl of Crawfurd* (1753).

A. Dick, 'A Journey from London to Paris in 1736', *Gentleman's Magazine*, 39 (1853), pp. 23–6, 159–65, 263–6, 579–83.

J. Douglas, 'Journal of a tour in Holland, Germany, France' in W. Macdonald (ed.), *Select Works* (Salisbury, 1820).

J. Essex in W. Fawcett (ed.), *Journal of a Tour through part of Flanders and France in August, 1773* (Cambridge, 1888).

Fife in A. and H. Taylor (eds.), *Lord Fife and his factor* (1925).

Gardenstone, *Travelling Memorandums made in a tour upon the Continent of Europe, in the years 1786, 1787 and 1788* (3 vols., 1791).

Garrick in R. C. Alexander (ed.), *The Diary of David Garric: being a record of his memorable trip to Paris in 1751* (New York, 1928).

Garrick in G. W. Stone (ed.), *The Journal of David Garrick Describing his visit to France and Italy in 1763* (New York, 1939).

Gibbon in G. A. Bonnard (ed.), *Gibbon's Journey from Geneva to Rome* (1961).

Grafton in W. P. Anson (ed.), *Autobiography and Political Correspondence of Augustus Henry Third Duke of Grafton* (1898).

R. Gray, *Letters during the course of a Tour Through Germany, Switzerland and Italy* (1794).

T. Gray in P. Toynbee and L. Whibley (eds.), *Correspondence of Thomas Gray* (3 vols., Oxford, 1935).

Harcourt in E. Harcourt (ed.), *The Harcourt Papers* (7 vols., Oxford, no date).

S. Ireland, *A Picturesque Tour through Holland, Brabant and part of France* (1790).

A. Jardine, *Letters from Barbary, France, Spain, Portugal* (1788).

252   *Selective Bibliography*

T. Jones, *Memoirs of Thomas Jones* (1951).
W. Jones, *Observations on a Journey to Paris in the month of August 1776* (1776).
Knight in E. F. Eliott-Drake (ed.), *Lady Knight's Letters from France and Italy 1776–1795* (1905).
W. Lucas, *A Five Weeks Tour to Paris* (1750).
Lyttleton in R. Phillimore (ed.), *Memoirs and Correspondence of George, Lord Lyttleton* (2 vols., 1845).
J. MacDonald, *Travels in various parts of Europe, Asia and Africa* (1790).
J. Mckay, *A Journey through the Austrian Netherlands* (1725).
T. Martyn, *The Gentleman's Guide in his tour through Italy* (1787).
T. Martyn, *The Gentleman's Guide in his Tour through France* (1787).
T. Martyn, *Sketch of a tour through Swisserland* (1787).
Melvilles and Levens in W. Fraser (ed.), *The Melvilles Earls of Melville and the Leslies Earls of Leven* (3 vols., Edinburgh, 1890).
J. Millard, *The Gentleman's Guide in his Tour through France* (1770). For alternative attribution *Factotum* 11 (1984).
A. Miller, *Letters from Italy* (3 vols., 1776).
J. Moore, *A View of Society and Manners in France, Switzerland and Germany* (1779).
L. Muirhead, *Journals of Travels in parts of the late Austrian Low Countries, France, the Pays de Vaud and Tuscany, in 1787 and 1789* (1803).
J. Northall, *Travels through Italy* (1766).
Northumberland in J. Greig (ed.), *The Diaries of a Duchess* (1926).
J. Northall, *Travels through Italy* (1766).
Orrery in Countess of Cork and Orrery (ed.), *Orrery Papers* (2 vols., 1903).
John, Earl of Orrery, *Letters from Italy* (1773).
J. Palmer, *A Four Months Tour through France* (2 vols., 1775).
J. Parminter in O. J. Reichel (ed.), 'Extracts from a Devonshire Lady's Notes of Travel in France 1784', *Transactions of the Devonshire Association for the Advancement of Science, Literature and Art* (34), 1802.
H. Peckham, *A Tour through Holland, Dutch Brabant, the Austrian Netherlands, and part of France* (1772).
T. Pennant, *Tour on the Continent 1765* (1948).
R. Poole, *A Journey from London to France and Holland* (2nd edn., 2 vols., 1746–50).
S. J. Pratt, *Gleanings through Wales, Holland and Westphalia* (3 vols., 1795).
Present State of Germany (2 vols., 1738).
A. Radcliffe, *A Journey made in the summer of 1794, through Holland and the Western Frontier of Germany* (2 vols., 1796).
J. Richard, *A Tour from London to Petersburg* (1780).
Richmond in Earl of March, *A Duke and his Friends. The life and letters of the second Duke of Richmond* (2 vols., 1911).
E. Rigby in Lady Eastlake (ed.), *Letters from France in 1789* (1880).
J. Russell, *Letters from a Young Painter abroad to his Friends in England* (1748).
J. St John, *Letters from France to a Gentleman in the South of Ireland written in 1787* (Dublin, 1788).
S. Sharp, *Letters from Italy* (1767).
J. Shaw, *Letters to a Nobleman* (1709).
M. Sherlock, *Letters from an English Traveller* (1780).
M. Sherlock, *New Letters from an English Traveller* (1781)
Smeaton, *John Smeaton's Diary of his Journey to the Low Countries* (Leamington Spa, 1938).
J. E. Smith, *A Sketch of a Tour on the Continent* (3 vols., 1793).
T. Smollett, *Travels through France and Italy* (1766).

M. Starke, *Letters from Italy* (2 vols., 1800).

L. Sterne, *A Sentimental Journey* (1768).

S. Stevens, *Miscellaneous Remarks made on the spot in a late Seven Years Tour through France, Italy, Germany and Holland* (no date).

J. Taylor, *The History of the Travels and Adventures of the Chevalier John Taylor* (2 vols., 1761–2).

P. Thicknesse, *A Year's Journey through France and part of Spain* (2 vols., Bath, 1777).

C. Thompson, *The Travels of the late Charles Thompson* (3 vols., Reading, 1744).

A. Thomson, *Letters of a Traveller* (1798).

J. Toland, *An Account of the Courts of Prussia and Hanover* (1705).

J. Townsend, *A Journey through Spain* (3 vols., 1791).

J. C. Villiers, *A Tour through part of France* (1789).

A. Walker, *Ideas suggested on the spot in a late excursion* (1790).

H. Walpole, *Paris Journals* in W. S. Lewis (ed.), *Horace Walpole's Correspondence* (1939)

T. Watkins, *Travels through Swisserland, Italy, Sicily the Greek Islands, to Constantinople* (2 vols., 1792).

Wharton in G. Rodmell, 'An Englishman's Impressions of France in 1775', *Durham University Journal*, new series, 30 (1969).

E. Wright, *Some Observations made in travelling through France, Italy, etc.* (1730).

A. Young, *Travels during the years 1787, 1788 and 1789* (2nd. edn., 2 vols., 1794).

Studies of Tourism and Books that Include Material on Eighteenth-century Tourists

P. Adams, *Travelers and Travel Liars 1660–1800* (Berkeley, 1962).

C. L. Batten, *Pleasurable Instruction: Form and Convention in Eighteenth-Century Travel Literature* (Berkeley, 1978).

R. Blunt (ed.), *Mrs Montagu 'Queen of the Blues'* (no date).

A. Bradshaw, 'William Van Mildert's visit to the Netherlands in 1792', *Durham University Journal* (1978–9).

J. Burke, 'The Grand Tour and the Rule of Taste', in R. F. Brissenden (ed.), *Studies in the Eighteenth Century* (Canberra, 1968).

J. D. Candaux, 'Du Mon-Cenis à Herculanum en 1752–53 ou les Débuts du "Tourisme" Genevois en Italie', in L. Monnier (ed.), *Genève et L'Italie* (Geneva, 1969).

W. H. Chaloner, 'The Egertons in Italy and the Netherlands, 1729–34', *Bulletin of the John Rylands Library*, 32 (1949–50).

B. Connell, *Portrait of a Whig Peer* (1957).

L. Cust, *Records of the Cust Family*, III (1927).

H. L. A. Dunthorne, 'British travellers in eighteenth-century Holland', *British Journal for Eighteenth-Century Studies*, 5 (1982).

J. Fleming, *Robert Adam and his Circle in Edinburgh and Rome* (1962).

J. Fleming, 'Lord Brudenell and his Bear-Leader' *English Miscellany* (1958).

B. Fothergill, *Sir William Hamilton* (1969).

B. Fothergill, *The Mitred Earl* (1974).

R. Halsband, *The Life of Lady Mary Wortley Montagu* (Oxford, 1956).

R. Halsband, *Lord Hervey* (Oxford, 1973).

L. Herbert, *The Pembroke Papers* (2 vols., 1939, 1950).

E. Hurd, *Dialogues on the Uses of Foreign Travel* (1764).

L. Lewis, *Connoisseurs and Secret Agents* (1961).

J. Lough, 'Letters from France, 1788–89' *Durham University Journal* 54 (1961).

C. Maxwell, *The English Traveller in France, 1698–1815* (1932).

W. E. Mead, *The Grand Tour in the Eighteenth Century* (New York, 1914).

H. A. Mildmay, *A Brief Account of the Mildmay Family* (1913).

H. J. Mullenbrock, 'The Political implications of the Grand Tour' *Trema* 9 (1984).

S. R. Roget (ed.), *Travel in the two last Centuries by three Generations* (1921).

M. Sacquin, 'Les Anglais à Montpellier et à Nice pendant la seconde moitié du siècle' *Dix-Huitième siecle* 13 (1981).

R. Shackleton, 'The Grand Tour in the Eighteenth Century' in L. T. Milic (ed.), *Studies in Eighteenth-Century Culture* (1971).

H. Schwarzwalder, 'Reisebeschreibungen des 18. Jahrhunderts über Norddeutschland', in W. Griep and H. Jager (eds.), *Reise und Soziale Realität am Ende des 18. Jahrhunderts* (Heidelberg, 1983).

O. Sitwell, *Sing High! Sing Low!* (1944).

B. Skinner, *Scots in Italy in the Eighteenth Century* (Edinburgh, 1966).

E. A. Smith, 'Lord Fitzwilliam's "grand tour"' *History Today* 17 (1967).

G. Stanhope, *The Life of Charles Third Earl Stanhope* (1914).

A. M. Stirling, *Annals of a Yorkshire House* (2 vols., 1911).

J. Stoye, *English Travellers Abroad, 1604–1667* (1952).

L. M. Wiggin, *The Faction of Cousins* (New Haven, 1958).

INDEX